Trade Union Development and Industrial Relations
in the British West Indies

A Publication of the
Institute of Industrial Relations
University of California

Trade Union Development
and Industrial Relations
in the British West Indies

WILLIAM H. KNOWLES

Berkeley and Los Angeles, 1959
UNIVERSITY OF CALIFORNIA PRESS

UNIVERSITY OF CALIFORNIA PRESS
BERKELEY AND LOS ANGELES
CALIFORNIA

CAMBRIDGE UNIVERSITY PRESS
LONDON, ENGLAND

Foreword

This study of labor relations in the British West Indies suggests that the characteristics of the evolving labor movements of underdeveloped areas deserve careful attention. Where unions have obtained a strong foothold and the great majority of voters belong to the working class, it is relatively easy for union leaders, or leaders of political parties that are closely affiliated with the labor movement, to gain political power. In such a situation the stability of the labor movement may be a crucial determinant of political stability.

In the West Indies, as in many underdeveloped areas, unions of the "job-conscious" variety have been slow to evolve, particularly in the dominant agricultural sector of the economy. Union leaders have frequently been more concerned with political action than with the development of collective-bargaining relationships, and would-be political leaders have been able to attract large followings by organizing unions which they sought to use as springboards to political power. The unions have sometimes been ephemeral and the leaders occasionally characterized by demagogic tendencies.

Yet more permanent unions are emerging and are beginning to play an important role. Probably the most significant contribution of this study lies in its analysis of the conflicting tendencies making for stable and unstable unionism. Of particular interest, also, is the discussion of the attitudes of management, union, and government leaders toward alternative methods of stimulating economic development in the face of a serious overpopulation problem.

Now that the Federation of the British West Indies is a going concern, the direction of development of the union movement assumes even more critical importance. The representatives of the Crown will have less opportunity to offer advice and assistance to the leaders of infant unions, while there will be an inevitable struggle for dominance between the political leaders of the larger islands and territories, many of whom have strong union ties. The outcome of this struggle will have an important bearing on the political stability of this strategic neighbor of the United States.

ARTHUR M. ROSS
Director

Acknowledgments

Since it is not feasible to acknowledge individually the assistance of the many West Indians whose friendly coöperation, helpful advice, and generosity in giving me time for interviews made this study possible, I wish to thank them collectively. In particular, I wish to express my gratitude to the staff of the Institute of Economic and Social Research, University College of the West Indies, for their aid in orienting me to the task; and to the labor officers of the British West Indies without whose invaluable assistance the study would have been impossible.

I am grateful also to the British Information Services for permission to reproduce two tables and the map of the Caribbean and adjacent countries from the Central Office of Information publication, *The West Indies: A Nation in the Making* (London, 1957).

Among those whose reading of the manuscript contributed many useful suggestions, I am indebted to my colleagues Margaret Gordon, Walter Galenson, and Joseph Garbarino. Finally, a note of appreciation must be given to Patrick McGillivray and Lee Neugent for their assistance in gathering statistical data, and to Gene Hay and my wife, Yereth, for their editorial assistance.

W. H. K.

Contents

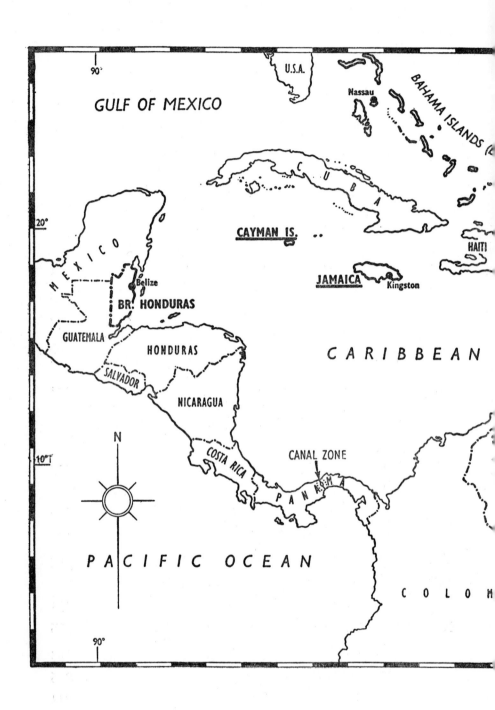

GULF OF MEXICO

U.S.A.

Nassau

BAHAMA ISLANDS

CUBA

90°

20°

CAYMAN IS.

HAITI

MEXICO

Belize

JAMAICA   Kingston

BR. HONDURAS

GUATEMALA

HONDURAS

CARIBBEAN

SALVADOR

NICARAGUA

N

COSTA RICA

CANAL ZONE

10°

PANAMA

COLOM

PACIFIC OCEAN

90°

THE CARIBBEAN
AND ADJACENT COUNTRIES

The British Caribbean territories are shown in heavy type
and those which form The West Indies federation are underlined

MILES

0   100   200   300

0   100   200   300   400   500

KILOMETRES

70°

20°

10°

CAICOS IS.

TURKS IS.

DOMINICAN REPUBLIC

VIRGIN·IS. (U.S.)

VIRGIN IS.

ANGUILLA

LEEWARD IS.

PUERTO RICO (U.S.)

ST. KITTS

NEVIS

ANTIGUA

MONTSERRAT

GUADELOUPE (Fr.)

DOMINICA

MARTINIQUE (Fr.)

S E A

ST. LUCIA

ST. VINCENT

BARBADOS

ARUBA (Neth)

BONAIRE (Neth)

CURAÇAO (Neth)

GRENADA

WINDWARD IS.

TOBAGO

Port-of-Spain

TRINIDAD

V E N E Z U E L A

Georgetown

BRITISH GUIANA

NETH GUIANA

FRENCH GUIANA

B I A

70°

B   R   A   Z   I   L

Introduction

The purpose of this study is to examine the social, economic, and political background of the labor movement of the British West Indies. Trade unionism in the British West Indies became a labor movement in 1939, is still a young movement, and has experienced a rapid growth. What caused its sudden growth and the direction of its development leads into an interesting and fruitful area of inquiry. It is frequently observed that labor movements are the products of their particular environments. In studying the environmental background of BWI union development, this monograph will take up the heritage of slavery, colonialism, and estate agriculture; the economic problems of marginal tropical agriculture, overpopulation, and general, chronic unemployment; problems of racial-ethnic groups, class structure, and social attitudes; community and family organization, worker attitudes and personality patterns; development of political parties, political issues, nationalism and anticolonialism; the policy of the colonial government toward unionism; and the attitudes of employers toward unionism. It was anticipated that such external forces as communism, socialism, British trade unionism, and the International Confederation of Free Trade Unions would have an influence on BWI union development. In the course of study it was learned that Harlem, United States military bases in the Caribbean, United States farm recruitment, American Jesuits, and American unions also have exercised a profound influence upon BWI union development.

This monograph may also be viewed as a case study in union development in underdeveloped areas. Many features of the BWI environment are similar to those of other underdeveloped areas—features such as the predominance of agriculture and lack of manufacturing industries, overpopulation and underemployment, rising nationalism and the decline of colonialism, quasi-feudal working relationships, lack of capital and entrepreneurial talent, and a complex social structure based on subtle racial discrimination. As with the peoples of underdeveloped areas the world over, the people of the BWI are in revolt against poverty, general unemployment, and lack of human dignity. This revolt takes many forms, and the labor unrest of the working class is different from that of the lower middle-class and the middle-class intellectuals. The type of labor movement that has evolved is also a factor in the revolt and, in the opinion of the writer, is characterized by two major directions of development; one irrational and unstable, and the other rational and stable.

Lacking union traditions and experience, and confronted with the multitude of problems of an underdeveloped area, it is to be expected that such a young labor movement would go through a period of chaos and confusion in its development. It is useful to know under what conditions unionism develops stability and a capacity to provide rational solutions of the problems of workers, and under what conditions it develops an instability which only frustrates worker goals and permits opportunists of all ideologies to gain control of the labor movement. The answers to these questions have important implications for the problems of economic development. To us in the United States, however, union development in the BWI must be more than just one case study among many, for they are among our nearest neighbors, guards the approaches to the Panama Canal, and is our major source of supply of aluminum ore (bauxite). The BWI were federated in 1958 and given a large measure of self-government, leading to eventual dominion status. The political stability of this newest of nations will depend in large part on the stability of its labor movement. One of the objectives of this monograph is to examine the relationship between unions and political parties.

The main findings and conclusions of the study are based on analyses of statements in interviews made during a 14-month period in 1953–54 with estate owners, secretaries of employers' associations, estate managers, colonial administrators, union leaders, and politicians. Labor officers in each colony were most coöperative in arranging interviews, and an attempt was made to interview all prominent leaders in the labor-relations field. With few exceptions the attempt was successful, although some labor leaders were out of the colony at the time of the survey; but this occurrence was not frequent enough to alter the findings. For the most part, the persons interviewed were friendly, coöperative, and candid. Not only were they anxious to discuss the problems of labor relations, but frequently they sought the writer's opinion and advice. Realizing that his opinion might bias the interview, the author adopted the role of the interested but uninformed friend. Sometime during the interview, after rapport had been established, more aggressive phrasing of questions would be tried in order to compare defensive responses with previous answers. Although the interviews were unstructured and persons were encouraged to develop those points they thought most relevant to an understanding of union development, questions were asked concerning twelve major areas of the economic, social, and political background of union development. Additional weight would be given the study if prominent West Indians could be directly quoted, but the interviews were to be confidential. Opinions, therefore, are summarized as majority and minority viewpoints of those interviewed.

There are two possibilities of bias in the findings. First, since the interviewer is white and an American, while most of the interviewed persons were nonwhite West Indians, perhaps some of them stressed points they thought a "Yankee" would like to have emphasized. In general, union leaders were very pro-American, while middle-class colored leaders tended to be critical because of racial discrimination in the United States. Attitudes of white employers and colonial officials toward a visiting American varied considerably. Second, few interviews were held with workers themselves, and the study depends largely upon what prominent leaders think of the attitudes and values of workers. Although it is desirable and useful to know the opinions of community leaders regarding the thoughts and aspirations of workers, further research among the workers themselves is needed.

Finally, there is a decided difference between the opinions recorded in interviews in 1953–54, and the opinions expressed by many of these same people as published in previous studies. Union leaders and politicians, for example, had become less socialistic and less anti-British, while employers were now more favorably disposed to unionism, self-government, and racial equality. The shift in opinion was not attributable to an attempt to put on a good front. Rather, the difference in attitudes reflects the revolutionary changes of the past twenty years which have all but ended autocracy. Just as there have been profound changes in attitudes in the United States within the past two decades on such matters as unionism, the role of government in economic development, and racial discrimination, the same trends have been evident in the BWI.

The interviews took place during the year 1953–54 while the author was on a Fulbright Research Fellowship to the University College of the West Indies. The itinerary included eighteen weeks in Jamaica, ten weeks in Trinidad, six weeks in British Guiana, two weeks in British Honduras, two weeks in Barbados, and one week each in St. Lucia, St. Vincent, Antigua, and St. Kitts. As Grenada was the family headquarters for the last half of the year, frequent visits were made to home base. Due to lack of time, transportation difficulties, and unimportance of union development in these colonies, the writer did not visit Monserrat or Dominica. In addition to the itinerary, the writer lived in Grenada for a year, 1951–52, during which time he visited St. Lucia, St. Vincent, Barbados, and Trinidad.

Chapter I	General
	Background

The British West Indies, which form a great arc across the Caribbean for some 2,500 miles, are hardly a distinct geographical territory. Yet this arc, which begins at British Honduras, sweeps northeast to Jamaica, skips over Hispaniola and Puerto Rico, then turns southeast toward the Leeward and Windward Islands, to Barbados, Trinidad, and British Guiana, has become a federation with a single governing body. (British Honduras and British Guiana, although considered part of the BWI, are not as yet part of the new federation.) The similarities of language, custom, and tradition which create group consciousness make federation possible. These factors also make possible an integrated study of the development of trade unions despite the physical separation of the islands. Within this arc there is more water than land. The distances between islands are great, and, until the advent of air travel, colonies were cut off from one another by the direction of the trade routes which all led to Great Britain and Canada rather than to interisland traffic. Nevertheless, because of a common background of natural resources, similarities in climate, the manner of island settlement, together with the system of agriculture, and the politics of sugar, there exists a cultural unity. Consequently, the development of trade unions in the British West Indies, though each union is separate and autonomous, has many important aspects in common.

Sugar and Slavery

In a discussion of any phase of West Indian life, sugar takes precedence in importance in the historical development.[1] The introduction of sugar production in the West Indies dates back to about 1640, and has since been a basic factor in the development of labor attitudes toward work, toward the land, and toward the employer-employee relationship. The cultivation of sugar required large-scale preindustrial capitalistic forms of agriculture. Although small farms, similar to those in the New England colonies, had been settled, they were soon replaced by large landed estates. As the cultivation of sugar required a large and disciplined labor force, and attempts to use debtors, criminals, and beggars from England were unsuccessful, slavery was brought to the West Indies.

For more than one hundred years sugar sales to Europe reaped great fortunes for those who held title to the estates. Even after the Indies lost their competitive position in the European markets, riches continued to flow from protected English markets. Had Europeans come to the West Indies to settle, as they had done in North America, some of the wealth might have stayed with the estates. However, those who came worked with the intention of making quick fortunes, then returning "home" to spend their money lavishly, building homes or buying seats in Parliament. They did not come to build or to develop, but to exploit. The more competent men took their fortunes and left. Usually their children did not return after an education in England. Thus, not having established roots or ties with the islands, it is not surprising that, although in some ways the West Indies were further advanced and more highly prized than the thirteen colonies of North America in the eighteenth century, there were no men in the West Indies of the caliber of the leaders of the American Revolution. Also, it is not surprising that little wealth from the growth and sale of sugar stayed in the colonies to promote economic and cultural development. (As examples, Harvard University, Massachusetts, was founded in 1639; University College of the West Indies, Jamaica, was founded in 1947.)

Successful estate management required skill and ability—quali-

---

[1] For notes to chapter i, see pp. 193–195.

ties which were frequently lacking. Absentee ownership became a burdensome and inefficient form of management. Financial affairs were often left in the hands of a town lawyer or doctor, who handled several absentee estates. Production management was left to an estate manager who operated through an unwieldy chain of command. This clumsy system of organization would have been strained even if the administrators had been men of ability. Since it was difficult to entice highly qualified men with experience in management to the West Indies, most of the estate managers were second rate. A tradition of high living and gambling, especially in Jamaica, depleted the estates of adequate capital and left most of them with burdensome debts.

Paralleling the development of wealth founded on sugar, there grew the fiction of the cultured (white) gentleman. Riches and culture were considered one and the same, and when the sugar industry declined, the fiction remained a part of West Indian life. The comparison of the West Indian estate owner with the English country gentleman is erroneous, contrary to historical fact. The basic difference was found in slavery. Although slavery enabled the white men to have some leisure time, the leisure was not used in the arts or the pursuit of learning, but, as the historians record, was used in the heavy consumption of alcohol, in gambling, and in the pursuit of women.

The decline of the sugar industry, which started as early as 1730 but was not seriously felt until after 1850, brought with it the decline of the British West Indies. New sugar areas were developed outside of the West Indies—areas which were more economical—and so by 1815 the British had lost the European sugar market. Further, the independence of the North American colonies created still another loss, as the new nation traded wherever terms were favorable. In addition, the West Indies lost the North American colonies as a low-cost supplier, as, by law the BWI were forced to trade within the British Empire. Then, in England, the industrial revolution caused interest to shift from sugar to cotton. With the opening of the African and Asian empires Britain turned its attention to the East, and away from the West. The decline of the mercantile economic doctrine in favor of laissez faire led to the abolition of a protected market for sugar in England. Subsidized sugar-beet production in Europe added to the competition, and, finally, the sugar economy received yet another blow from the abolition of slavery in 1833.

Colonialism

Great Britain's experiments with various forms of colonial government represent another feature of West Indian history.[2] None of the experiments worked well. Slaves, who were to become the legally free working class, constituting the bulk of the population, did not participate in government affairs, nor were they provided with the education necessary for participation. Except in Barbados and Antigua, the local "whites" serving as elected or appointed advisors to the governor present a sorry record of apathy, incompetence, corruption, and irresponsibility. With the most able men quitting the colonies, the quality of the legislative councils was not high. England was considered "home," creating a rapid turnover in white population. As the council members were only advisory to the governor, and often unenthusiastic, their tactic was to harass the governor and colonial administration. Since they were in no way responsible for decisions, most of which came through the colonial office, the elected men expressed themselves in extremes. The governor was theoretically responsible for carrying out colonial policy, yet he could not function without the coöperation of the local plantocracy. Thus, caught in the middle, governors quickly learned that the safest course was to do nothing. The choicest positions in the colonial service were in the eastern Empire, and therefore the West Indies often were not served by the most able administrators. Finally an expensive and unwieldy bureaucracy developed which has a long and inauspicious history of doing practically nothing.

With the decline of the sugar industry and with the parliamentary decree ending slavery, neither the estate system nor the colonial government were prepared to cope with the changes or the problems that were created. The estate owners lacked entrepreneurial talent and the capital necessary to exploit the limited resources of the West Indies, while the United Kingdom turned its attention elsewhere. The laissez-faire doctrine held that the West Indies could work out their own destiny with optimum efficiency if the colonial administrators merely preserved the necessary law and order. Further, the local government did not offer the minimum social service necessary to economic reorientation. The administration claimed that it could do nothing without additional tax revenue. The planters, already pressed by debts, higher costs, and lower profits, replied that higher taxes would only lead to greater bureaucratic waste. One historian describes the government of the 1890's as "luxurious ossification." [3]

In desperation, with the decline of sugar, the estates finally experimented with new crops. Cotton became important, but its planters had difficulty in competing with American cotton production. In the high rugged mountains coffee, cocoa, bananas, arrowroot, nutmeg, and citrus fruit were planted. Yet, in spite of the experimentation with other crops, sugar has maintained itself as the most profitable for flat-land cultivation, and sugar continues to dominate the economy of the BWI today. Whether it is cocoa, bananas, or sugar, however, the BWI is a marginal producer in the competitive world markets.

The abolition of slavery by parliamentary act in 1833 did not appreciably alter the economic decline, but it did create new problems for the estate managers—problems of instituting new work relationships. The theory behind the Apprenticeship Law of 1833 seemed laudatory; however, the plan did not work out. The actual abolition of slavery was to be invoked in 1836, while the intervening years were to be used as a period of apprenticeship during which time the slaves were to be taught a trade and given a garden spot, as well as clothing and medical care, in return for their labor on the estate. The spirit of the law was absent, as the slave owners were reluctant and resentful. With rare exceptions they felt no obligation to teach the slaves. In some instances, knowing that their chattel was soon to be free of supervision, and no longer regarding the slaves as expensive investment property, the estate owners proceeded to work them harder and without concern for their health. On the other hand, the slaves associated abolition with the right *not* to work and therefore were not eager to learn. As a result, abolitionists feared the growth of slavery disguised in a new form. The visionary hopes that a yeomanry of independent Negro freeholders would arise from an uneducated mass of slaves proved to be overoptimistic. Once having decreed freedom, the British government left the matter to the natural laws of human nature and of the market—as they were then understood. In spite of the failure of the plan, it is noteworthy that the slaves received their freedom thirty years before the American Civil War, and that the transition, though sadly inadequate, was relatively peaceful. The local governments of the West Indies lacked the interest, revenue, imagination, and ambition to assist in the transition to a free society.

Religious leaders, who had been active in the struggle for emancipation, attempted to aid in this transition, but often were overwhelmed by the task and were ill equipped to cope with the problems. Much of their effort was frustrated by the rise of "native baptists" sects led by illiterate men preaching a babble of Bible stories commingled with ancient superstitions. The crude and highly emotional religious groups could not meet the needs. Contrary to the hopes of the abolitionists, emancipation for the slave did not connotate freedom in the British sense—freedom for individual pursuit—but one which, to the slave, meant freedom from work entirely. The example of the estate owner, or the manager, was the slave's concept of the Englishman and his use of freedom. The slave, in his innocence, believed that he would live a life such as those he had seen; he would emulate the leisure of the white man. It is important to an understanding of the entire work relationship of the West Indies to recognize that the idea of manual labor became generally associated with slavery. The work of the field hand was considered lowest-grade slave labor, and is still considered as such by working people of the West Indies. Except in the Leeward Islands and in Barbados where all land was under cultivation, large numbers of former slaves took to the "bush" and became "squatters" on crown land. Thus, in an area where labor supply was already a problem, the shortage became acute, and it became difficult for the managers to induce these free men to work for wages. The result was the creation of a haphazard work relationship born of a confusing combination of threats and bribery, which were purposely vague in order to avoid accusations from abroad of continued slavery or peonage. Except for the squatters, legally free, the Negro remained a slave to sugar.[4] Without adequate understanding and education, the Negro was unable to pull himself into the new freedom. In 1861 William F. Sewell of Columbia University,[5] wrote: "Without instituting a mass education system for the free laborers, there would be little change, while education could make progress go on at the rate it had since the end of slavery."

For almost one hundred years the British West Indian society, economy, and political situation remained virtually static. Except for periods of prosperity in the 1860's and in 1914–1920, the economy was in a chronically depressed state. Education remained dormant. A high infant mortality rate and emigration to North, Central, and South America held the population fairly constant. Even with the end of slavery, the semifeudal estate system of agriculture continued to dominate the economy. Although it was an inefficient and unimaginative method, it was more efficient than any known alternative. The attitudes toward work, recreation, and race which had been nurtured under slavery, were perpetuated and became an integral part of the employer-employee relationship. An element in the continuum was the colonial administration and bureaucracy which perpetuated the complaisant stalemate between conflicting interests. Although numerous commissions of inquiry were sent out, making reports and recommendations, and although subsidies in the form of imperial tariff preferences began in 1919, it was not until World War II that the BWI emerged from a century of slumber.

Economic Background

Agriculture.—As already indicated, the main source of income and employment in the BWI is agriculture, with sugar cane predominating. The 79 sugar factories of the BWI employ 130,-000, another 180,000 are employed in cane cultivation on estates, and, in addition, there are 50,000 small-scale cane farmers.[6] Despite the economic decline, no substitute for sugar has yet been found. Sugar represents 76 per cent of agricultural exports and one-half of all agricultural production. Dependent on cane, the West Indian planter has been further harassed by cane disease, periodic hurricanes, the rugged terrain, and the watershed and irrigation problems, as well as, in some areas, the poor soil. One writer describes sugar cultivation in some of the colonies as a combination of sunshine, rain, and fertilizer with the soil serving only as anchor for the cane plant.[7] The Venn Commission studying the sugar industry in British Guiana indicated at the very outset that British Guiana was a high-cost, low-yield producer. In spite of increased tonnage per acre as a result of improved techniques of cultivation, the sucrose content was low; 10.5 tons of cane to one ton of sugar in British Guiana compared to 5 tons of cane in Hawaii and 4 tons in Java.[8] A similar observation was made in inquiring into the background of the Trinidad and Tobago labor disturbances of 1938.[9]

A large unskilled labor force, high revenue per acre, the absence of soil exhaustion, and rapid recuperation from hurricane damage are important factors contributing to economical sugar-cane cultivation. Arthur Lewis observes that a single acre planted in sugar cane in the West Indies produces more wealth than an acre of any other staple crop in the world. Although sugar cane is therefore the major source of employment with one man-year of labor required to produce two acres of cane, Lewis correctly concludes that it is impossible for the laborer to earn a decent living from two acres of land. It is important to an understanding of the development of trade unionism to recognize that, though sugar provides most of the jobs, it does not provide the standard of living which is currently demanded by the West Indian worker.[10] In part, the association of sugar with poverty can be eliminated by further mechanization of the industry, thereby increasing the productivity of labor. Yet, the experts agree, the industrial areas of the world must pay higher prices for sugar if the cane workers are to attain a higher standard of living.[11] Attempts to support the price of sugar in the 1930 Empire Preference Agreement failed because the formula for fixing prices tied the support price of sugar to the free-market price. Since there was no truly free market for sugar, prices fell. The International Sugar Agreement of 1937 was never operative because of the start of World War II. During the war the United Kingdom undertook to buy the Empire's sugar production at fixed prices for distribution throughout the Empire. For the first time, the cost of production, including a consideration of wage rates, was made part of the price formula. In 1952 the United Kingdom entered into a long-term bulk-purchase agreement with sugar producing areas in the Empire running until 1964, which did not meet West Indian approval, but nevertheless has afforded higher income and

Table 1

QUANTITY AND VALUE OF MAJOR BWI EXPORTS (1956–1957)

Colony	Industry	Quantity	Value in BWI dollars
Jamaica	Sugar (tons) Bauxite-Alumina	396,551[a] 2,063,000[a]	51,741,283[a] 41,000,000[a]
Trinidad	Oil (bls.) Sugar (tons)	28,929,000 160,000	262,296,300 25,698,583
Barbados	Sugar (tons) —[b]	171,010[a] —[b]	22,744,030[a] —[b]
Antigua	Sugar (tons) Cotton (lbs.)	28,713 1,209,461	5,253,300 1,386,911
St. Kitts-Nevis	Sugar (tons) Cotton (lbs.)	50,371 695,036	—[c] —[c]
Grenada	Cocoa (lbs.) Nutmeg (lbs.)	1,276,800 3,990,113[d]	—[c] —[c]
St. Lucia	Sugar (tons) Copra (lbs.)	11,617 2,931,926	1,545,061 —[c]
St. Vincent	Arrowroot (lbs.) Copra (lbs.)	10,012,480 4,578,000	—[c] —[c]
British Guiana	Sugar (tons) Bauxite (tons)	263,333 2,435,282	41,622,197 —[c]
British Honduras	Timber (cu. ft.) Citrus Fruit (boxes)	14,514,270 222,800	3,018,029 961,900

[a] 1955–1956 figure.
[b] There is no major agricultural or industrial product in Barbados other than sugar.
[c] Information not given in the source.
[d] The 1955 hurricane severely reduced crop yields.

NOTE—Some colonies have substantial incomes from other commodities; others rely solely on the major commodity. See Table 2.

SOURCE—*The West Indies Yearbook, 1956–1957* and *1957–1958*. Montreal: Thomas Skinner of Canada, Ltd., 1957 and 1958.

stability in the sugar industry. Since World War II sugar production has increased steadily, reaching a record output of a million tons in 1955. Two-thirds of this output benefit from the negotiated price under the Commonwealth Sugar Agreement of £ 43–16–8 a ton for the 1958 crop, as compared with £ 12 before

Table 2

BWI IMPORTS AND EXPORTS (1954)

Colony	Imports (BWI dollars)	Exports (BWI dollars)
Antigua	7,865,976	6,311,731
Barbados	48,610,328	40,396,991
Grenada	8,108,669	8,473,288
Jamaica	178,339,200	147,196,800
St. Kitts	9,928,689	8,777,832
St. Lucia	4,416,561	3,139,862
St. Vincent	5,456,000	4,270,000
Trinidad	249,529,402	261,629,242
British Honduras	11,409,568	7,827,826

NOTE—The difference between exports and imports is made up by the tourist trade, subsidies, and remittances from abroad.

SOURCE—*Trinidad and Tobago Yearbook,* 1957, compiled by Henry Dow, Yuille's Printeries, Port of Spain.

the war.[12] Unfortunately, however, wage gains to the workers have been wiped out by the postwar inflation.[13]

Citrus is, for the moment, in a favorable position. A ten year bulk-purchase agreement has been established between the United Kingdom and Trinidad, Jamaica, and British Honduras, a plan which offers stability for the growth and development of citrus production. British Honduras, however, presents an example of the difficulties involved in tropical agriculture which is important in the understanding of the development of the area. The British Honduras grapefruit has won world prizes for taste and texture, and the crop ripens at a time which gives it a competitive advantage. These advantages are offset by raids on the orchards by tropical insects, parrots, and monkeys. Further, no port facilities exist, resulting in high handling costs. Then, British Honduras is located off the main shipping lanes, increasing the cost of freight charges, as well as expenses of tin cans, crates, and fuel oil, all of which must be imported. Despite the low wage rates afforded the British Honduras worker, the citrus industry cannot compete with California or Florida in production.

Bananas and other agricultural products have similar disadvantages. At one time bananas were the mainstay of Jamaica's economy; then Panama and leafspot diseases destroyed the crops and the industry. A new disease-resistant banana (the lacatan) has been developed, restoring production in Jamaica, and adding considerably to the postwar prosperity not only of Jamaica, but also of Trinidad, Grenada, St. Lucia, and Dominica. Between 1890 and 1929 cocoa was a major Trinidad crop, but the competition from Brazil and the Gold Coast, along with the advance of witches'-broom disease, caused failure. Grenada had a postwar boom in cocoa, though prices have since declined, and the trees were seriously damaged in the 1955 hurricane. BWI cocoa production is 50 per cent below prewar levels. Sea island cotton contributes to the economies of St. Vincent and the Leeward Islands. This cotton has the world's finest long fiber and commands a premium price, yet the supply is very small and can yield only a negligible profit.

Grenada produces 25 per cent of the world's supply of nutmeg, but it is at a cost disadvantage in relation to Java, the major producer. During the Japanese occupation of Java, Grenada nutmeg sold at a premium; however, following the war, prices fell precipitously. Pimento, a minor product of Jamaica, and arrowroot, which is grown in St. Vincent, are the only products in which the BWI has a world monopoly. Even with monopoly advantage, revenue from pimento is small, and in recent years the supply has been reduced by the ravages of disease. As there is but one buyer for arrowroot, an American company, and as other starches serve as an adequate substitute, St. Vincent's monopolistic advantage is reduced to minor importance. Before Brazil became an important competitor, coffee was an important West Indian crop. Now Brazil dominates the market, without any serious challenge from the West Indies. Chicle, the base for the making of chewing gum, is a major source of revenue and employment in British Honduras. However, British Honduras is a high-cost producer, and since the war the development of synthetic gum has depressed the prices and reduced the demand.

Until World War II the agriculture of the British West Indies was oriented to export of cash crops. Food was imported because estate owners did not look upon the low-income local population as a profitable market; also because praedial larceny made food crops unprofitable.[14] Food production has been a peasant enterprise, but has been impeded by lack of skills, capital, and credit, as well as by uneconomic land units, insecure tenure, and poor transport and marketing facilities. Agriculturists point out that it would be more economical to switch marginal cane acreage to food production and reduce imports of high-cost food. Rice-development schemes in British Guiana, British Honduras, and Jamaica are moves in this direction. Estate owners are being persuaded by departments of agriculture to consider the cow as a source of meat and dairy products rather than only as a manure producer. Even if the local fishing industry were better organized and perhaps could give higher yields, the Caribbean does not produce bountiful catches, and even fish is an import.

On the average, agricultural production has increased 8 per cent a year for the past ten years, but as output has yet to recover from World War II lows, this progress is not a net gain. Commenting on the current status of agriculture in the BWI, A. L. Jolley of the Trinidad College of Tropical Agriculture, states that since World War II only the sugar industry has improved its position while all other sectors have lagged in development. Describing BWI agriculture as "strikingly inefficient," he places the blame primarily on poor management. Estates specializing in tree crops are undermanaged, carry too much labor, and have insufficient equipment. Jolley concludes that unless agricultural efficiency improves, the average wage for agricultural labor will remain about $500 a year.[15]

Industry.—The predominant labor group in the West Indies is in agriculture. Industry's contribution to total revenue is small and to employment opportunities still smaller. British Honduras and British Guiana forests contain valuable timber; with mahogany as the main resource for British Honduras, and greenheart, purpleheart, and walaba as minor exports of British Guiana. The demand for mahogany is subject to wide fluctuations; it enjoyed a short post-war boom as a useful material in the production of television cabinets. Tropical forests are not stands of timber but isolated individual trees amid thick tangles of bush. Thus, logging costs are high and transport costs through roadless swamps and sand dunes even higher. The huge expanses of rain forest do not yield large amounts of merchantable timber, and therefore the logging industry remains of limited importance. Oil has become a major industry which provides an above-average BWI standard of living for the island of Trinidad and is therefore coveted by the laborers. Crude-oil production for 1955 was 24,896,000 barrels, and the industry employed 21,000 workers.[16] Bauxite is a major revenue producer for British Guiana, and in more recent years for Jamaica. Again, however, the employment opportunities are relatively small. Jamaica possesses the greatest bauxite deposit in the world, an estimated known quantity of 315,000,000 metric tons. The British Caribbean supplies 80 per cent of the bauxite ore for the North American aluminum industry.[17] The fact that the bulk of the free world supply of bauxite comes from these two sources has, more than any other factor, reawakened world interest in the BWI. There is also gold and diamond mining in British Guiana and gypsum mining in Jamaica, but these are lesser industries. An American company has secured a 37,000-acre manganese mining lease in British Guiana and ore shipments are to begin in 1959.[18] Because of the lack of resources or internal markets, manufacturing industries are not important in the West Indies. Beyond these fundamental limitations there are inadequate, unreliable, and expensive power supplies, poor public utilities, inadequate roads and harbor facilities, high freight rates, lethargy of the government bureacracy, and the shortage of skilled labor. Despite these overwhelming handicaps light manufacturing got a start during World War II. In a modest way the BWI fabricates shoes, clothing, foodstuffs, and construction materials. The most hopeful development on the economic front is the postwar tourist boom. Whereas prewar tourist trade was negligible, 551,000 American tourists spent $117,000,000 in the BWI in 1956.[19] Revenues from the tourist industry are now second only to those of sugar in Jamaica and Barbados. With the increase of prosperity and leisure time in the United States and the expansion of air routes, the West Indies are destined to become the Riviera of America. This development will undoubtedly have its effect on the trade-union movement through increased employment in the tourist industry.

Population and Unemployment.—The limited natural resources of the area become more meaningful when measured against the population pressures. The British West Indies have a population of more than three and a half million. It is growing at the rate of about 2½ per cent per annum, doubling every 33 years. Bearing in mind that it is not industrial, and that more than half of the land is not arable, the BWI has one of the highest population densities in the world. Arthur Lewis estimates that a density of 60 persons per square mile would support the entire population at European peasant standards. The Leeward Islands have 257 persons per square mile; Trinidad and Tobago, 282 per square mile; Jamaica, 294 per square mile; the Windward Islands, 306 per square mile, and Barbados, the most impressive, 1,159 per square mile (now estimated at 1,400).[20] A survey by the Foundation for Scientific Research in Surinam and the Netherland Antilles estimated the total available area of potentially arable land per person as follows: Barbados 0.3 acres; Jamaica 0.5 acres; Leeward Islands 0.55 acres; Trinidad and Tobago, 0.6 acres; Windwards 0.55 acres. To provide an adequate diet for one person, two and a half acres is considered a minimum.[21]

Table 3

AREAS, POPULATIONS OF BRITISH CARIBBEAN DEPENDENCIES

Territory	Total Area (sq. miles)	Population (mid-1956 estimate)
Barbados	166	228,000
British Guiana	83,000	499,000
British Honduras	8,867	82,000
Jamaica and Dependencies	4,677	1,577,410
Leeward Islands:		
Antigua	171	53,000
St. Kitts-Nevis	153	54,800
Trinidad and Tobago	1,980	743,000
Windward Islands:		
Dominica	305	63,800
Grenada	133	89,100
St. Lucia	238	89,000
St. Vincent	150	77,600

SOURCE—British Information Services.

During the 1930's, the time in which workers became conscious of themselves as a group, the pressure of population became acute. First, outward migration was cut off, and many former migrants were forced to return. Second, improved sanitation, medical care, and, following the war, malaria control drastically reduced the death rate. Agriculture had already reached the limit of its capacity to support the population. Further, the number of people employed in agriculture is slowly declining as mechanization has increased. Between 1947 and 1954 the population of Barbados increased by 30,000—a greater number than that of the entire already existing labor force of its sugar industry. The head of the Industrial Development and Welfare Corporation of Antigua told the writer that 1,100 new jobs had to be created every year just to prevent the already seriously high unemployment figure from rising further in a one-crop economy. St. Kitts-Nevis, with a population of 30,000, offers 7,000 jobs during harvest in the sugar industry, which, again, is the only industry of that island. With a population growth of 1,000 per year, the labor force will double itself every seven years. Commenting on the population problem in British Guiana, the Venn Report stated that 30 per cent more jobs would have to be created within twelve years just to maintain the status quo of the present unemployment figure.[22] The World Bank's report on Jamaica estimated that 100,000 jobs would have to be found by 1962 to keep the status quo; and jobs for 180,000 to 210,000 would have to be found to reduce unemployment by 5 per cent.[23]

In St. Lucia and Trinidad and Tobago there is some idle land, it is true. There are swamps that could be reclaimed in many colonies. British Honduras and British Guiana have large areas of underdeveloped land—back in the bush where rain forests and jungles are problems, and where travel is by rivers only. Possibly these areas can be developed. More than offsetting these possibilities, however, is the large population, which is getting larger and at the same time demanding higher standards of living. Already there are too many people engaged in the estate and peasant agriculture for the good of the land, or for that of the general economy. British Guiana, for example, has a relatively low population density, to which many look for potential population-pressure relief. However, British Guiana's narrow coastal belt of agricultural land is already overcrowded, with only the interior left with its unproductive rain forests. Underdeveloped coastal lands may possibly provide employment for its rapidly growing population if large capital requirements can be met. An enigma still, the agricultural potential of British Honduras will remain unknown until soil studies are made.

Since the land will not support the overflowing population, the question is obvious of where the people will earn their living. First, the result of population pressures has been to force women out of agricultural employment. Second, although statistics are unavailable or at best fragmentary, unemployment is endemic. The extent of unemployment can be reckoned from the following estimates of employment opportunities in Jamaica:[24]

Per Cent of Labor Force	Number of Weeks Employed Each Year
35	11
36	12–27
17	28–39
9	40–51

Third, overpopulation can be measured by the amount of disguised unemployment. In Jamaica, for example, 16 per cent of the labor force is in domestic service. Servants at the top who are higher up on the wage scale themselves hire servants, who, in turn, hire servants who are on the lower rung of the wage scale. "Yard boys," porters, and others doing menial work are in abundance. According to union officers, there are stores in Port of Spain so overstaffed with shop clerks that wages are not paid, except in the form of commissions on sales. The sidewalks of capital cities are crowded with peddlers. Men and women—even children—"scuffle" for subsistence living, which includes activities such as peddling small wares, begging, running errands, and petty theft. Country lanes on all the islands are lined with shacks or "stores" whose inventories consist of a few cans of corned beef, a crate of salt fish, and a sack of rice.

Fourth, a large measure of the population pressure is the result of the growth of cities. The capital city contains about half the population of each of the colonies (except for Kingston, Jamaica), and such city populations are not justified in an agricultural nonindustrial area. In many places they are functionless in terms of the modern urban centers of the Western world. Although some colonial officers condemn the "abandonment of the land" (which also still remains overcrowded) and call for improved amenities in the rural areas to stop the "drift to the cities," the fact remains that people are being crowded out of the rural areas and therefore congregate in the cities simply because there is no alternative.[25]

The problems created by rapid growth of the urban proletariat have been described as follows:[26]

In Kingston, Jamaica, for instance, hundreds upon hundreds of families live crowded side by side in minute shacks made of old car bodies, pieces of boarding, sometimes just cardboard. In some of the slum areas where the people are squatters upon private land there is neither water nor light nor roads. The inhabitants live mainly by crime, preying upon the life of the urban area proper. Few residents of Kingston would go unaccompanied into the slums. The police are most reluctant to penetrate into them, and usually when they go at all they go in force. Very little attempt has been made by missionaries or social workers to touch these people who have become too intractable a problem for anybody to tackle. . . . In the slums even small children fight with knives and stones and pieces of broken glass. Quarrels which develop with lightning speed into quite serious disturbances are very frequent. Crime of every kind is rife.

The pressure of population on limited resources is the most crucial social, economic, and political problem in the British West Indies. The solution is neither immediate nor easy. Students of the problems agree that emigration is not the answer. The United States Farm Labor Recruitment program and the postwar influx of West Indians to the United Kingdom are insignificant in comparison with the magnitude of the problem. Emigration to the relatively undeveloped British Guiana and British Honduras would be of little assistance, and, moreover, these colonies tend to restrict immigration from the rest of the colonies. Relatively prosperous, Trinidad and Jamaica also restrict immigration from other West Indian territories. North, South, and Central America, Cuba, and the Dominican Republic curtail entrance of Negroes under one pretext or another. The possibility of creating jobs through industrialization and the limiting of further population growth by contraceptives will be discussed in the chapter on trade-union policies.

Race, Class Structure, Social Attitudes

Racial and Ethnic Groups.—Union development in the British West Indies has taken its own course based on the agricultural nature of the economy, the estate system, and the fact that most inhabitants are the descendants of African slaves. The attitudes resulting from the slave economy have had a place in the social, economic, and political development of the area. The largest racial group is Negro; the second largest East Indian. In British Guiana the East Indians are by a slight margin the largest group, and in Trinidad the second to the largest, but in most other colonies there are few East Indians. From the standpoint of economic power and social status, the most important minority is the European white group. There are also Chinese, who constitute a large group in Trinidad and Jamaica; and Syrians, Sephardic Jews, and Portuguese. (The Portuguese, because they came as indentured servants and primarily from the island of Madeira, are not considered as "white" by the local people, nor are they considered as European and are not so counted in the census.) In British Honduras and British Guiana there are indigenous (American) Indian tribes who lead a separate tribal existence and do not take part in the main stream of West Indian life.

Table 4

DISTRIBUTION BY RACIAL ORIGIN AT LAST CENSUS (1946)
(in thousands)

	Total	African	East Indian	American Indian	European	Mixed	Others
Barbados	192.8	148.9	0.1	—	9.8	33.8	0.1
British Guiana	375.7	143.4	163.4	16.3	11.0	37.7	3.9
British Honduras	59.2	22.7	1.4	10.0	2.3	18.4	4.4
Jamaica and Dependencies (1943)	1,249.9	971.4	21.4	—	16.0	232.2	8.8
Leeward Islands:							
Antigua	41.8	35.4	—	—	0.7	5.4	0.2
	14.3	13.3	—	—	0.1	0.9	—
St. Kitts-Nevis	46.2	40.0	0.1	—	0.9	5.1	0.1
	6.5	5.7	—	—	—	0.8	—
Trinidad and Tobago	558.0	261.5	195.7	—	15.3	78.8	6.7
Windward Islands:							
Dominica	47.6	11.9	—	—	0.1	35.5	0.1
Grenada	72.4	53.3	3.5	—	0.6	14.8	0.2
St. Lucia	70.1	40.6	2.6	—	0.3	26.3	0.2
St. Vincent	61.6	45.0	1.8	—	1.9	12.6	0.3

SOURCE—British Information Services.

Significant to the West Indian order are those of mixed origin. The "colored people" as they are called in the West Indies, are principally from white European and Negro heritage, though there are many of varied racial origin. Race differentiation is difficult to define because of the integral relation of race to class to social attitude. As a result the statistics on the size of the "colored" population are not reliable.

Class Structure.—To a large degree racial distinctions are related to differences in economic and social position.[27] European "white people" are at the apex of the pyramid because of their ownership of the estates, control of commerce, dominance in the professions, and high positions in civil service and the colonial administration, as well as the historical development from the slave economic-social system. The term "white" symbolizes the power and prestige derived from European culture and social status. The supposed superiority was assumed and often emulated. However, as will be further commented upon, the white race, as such, is rapidly losing its dominant position in politics, and even in the social structure. The change has been more rapid since the end of World War II, though psychologically "white" remains the measure of "good" or the "best" in the minds of many West Indians. The Negro workers are at the base of the class structure. These are mostly unskilled field hands living at a subsistence level, poorly educated, and with values and a way of life generally at variance with European standards. Hence, in the social concept, "black" became associated with "primitive," or "African" with poverty and superstition. Between the top and the bottom is the "colored" middle class who hold the clerical, professional, and junior administrative positions. This class, educated and with European values, aspires to things "white" and disdains things associated with "black." The East Indians of Trinidad and British Guiana are mostly field hands, though in recent years there has arisen an East Indian middle class. Other minority groups tend to lead a separate social existence and tend toward economic specialization, though in general there has been a loosening of the barriers since the war. The West Indian thinks of the Jew as the merchant, the Syrian as the dealer in dry goods, the Portuguese as the operator of the rum shop, and the Chinese as the owner of the corner grocery. The West Indian conglomeration of races, as in Trinidad, cannot yet be called a melting pot, but rather a bowl of the still unmixed salad.

Social Attitudes.—Compared to most of the world, race relations in the BWI are good. There is no Jim Crow. There are no discriminatory laws based on race, and people with a degree of Negro heritage are not all lumped together under the single classification of Negro as in the United States. At first glance, the visitor observes people of every hue and race occupying all kinds of jobs, holding all levels of political office, and participating in every facet of West Indian life. Yet, this first impression is misleading, for racial and social discrimination in the West Indies exists, but is highly evanescent. There are no signs, "For Whites Only," for the basis of discrimination is not "black versus white." Instead, everyone subtly discriminates and is subtly discriminated against.[28]

Of all groups the "white" upper class has the strongest racial and class feelings; although they do not say so publicly, many of them privately declare that the Negro race is inherently inferior and that the English race is predestined to rule. There were some, interviewed by the writer in 1953–54, who claimed that the English upper classes are biologically superior to other classes even among the English "race" itself. The concepts of race, nationality, and class become confused when the West Indian "white" man proceeds to explain why the German or French "races" are incapable of ruling properly, when the Australians, New Zealanders, and Americans who have been guided by the English "race" are capable of self-government. There were some who believed they were still carrying the "white man's burden," the defenders of civilization against impossible odds. This group, a recognized minority, felt that the home government had erred in granting an increased measure of self-government in the colonies. Using Haiti as the example, they predicted self-government would end in corruption and chaos. Further, they believed that self-government and the increase of trade-union strength would drive the white man from the islands, and it was only the white man who could save the Negroes from themselves. The reasoning of this group is not new, and is perhaps the reasoning that prevented the installation of an educational system at the termination of slavery.

There were those from other racial groups, and even some whites who were critical of the attitudes of the white upper class, and considered them detrimental to the welfare of the BWI. George Woodcock, a member of the Constitutional Commission in British Guiana, 1953–54, typified this point of view. He believed that the attitude of the white West Indians was a basic cause of labor unrest. In brief, he criticized them for class snobbery; for calling England "home" (even though many of them and their families had been in the colonies for several generations); for having no loyalties to the colonies; for being educated, vacationing, and retiring in England.[29] A similar position was taken by the Archbishop Alan John Knight, of the West Indies, when he said that while poverty and squalor had intensified popular revolt against the existing order in the colony (British Guiana) the rebellion itself was directed mainly against the grave abuses of wealth and privilege. He said:

Upper and middle classes nurse no strong grievance because they do not suffer unduly and often stand to benefit from the present system. And because many of the more fortunate folks have no knowledge of the conditions under which others have to live, they sometimes find it difficult to understand the resentment towards them felt and sometimes shown by their less fortunate neighbors. The situation is further aggravated by the existence among us of select clubs and associations which either by their constitution or by the whim of members are restricted in membership to one race, class, or color.[30]

Consistent with his class beliefs, the West Indian employer when dealing with labor finds it difficult to acknowledge that he is bargaining with his equal, and is often convinced that he can better serve the interests of the worker than the union representative can. Rottenberg summarized the white employer's viewpoint as follows:

Employers are 'cultured' and workers are 'primitive.' Employers have created a father image of themselves and believe that they know what is good for the people; workers are children, irresponsible, indolent and prodigal, who prefer leisure and rum to worthy material goods. Therefore a paternal relationship between workers and planters in which the power of decision is a monopoly of the 'better' classes is a condition set for a stable society and well being of the workers.[31]

Some of the interviewed planters regarded themselves as a martyred class. In the view of one such estate owner, the colonial government is against the planters because it is afraid of the peasants while politicians win votes by attacking the planters. Estate owners, he felt, are lethargic because of unfair taxation, because of lack of credit or roads, absence of marketing facilities and price supports, and because of the undependable pilfering laborers. "The English and the peasants are imperialists who are milking the estate owners," he said with grim finality.

Until recently those of the colored middle class generally sought to identify themselves with the white upper class. In emulation of the whites, they too declared that anyone darker than themselves was inherently inferior. As a consequence there developed a complicated and subtle social structure based primarily on the shade of color and the family background.[32] As a Jamaican union leader and politician described this situation to the writer, the West Indies suffer from pigmentation discrimination rather than from absolute racial discrimination. Along with the social structure, a job hierarchy emerged which has tended to be based upon the shade of the skin, the darker laborer at the bottom, and the white employer and colonial administrator at the top. People of various hues of brown skin hold the clerical, office, and professional jobs. Social status and membership in social and recreational clubs are based upon the delicate nuances of shade on the one hand and family background coupled with economic success on the other.[33] The result of this social structure gives the West Indian middle class its dominant personality types, namely the aggressive, often even belligerent, or the coldly correct, distant, and formal personality; or the excessively friendly, insecure person desperately seeking the recognition he feels is due him.[34]

The attitude of this colored middle class is changing, however, because though the "white" people still hold the better jobs and receive higher pay for comparable work, the trained and educated darker-skinned professional people and administrators are no longer willing to accept second-best positions, when they are

qualified. Also, social distinctions which have tended to be structured by shade-color stratification are breaking down as the
middle class demands admission into clubs on the basis of education and income, rather than color and family history. Further, it
is important to note that there are now more "brown"-skinned
people than there are middle-class jobs.[35] Educated to European
attitudes and values, these people will not accept the indignity of
field-hand status or of living among the working class, whose way
of life is entirely different from theirs. The problem is further
aggravated by the fact that many of the lower class darker-skinned
children are receiving senior Cambridge Certificates (high school
diplomas) which, according to tradition, entitle the holders to
civil-service or shop-assistant positions. Among the lower middle
class which is struggling to find its way up from the working
class, the racial and class hatred is most intense.

On the other hand, workers have no really strong racial or class
feelings. The consensus among those interviewed was that workers
are so downtrodden, and the social hierarchy so marked, that the
feelings that stimulate class hatred do not influence them. This is
not to imply that the Negro workers have no feelings of class or
race, but rather that their resentment is not strong enough to be
the basis of organized protest. Social anthropologists have observed that West Indian workers make a personality adjustment
to this almost impossible situation with a protective camouflage
of withdrawal and passivity, a behavior which the employers
usually describe as inherent laziness and lack of ambition.[36] It
might be concluded that workers are too passive to hate; too
submissive to aspire to higher status in their society.[37]

That the West Indian workers react to the static social and
economic status with excessive absenteeism and tardiness, lack
of initiative, and stealing, rather than seeking positive solutions
was pointed out by Simey.[38] Madeline Kerr, a social anthropologist
who studied three Jamaican communities, attributes the absence
of strong resentment against racial discrimination to the ambiv-
alent attitude toward color found in the West Indian worker.
That is, although there are moments when such a person attributes
all his troubles to the domination of the society by the white
people, at another time, in another mood, the same person blames
himself and his fellow Negroes for what he considers their inherent

inferiority. These conflicting, sometimes contradictory, attitudes tend to neutralize each other, leaving the person confused and inactive.[39] The working class suffers from superstition, lack of education and opportunity, along with the psychological handicap of believing that things white are, in fact, superior. As a result, the Negro working class tends toward timidity, malice, and prejudice, resulting in irrational and unreliable behavior.[40]

Despite the absence of a strong racial and class feeling in daily life, in the field of politics the topics of class and color have become major campaign issues. Where universal adult suffrage is five to ten years old, and where most of the working population is semiliterate, campaign issues are necessarily reduced to the lowest common denominator, which in the West Indies is race and color. Demagogic Negroes campaign against both white and colored politicians. An ebony skin becomes a political asset, as 90 per cent of the electorate have dark pigmentation. Lighter skinned politicians may have exploited the color issue, yet at the outset they are at a statistical disadvantage. It is likely that the illiterate worker is not fooled by the wild promises of the demagogue. Instead, workers support irresponsible politicians in order to strike fear into the hearts of the colonial administrators, thereby obtaining improved government services. Henriques, an English sociologist and native of Jamaica, observes that though prejudice exists, there has been no rally to the black banner.[41]

Since the use of the scapegoat in politics is a strategy in channelizing emotions, Madeline Kerr asks why the wealthy whites have not been made a scapegoat in Jamaican politics, particularly as the contrast between the riches of the few and the poverty of the many is so painfully obvious. Two answers are offered: first, that politicians and many others blame a mysterious "they" for the ills of the country, and a vague "they" does not crystallize into a solid scapegoat; and second, the long road of hopeless inevitable poverty, so accepted as a part of life, has created an "every man for himself" philosophy—a philosophy of the jungle—which prevents effective collective action against either real or imagined enemies.[42] This attitude, born of poverty, has had its effect on the development of trade unions. Many observers believe that the racial issues in politics will die down when the demagogue is unable to carry out his promises, or demonstrates his ability as an administrator; that then there will emerge a responsible type of politician who will honestly represent the interests of the working-class electorate, regardless of racial characteristics. The political success of Norman Manley in Jamaica, Grantley Adams in Barbados, and Eric Williams in Trinidad, all of whom stress the unity of West Indians as a national group, suggests that racial issues will not become major political weapons.

In British Guiana and in Trinidad, however, there is a special and separate racial problem, resulting from the disharmony between the East Indians and the Negroes.[43] The East Indians, who came to the West Indies between 1851 and 1917 as indentured servants, now outnumber the Negroes in British Guiana and make up one-third of the population in Trinidad. Educated Negroes whose cultural ties are with Europe expressed a fear when interviewed that the East Indian with his Eastern culture would change the colonies. In recent years a powerful East Indian middle class developed. Following the independence of India and Pakistan many East Indians hoped to turn British Guiana and Trinidad into East-Indian-influenced states. The underlying conflict between Negroes and East Indians, ever present, manifests itself in different ways—for example, the Negro group was against, and succeeded in obstructing, public subsidies to Hindu and Moslem schools, although it encouraged subsidies for Anglican and Catholic schools. Frequently East Indians have difficulty in securing positions as teachers. In British Guiana the middle-class Negro has long dominated most civil-service positions, and now is resentful of the new East Indian middle class which is edging into these jobs. Another source of conflict is cremation, an East Indian custom, which is illegal in Guiana and Trinidad. Still another is linguistic: only since the disturbances of 1953 have government communications been made available in the languages of the East Indians.

A cultural difference, often resented by members of both groups, derives from the attempt of middle-class colored people to maintain social appearances. They are therefore debt-ridden, while the East Indian lives in poverty, stinting himself with amazing self-discipline, often even going hungry in order to accumulate anything from a meager to an often large savings fund. The colored middle class fears what it regards as the alienation of the land, as the East Indians are purchasing more and more land with their savings. The race-ethnic situation is further complicated in both British Guiana and Trinidad by the national rivalry between Pakistan and India, which finds its counterpart locally in the growing conflict between Hindu and Moslem groups.

Superficially, the Negro working class gets along well with the East Indian working class. Actually, however, the two groups do not intermingle. Negro workers resent the "coolies," who, they claim, undermined wage rates after the ending of slavery. This resentment is a basic consideration in the study of trade unionism in the area, and has resulted in separate growths of the unions. The East Indian's frugality, his willingness to toil, are markedly different from the pattern of work of the West Indian Negro. Though conflict exists between the middle classes, there is little open conflict between the workers of each national group, because the Negroes have left the sugar fields, and are employed only in the higher-paying cane-cutting jobs (the East Indian lacks the physical stamina for this heavy labor). This has resulted in a division of labor, the East Indians working as field hands, and the Negroes as factory maintenance and service men in the towns.

Thus the antagonism between Negro and East Indian is, for the most part, latent. Population gains of the latter group together with growing nationalism, however, could increase racial and national tensions. Politicians might exploit dormant antagonisms for personal gain. At present in Trinidad the successful political party, the People's National Movement, stresses West Indian nationalism and identification with place of birth, rather than place of ancestral origin. Some Trinidad politicians continue to appeal to racial interests as a campaign tactic. The question remains open as to whether all Trinidadians will come to regard themselves as West Indians. The problem is more acute in British Guiana where Cheddi Jagan's People's Progress party has solid East Indian support whereas other groups remain politically divided. (See chapter III on British Guiana.) Responsible union leaders appeal to the unity of all workers, regardless of race or national origin, though they readily concede that this appeal is difficult to put across.

Working Conditions on Estates

It is remarkable that despite distances between these islands, with communication fragmentary until recently, there are genuine similarities in the social and economic patterns between them.[44] These can best be explained by the common background born of the British plantation economy with a labor force of slaves. The estate system of agriculture and the society around it continue to dominate, as the sharecropping and independent peasant proprietorship system substitutes are not sufficiently far-reaching to have altered the ways of life. Nevertheless, the stereotyped concept of the sugar estate is true only of the islands of Barbados, St. Kitts, and Antigua, where 70 per cent of the land is controlled by 0.1 per cent of the people. This large-scale land control does not apply to three-fourths of the people of the West Indies. Instead there are all kinds of employer-employee, landlord-tenant, landowner-sharecropper relationships.[45] Further, no generalizations can be made concerning estate size or the extent of absentee ownership because of the wide variety of individual situations, from the small family-owned and -operated estates of Barbados to the twelve estates of Booker Brothers of British Guiana. As might be expected, the smaller estates and the family-operated ones have better labor relations than the big estates owned by absentee corporations. Even as to size, however, it is difficult to generalize, for the small estates, particularly in Grenada, have had their share of labor disturbances. But it is also true that estates which house workers on the land have more difficulty than those which recruit labor from nearby villages. Owners, managers, union leaders, and government officials are unanimous in stating the desirability of creating independent villages apart from the estate land.

On estates where the workers are housed, the employee-employer relationship is quasi-feudal. By tradition, from the days of slavery, the worker is entitled to a "house spot," usually supplying his own "prefab" hut. At the time of slavery the "great house" occupied the center, the highest point on the hill. Beyond were the shacks or huts of the slaves—first the "head man's" abode with a garden spot, and then the homes of the others, according to the hierarchy. Today, as then, a garden spot, livestock grazing rights, and the right to sell manure to the estate, as well as firewood-gathering rights, are included among the nonmonetary benefits of estate workers. A survey of working conditions in the sugar industry of Jamaica, for example, indicated that about 40 per cent of the labor force was housed on estate land and that the average garden spot was one-third of an acre per worker.[46]

Born of slavery, developed through tradition, these rights, though they exist, are not clearly defined, and as a result lead to abuses on both sides. The system was based on paternalism, and since the worker is in the weaker bargaining position the element of paternalism is reënforced. Discharge from a job not only means loss of position, but of house, garden spot, and whatever small side income the worker has earned from the land. Some estate owners assured the writer that they seldom fired anyone. By custom it was nearly impossible, and therefore the owner was forced to carry the lazy, the aged, the infirm; and some independent farmers using the rent-free land merely masqueraded as workers for the estate. One estate owner on the island of St. Vincent assured the writer that the only residents of his estate whom he ordered off the land were "sweet men" (young men who play gigolo to the women field hands), because the women fought over the men. On the other hand, union officers were as positive that employers frequently abused their power as landlords in order to victimize union members and to dispossess the useless aged and infirm, who often had given the best years of their lives in service to the estate.

In point of fact, probably it is not the actual abuse of the right to dispossess workers from their homes and garden spots that is at issue, but rather the possibility of arbitrary dismissal which strikes fear into the minds of the workers. The situation is further intensified when the owner or manager of the estate is also the local justice of the peace. In some colonies the estate owner holds "estate court" in which he serves as the arbitrator of family and neighborhood quarrels. On one estate in British Guiana which the writer visited, there were ten thousand employees housed on estate grounds. In answer to the inquiry who was the mayor, or the justice of the peace, or in charge of community affairs, the manager replied that all these offices were under his jurisdiction.

Hence, the worker finds himself confronted with an employer who is also the landlord and the law.

During the time of slavery, labor was scarce and the purchase price for the slave was high. As a consequence, the manager felt at least a monetary compulsion to care for the basic subsistence needs of the slave. The custom developed that anyone born on the estate was part of the work force; custom entitled these workers to share in the job opportunities, however limited, and in the nonwage benefits as well. Labor is no longer scarce, and estate owners are therefore saddled with a surplus working force constituting hidden fixed charges in the form of special rights, even when actual wage payment may be low.[47] Since the estate owner supplies assorted community services which would normally be taken care of by local government, a labor surplus without alternative employment opportunities increases the employer's cost regardless of the amount of wages or the inadequacy of the nonmonetary benefits. Hidden labor costs include social services and the high-cost labor of the aged or infirm, whom the estate management is reluctant to order off the grounds. Union pressure for higher wages makes it impossible for management to carry marginal workers and has caused owners to join with the unions in requesting government-sponsored social-security programs.[48]

Workers, moreover, are not compelled to work all the time on the estate (especially as there are not that many jobs) and some devote more time to their own crops than to those of the estates; thus in effect they are squatters. In British Guiana many workers are acquiring sizeable land for rice cultivation, and in Trinidad there are workers who sharecrop marginal cane fields. The growing and harvest seasons coincide, for the estate crops and the garden crops. Therefore when the labor is most needed, employers are often faced with a shortage, for the worker is harvesting his own crops. For this reason bonuses are given for full-time work during the harvest. In expectation of such labor shortages, the estate owner solves the problem by encouraging a labor surplus on and around the estates. An overseer on one estate explained the informal nature of the work arrangement as follows: there is no work scheduling; work is shared by whoever shows up each day, though estate residents have priority over nonresidents; a system of bonuses assures steady work during the crop season, but the estate does not promise regular employment. This situation was demonstrated when our inspection party encountered a gang of workers who complained to the supervisor that they had walked "aback" (toward the jungle) some five miles only to find that there was no work for them that day. The overseer apologized, explaining that the management had erred in the work-scheduling plans, that they were further behind in the cane burning than was anticipated. Within the framework of estate operation, the workers had no grievance.

The friction of the gentleman planter still prevails. It does not contribute to good relations between estate management and labor. Often the owner turns the business of the estate over to a town lawyer, and a hired manager is in charge of functional management of the estate. The manager, in turn, delegates authority to the overseers, which is then passed on to the headman and to the drivers. This practice is long rooted in the absentee ownership of the slave days, and is almost as inefficient today as it was then. It is inefficient as a business operation and dangerous as a system of authority. The driver, before emancipation, was a slave, yet he was the power over the fields, with the right to assign jobs. Today the driver can still assign the best and easiest tasks to his friends. Workers who incur his wrath may find their task rates arbitrarily slashed, may be told that the work is unsatisfactory, and that it has to be done over again before pay can be collected. The kick-back racket is a universal evil. To be assured of steady work at fair task rates, the worker contributes garden produce to his supervisors or gives his free time working in their garden spots.[49] Women field hands frequently gain job security by living with the drivers or headmen. Some drivers have as many as five or six women contributing to their affluence. In extreme cases, job security is bought by contributing a daughter to the estate manager as a concubine, another derivative of slave society.

To a large extent the labor problem in the BWI grows out of poor supervision. The Venn Report pointed out that the future of labor relations, and perhaps the future of British Guiana itself, was in the hands of the overseers, men who lacked experience in either the tropics or in agriculture, who were not an integral part of the society of the country, and who were unaware of the racial issues and the religious needs of the people. The report also observed that the low pay, the humdrum way of life, the end of past high living on the estates, did not make supervisory jobs sufficiently attractive to bring in good-caliber men.[50] Spokesmen for the large sugar estates of Jamaica, Trinidad, and British Guiana complained that they have been unable to secure qualified supervisors from England since the end of the war. Further, they attributed much of their labor trouble to the poor qualifications of the employees from England. Socialism and social security in the British Isles, they felt, had caused the more competent young Englishmen to lose interest in furthering the Empire, and therefore the "natives" would take over by default.[51] One personnel officer went further, maintaining that the West Indies were always a backwater of the Empire, and that most of the able men went to Southeast Asia where opportunities were more enticing. It was his belief that poor supervision was the long-standing cause of labor unrest on the large estates. None of those interviewed, however, seemed ready to reconcile themselves to the need for solving the problem by training West Indians as supervisors.

The nature of agricultural employment, coupled with the general aversion to manual labor, results in an unusual pattern of employment. Agricultural employment is seasonal. There is, therefore, a group of workers who are regularly unemployed. While year-around work is provided for some estate workers, many work from a five- to a seven-month year, depending on the crop. This seasonal and casual nature of employment contributes to general internal migration. The uprooting of meager homes; the drifting from one estate to another; the shifting between the capital city of the colony and estates of birth,[52] all contribute to a vague, uneasy sense of not belonging to any particular place.

Mechanization of tropical agriculture has not progressed much. Most work is still done with the hoe and the cutlass. Since manual labor (particularly on the sugar estates) is largely associated with slave labor, field hands have the lowest status in the (working class) social scale, as already pointed out. Negroes seek to improve their status by emulating the pattern of the whites—avoiding physical labor. Paradoxically, therefore, a labor shortage exists hand in hand with an overwhelming surplus.

In a survey of the unemployed in Antigua, an island which suffers from wholesale unemployment, it was found that:

Most of the unemployed expressed reservations with respect to the kind of work they would accept. Only 20 per cent said they would accept 'any kind of work.' Only one unemployed person in 20 was looking for work in agriculture. When unemployed persons were asked specifically whether they would accept cane field employment, only 1 in 3 replied in the affirmative. . . . By and large, the survey confirmed that the people of Antigua attempt to escape work in the fields by holding out for other jobs for which they consider themselves qualified.[53]

The distaste for field work, the desire to share the limited existing employment opportunities, the need to attend to the worker's own garden crop, and tradition have resulted in the short work week. A survey made by the Antigua Labor Department showed that most workers on sugar estates work four days or less each week. Figures submitted by the main cane-growing estates showed that in 1951 cane cutters worked an average of 30.5 days per man out of a possible 120 working days during the height of the crop. The average number of days worked per week by field workers varied from 2.5 to 4.6 days in the harvesting season and from 2.7 to 3.7 in the out-of-crop period.[54] A survey of 5,000 field workers made by the Jamaica Department of Labor in 1944 showed that the average number of days per week worked by field hands throughout the year was 3½.[55] On a sugar estate visited in British Guiana the estate manager reported that of the ten thousand residents on the estate, so few were on the job that he had to import labor from neighboring communities. The residents did not want to work the regular full week. "Too busy farming their own land or sleeping," was his surmise, but he added that technological change would soon end the shortage. Commenting on the pattern of work in British Guiana, the Venn Report noted that more men asked for work than there were jobs available during the middle of the week, but the factories were short of cane requirements by 26 per cent on Mondays, 13 per cent on Tuesdays, and 52 per cent on Saturdays. There were 3.66 days per week of employment available for male employees and these employees actually worked 2.3 days per week during the year.[56]

In the typical work week on the island of St. Lucia, the worker uses Monday to mark out the size of the task he will do during the week. Tuesday, Wednesday, and Thursday are work days. Friday, Saturday, and Sunday are given over to the cultivation of the worker's own crop, to the care of livestock, or fishing, or to a little "spreeing" and leisure. Major Orde Browne, in his discussion of the pattern of work, wrote: "Part-time employment is very common, and while it is in some cases a hardship, in others it accords well with the needs of the worker. Men who have a plot on which to grow a portion of their requirements may well appreciate a position where they earn wages three days a week and till their own ground for the remainder of the time." [57] In addition to these reasons for voluntary unemployment, Madeline Kerr indicates that workers generally believe that their employers derive large profits from their labor and are cheating them, hence they should do as little as possible. The workers, often pictured as the "gay" West Indians, are far from being compliant and servile. Voluntary unemployment is not only convenient for their own gardening and leisure needs, but the low productivity is their passive weapon against superior economic forces.[58] The decision not to work, as well as the choice of a particular kind of work, expresses, to a degree, personal freedom and limited power. The organization of trade unions, still of recent vintage, may change this attitude.

The rates of pay vary from colony to colony and even from one estate to another. Wage rates are calculated by the day rather than the hour. Whenever possible wages are paid according to the tasks which are regarded to be one day's work. The nature of the tasks to be performed was established during slavery. During a hundred years, when the worker was not able to bargain over the task rate, he was able to beat down the standards until most tasks could be done in four to six hours. To summarize the pattern of agricultural employment: many workers are employed during a five- to seven-month growing season, the typical work week is about three days, and a day's task is from four to six hours.

The wage rate fluctuates according to the age, sex, and physical fitness of the worker. In British Guiana the breakdown is as follows: The workers of the "Creole" gang are very young or very old, performing light work; the "weed" gang is made up of able-bodied women and boys, the "shovel-and-fork" gang uses the stronger grown men. The estate laborer is neither a full-fledged wage earner nor an independent farmer. On the one hand he refuses regular steady work, and on the other he lacks the means of becoming a full-time independent farmer. The dichotomy of his existence leaves him a divided man—he is not fully conscious of his greatest wants and difficult to organize into unions.

Social Disorganization

Poverty, underemployment, estate agriculture, and class-color stratification reënforce one another to produce social disorganization,[59] particularly among the working class. Social disorganization, in turn, is important to an understanding of trade-union development as well as the problems of self-government and economic development. Social anthropologists and social psychologists have documented in detail the extent of social disorganization in the BWI, but for an appreciation of the background to union development the following measures of disorganization should be listed:

The prevalence of unemployment, seasonal employment, and casual employment causes migration between estates, between city and country, and between colonies. As a consequence of almost aimless drifting, many workers lack roots in a particular community and a sense of belonging.

Peasant villages and estate "compounds" lack a community organization. If the employer or the central government did not repair the roads and water catchments, clean the drains and control malaria, it would not be done. One anthropologist described a peasant community as a geographical location rather than as a community because the community connotes a "togetherness" that does not exist.

Lack of cohesiveness among agricultural workers is also observed in the absence of social and recreational activities. If an outsider does not do the planning and organizing, leisure time is spent in idleness.

Although West Indian workers are enthusiastic church goers, the government-supported Christian churches remain foreign institutions run by white men, and the population is only nominally Christian. Native religion is the one institution close to the people and serves an important psychological need in providing emotional release and a sense of belonging, but, at the same time, any one native church has an uncertain existence. Small religious groups come and disappear frequently.

Just as the worker does not regard the established church as "his church," he does not regard the educational system and government as belonging to him. School and government are operated by foreigners from a distance and are not part of the life of the average worker.

A measure of social disorganization is also indicated by the extent of praedial larceny. Peasants and workers steal each others' crops, thereby discouraging extensive gardening. Jamaica has reinstituted the use of the cat-o'-nine-tails as punishment for praedial larceny, but to no avail.

Absence of community organization extends to absence of family unity. West Indian workers generally do not marry; both men and women must work; children are usually raised by their maternal grandmother. Such an extended family organization is common to many cultures and may provide love and security for both parents and children. The BWI working-class family, however, is both extended and seriously disorganized. The family pattern is one of fear, mistrust, competitiveness, and isolation.

Working-class personality patterns are a direct consequence of the economic and social environment, reflecting and reënforcing social disorganization. The agricultural worker finds his opportunities for social and economic advancement little different from those of his forefathers under slavery and, until recently, has adjusted to his environment in much the same manner as the slaves did. Since ambition leads only to frustration (as it does for the lower middle class) the worker adopts a passive, dependent, accommodating, deferential personality. Such adjustment accounts for the lack of race- or class-directed aggressiveness among West Indian workers. Psychological tests indicate that working-class children suffer a lack of a feeling of belonging (whereas middle-class children are insecure because of the color bar), which results in impairment of intellectual development, in emotional imbalance, and in difficulties in social relations. Energy which is normally used in creative work is expressed in religious dancing, hysteria, and spasmodic violence. Apathy, which is normally shown in absenteeism and low productivity, can suddenly change to senseless violence or spontaneous strikes of riot proportions. In brief, difficult family relations, economic stagnation, lack of patterned behavior, inadequate schooling, magic, and apathy-violence patterns tend to amplify and reënforce one another to produce nonintegrated personalities.

Nationalism and Anticolonialism

Transition in social attitudes[60] is not a single phenomenon, but a complex outgrowth of historical factors that affect the entire population of a country. Some developments have been directly affected by the disturbances of the 'thirties and by the impact of the war, others indirectly. In the BWI most white upper-class people have always considered themselves English rather than West Indian. Except for the white Barbadians who feel a local patriotism, most West Indian whites regard themselves somewhat as transients—even those whose families have been in the colonies for several generations. As self-styled transients they take little interest in local affairs. Many planters and businessmen complain of monetary controls and the inferiority of British manufactured goods, though they do not as a rule think in terms of colonial exploitation. Almost all interviewed white people feared terrible consequences from measures increasing the degree of self-government. Of all the groups, the colored middle class is the most nationalistic; its members speak most of colonial exploitation and were the most vocal, in interviews made in 1953–54 in expressing a need for more self-government and political independence.[61] At the least, the middle class looks for more opportunities and improved social status arising from independence. Many believe that the English have not pushed economic development vigorously enough and that self-government will provide the environment in which this development and better job opportunities could be created. Finally, many of the middle class argue that true dignity and self-respect will be achieved with independence. The new government, they believe, will inspire an entrepreneurial elite to take initiative and flourish. In general, West Indian workers do not have strong feelings of nationalism or resentment of colonial exploitation.[62] Too submerged in the effort of making a daily living, the workers do not think about future issues. Since there is little sense of family or community feeling, it is not surprising that they do not identify with the colony or with the West Indies as a whole. Although almost all West Indians are skeptical and critical of the local colonial administrators, they are, nevertheless, intensely loyal to their queen.[63]

In interviews with West Indian workers—a relatively small sampling, to be sure—the workers never explained their poverty or unemployed state in terms of colonial exploitation. The typical complaint was that the British government did not subsidize or donate enough. The feeling frequently expressed was that as descendants of slaves, through no fault of their own, the workers find themselves living under poor conditions and, therefore, the British people whose forefathers brought them to the West Indies have the responsibility for their present welfare. Conceptual difficulties of peasants, as discussed by Madeline Kerr, result in a view of government as a remote source of an inexhaustible supply of money, and it is only the crooked scheming local politician who prevents the workers from getting their share.[64]

Summary

The British West Indies are a cultural unit with a common history and development. An understanding of the BWI labor movement begins with an appreciation of the fact that slavery, colonialism, and the estate system of agriculture have left a deep imprint on the culture of the BWI. The psychological effects of slavery touch both the employer and employee in their attitudes toward work, leisure, savings, employment relations, and class structure. Colonialism combined with a laissez-faire philosophy have resulted in a stalemate between interest groups, inviting a special kind of irresponsibility in government performance. Further, the governments of each colony failed to plan for the transition from slavery to freedom, or for the social and educational services and adequate public utilities necessary for the encouragement of private enterprise.

The absence of natural resources and the inability to cushion the economy following the decline of the sugar industry have left the existing estate system of agriculture only as the best of poor alternatives. Under the system, the employee-employer relationship was quasi-feudal and born of custom, therefore the rights and duties of each are still hazy and difficult to define.

Side by side, underemployment and labor shortage exist, since, as an outgrowth of slavery, employers and employees alike consider manual work undignified. Most existing work is unskilled and beast-of-burden variety, supporting in fact this concept of indignity. Further, workers are superstitious and semiliterate. Under these adverse conditions it is remarkable that union development in the BWI has progressed as far as it has.

In the hundred or more years since the end of slavery, the BWI society has been virtually static, a condition which has created an ever-widening gap between the West Indies and the industrial nations of the world. The only great change over the years has been the increase in population, which has worsened economic difficulties for the much larger number of people who now have to face chronic unemployment and underemployment. From the period following emancipation to the 1930's, the workers responded to the social environment with passive resistance, thereby creating the passive personality that is considered typical of the West Indian worker and that handicaps union development. However, since the depression of the 1930's, the personality pattern has been undergoing a change, and the workers are no longer willing to accept a standard of living, a work situation, and a way of life too closely akin to slavery. The increasing aggressiveness of the workers contributes to the development of unions, but it hampers stable growth of unions when it is expressed in irrational outbursts. The unions have given workers a positive means of combatting the severe frustrations of poverty, and are thereby overcoming the lack of industrial discipline which has been a serious barrier to economic development.

The studies of social anthropologists and investigators in government commissions, and the opinions of the interviewed West Indians were almost unanimous regarding the absence of community organization among the workers. This lacking communal spirit, either on the estate or in the peasant community, has been pointed out as a deterrent to positive individual behavior. Even the most rudimentary forms of social and recreational organization remain unstable unless given outside direction. The inability to organize for collective action and the extreme individualism are rooted in family patterns. Finally, BWI workers do not strongly identify themselves with the government or with established churches, and a lack of sense of belonging pervades the entire working-class society, adding to the other handicaps met in union development.

In a society structured along fairly rigid racial lines, the few white people occupying positions of economic and social power are separated from the great mass of Negroes by the small middle-class mulatto group. The middle group tends to serve as a buffer between the extremes, and racial issues are not used as a basis for the formation of trade unions. The working-class groups, rather than resenting the upper classes, seem to have more antipathy toward the colored middle class, whose members, because of their own insecurity, are often harsher with workers than are the white employers. At present, therefore, there is no perceptible basis for the use of racial hatred in the trade unions. The antagonisms which are strong among the lower middle class may develop further among the working class when the latter becomes more aggressive and assumes more middle-class values. At this time the most serious racial issue facing the unions is the disharmony between Negro and East Indian groups in British Guiana and Trinidad.

Suffering from the extremes of poverty, unemployment, and underemployment, the people of the West Indies might have placed the blame on the colonial government, and the trade unions might have built themselves up through attacks upon colonialism and exploitation. However, this has not been the case. The general opinion, reviewed above, is that the workers have been so submerged in the struggle for daily existence that the government is remote in their lives, and it is not likely to be much of an influence on their thinking. They do not regard the British government responsible for their difficulties. Poverty is a habit of mind and body, not something analyzed in historic perspective. Paternalism is so much a part of the culture that the principal complaint is that the British should do more for them in the way of material giving. The only stirrings of nationalism and the demand for self-government originated in the middle class.

| Chapter II | Recent Background |

The 1935–1939 Riots

Although there had been attempts at various times to form labor unions, there was no significant progress until the riots of 1935–1939. Spontaneous general rioting broke out without the benefit of organization or effective leadership. In 1935 during the rioting on the sugar estates in Trinidad and in St. Kitts, the waterfront workers of British Guiana and Jamaica were also on strike. There were general disturbances in Kingston, Jamaica, in 1937, and again, in 1938, throughout Trinidad, Barbados, and in the Frome area of Jamaica. In 1939 rioting occurred on the sugar estates of British Guiana and in Jamaica.[1] The riots led directly to the formation of many unions, and to a quickening of interest in unionism generally and a colonial policy of positive encouragement to union development.

As these labor disturbances, at first isolated, spread from one end of the West Indies to the other, a Royal Commission was appointed to investigate the conditions which produced them. In addition, Major Orde Browne was commissioned to make a special report on the labor situation.[2] The report of the Royal Commission (Moyne Report) was considered to be so critical of the colonial administration that its publication was held up for the duration of the war for fear that its contents might be used as enemy propaganda. Both reports outlined the social, economic, and political background of the riots as described in chapter i

---

[1] For notes to chapter ii, see pp. 195–197.

and listed the following conditions as weaknesses in social organization which led up to the disturbances:

Inadequate community services of all kinds.

The quasi-feudal relationship between employers and employees on estates.

The basic problems arising from underemployment and overpopulation.

The instability and risk of tropical agriculture.

The lack of protective or regulatory labor legislation.

The conclusion of the Royal Commission report was that the riots grew out of minor grievances and frustrations over a period of years which in turn had led to feelings of utter futility among the workers. No one single cause or group of major causes could be listed as reasons for the riots. The Royal Commission made the following recommendations to remove the basic causes of labor unrest in the West Indies:

Tropical agriculture must be subsidized. (This recommendation together with special problems growing out of World War II led to the Sugar Agreement which is based upon long-term guaranteed bulk purchases at guaranteed prices.)

The colonial government should take over community services which were being inadequately supplied by estate management and bring these services up to date. (This recommendation led to the creation of the Colonial Development and Welfare Corporation with funds appropriated by the British Parliament to get these social services started.)

Labor departments should be created in all colonies, protective labor legislation enacted, and factory inspection standards made explicit and enforceable. (Whereas previous recommendations on these matters by other commissions had been ignored, the above recommendations were adopted.)

A system of subsistent agriculture should be developed as an adequate though humble way of life, since industrial development was virtually impossible because of lack of basic resources.[3] (This recommendation may have made sense at the time it was made, during the great depression, but it is unacceptable to West Indians today.)

The recommendations of the Royal Commission resulted in a major change in colonial policy not only in the West Indies but throughout the British Empire. In considering the importance of the commission in its contribution to union development the fact should be stressed that Sir Walter Citrine was a member of it. He acted as investigator, but also gave encouragement, advice, and assistance to the organization of new trade unions. Without his assistance many of the fledgling unions might have died.[4]

Recent Economic Development

Although the riots of the late 1930's provided the spark for union organization, and although colonial policy was modified toward encouraging and fostering union growth, wartime and postwar economic changes have given an important additional impetus to the movement.[5] The entire economy dependent on shipping and general wartime shipping shortages, led to a shortage of imported foods and export difficulties, which provided an incentive to the BWI to become more nearly self-sufficient. Development of a rice crop offset the loss of rice from Asia, and the creation of a local fishing industry partially compensated for the lack of imports from Canada. Factories for the manufacture of clothing, shoes, building materials, cigarettes, and food processing were established. Postwar inflation made terms of trade less favorable and further encouraged the development of local consumer-goods industries. The long-term bulk-purchase agreement affecting sugar and other crops made by the United Kingdom has given the West Indian economy assured income and price stability. The construction of American bases created new jobs (posing a new problem of labor shortages in Trinidad), resulting in unprecedented prosperity for small shopkeepers. Large numbers of West Indians were recruited for both agricultural and factory work in the United States. The development of the bauxite industry in Jamaica, the rapid expansion of the tourist industry, and the postwar concern of the colonial government for economic development have contributed to the improvement of the economic position of the BWI.[6] Wartime and postwar economic developments have not been great if measured against the huge task of raising living standards and providing jobs, yet they have been significant compared to the progress of the previous hundred years.[7] The developments have in three ways provided a favorable climate for union growth. First, they have increased the tendency of the colored middle class to champion the cause of the workers. In interviews with prominent members of the colored middle class the observation was invariably made that the increased prosperity of the working class had also materially improved that of the middle class. In particular, mention was frequently made of the growth of small business based on increased purchasing power created by employment at United States military bases. As a result, many of the colored middle class no longer identify themselves with the white upper class, reasoning that the upper classes drain the economy of purchasing power through travel and expenditures abroad, while a greater share of the national income in the hands of workers would directly benefit the mercantile and professional middle class. For this reason the colored middle class is friendly toward trade unionism.

Second, union growth is encouraged because recent economic development has contributed to the changes in attitude of all workers whether or not they hold industrial jobs. Although only a small percentage of the total work force served in the armed forces, joined the merchant marine, worked on U. S. bases in the Caribbean and in the Panama Canal Zone, or came to the United States as war workers, enough of them had this experience to inform the entire working class of the standards of living enjoyed by workers outside the BWI. This also happened after World War I, but on a smaller scale and therefore with a lesser impact. All workers, no longer content with what they once considered to be the natural or normal way of life, now demand a better standard of living. What was once the dream world of the cinema now became a real life goal. Workers do not take kindly to the explanation that the wealth of goods they saw during the war was produced only by emergency conditions. Their response to the author's comment on wartime emergency was that if abundance can be created for war, it can also be created for them in peacetime. If not, they will start a war. Unions are benefited by stirrings of the working class from its lethargy and passivity.

In addition to a desire for consumer goods, increased contact with the outside world has caused the word to be spread that elsewhere workers have superior equipment. Standard tools in the BWI are the cutlass and hoe, which have been associated with slavery. West Indians now want power tools, not just to lighten their work, but to eliminate the beast-of-burden jobs and gain for themselves a new sense of power and dignity. Having seen the work accomplished on U. S. bases, West Indians have joined the "cult of the bulldozer." In building bases, American construction crews eliminated malaria in swamp lands; opened new land for cultivation; built roads over rough mountains and through what heretofore had been called impenetrable jungle; developed water supplies and sewage systems and provided lighting and refrigeration on a scale previously undreamed of by the inhabitants of the Caribbean. The sense of futility felt by West Indians in attempting to beat back the jungle with the cutlass and to build mountain roads with shovels, is giving way as power equipment is being demanded. Again, this change in attitude of the workers contributes to their heightened interest in trade unionism.

Finally, events during World War II aided trade unionism because exposure to conditions in the outside world impressed upon workers the fact that the employee-employer relationship need not be humiliating. In spite of racial prejudice encountered both on U. S. bases and in the U. S. itself, workers interviewed by the author stressed the superior treatment accorded them by American supervisors. They emphasized that it was the first time that they had ever seen white men doing physical work; that their supervisors instructed them and worked with them rather than giving orders; that trucks were provided to transport them from the work camp to the work site; that drinking water was available on the job; and that hot showers were available at the end of a day's work. The same comments were made regarding employment by the bauxite, oil, and airline companies operating in the Caribbean. Consequently, workers are no longer satisfied with the type of employment relationship found on most West Indian estates. Many of the rank-and-file leaders of the union movement gained their inspiration from employment abroad. As one union organizer told the author: "We are a poor country and can never have an American standard of living, but our employers can at least treat us like the Americans did."

Industrial employment at skilled and semiskilled jobs with job tenure and above-average wages has created a small aristocracy of labor. This group has broken with the traditions of the rural peasant communities to assume middle-class values. The hard core of loyal, dues-paying members is provided by this group of industrial workers; rank-and-file union leaders, without political ambitions, are now emerging from it. Accordingly, recent economic development has created a small, but firm, base for greater union stability.

The Role of the Colonial Government in Union Development

As a result of the Moyne Report, colonial government in the British West Indies began a policy of actively encouraging unions.[8] The former government attitude of fear of unions as dangerous to the economic well-being of the colonies and a threat to the Empire was completely changed, and the administration began to consider unions as bulwarks of democracy, necessary to the survival of the Empire. As many English administrators told the writer, democratic self-government cannot start at the top but must develop in all institutions of a society. Accordingly, union development as a democratic grassroots movement was considered necessary to eventual granting of full political democracy. Government encouragement of unions has been a major cause of their rapid postwar development.

Obstacles to union organization, such as liability for torts and antipicketing laws, were removed in a law modeled after the British trade-union law. Departments of labor were established in each colony. The functions of these labor departments are summarized in a typical report:

> The Department functions include the fostering of good industrial relations, including the prevention and settlement of labour disputes, and assistance to industry in establishment of voluntary negotiating machinery; the collection, preparation, and publication of Labour Statistics which include wages, hours of work, and conditions of employment, also of the cost of living indices; the operation of the Bureau of Employment and Emigration; the supervision of the weighing of sugar cane; the inspection of factories, quarries, shops and work places in general; the recruitment of workers for employment overseas; and the administration of labour legislation.[9]

Some departments of labor have attempted to operate employment offices but the results have not been promising. Where there is chronic unemployment and few employers, a placement office is of little value to either job seekers or employers. The most useful employment service provided by departments of labor is in the recruitment of workers for agricultural employment in the U. S. The departments of labor are also handicapped in their collection of labor statistics. They have given up attempting to measure unemployment because of the prevalence of underemployment and share-the-work schemes. Wage studies are not meaningful when nonmonetary benefits are an important part of the wage structure. Variations in nonmonetary benefits together with difficulty in defining a family unit make cost-of-living studies problematical.

Labor officers give advice to groups of workers and to union leaders on the formation and organization of unions. They have stressed traditional union goals, avoidance of political entanglements, and the need to respect jurisdictional lines. They have not been entirely successful in shaping unions to the British model, but union organization would have been even more confused without the guidance of the British trained labor officers. Moreover, labor officers have not hesitated to advise workers against unions whose leadership was of questionable integrity and those whose politics were extremely anti-British. In some instances, the advice of the labor officer was respected, in others rejected. There were instances of labor officers going beyond mere technical advice to interfere with the internal affairs of unions. The propriety of such actions even under emergency conditions is open to question. In several colonies where unions are weak or where sectors of the economy are unorganized, labor officers handle individual grievances of unorganized workers. Union service supplied by government fosters further dependence upon the administration rather than development of autonomous unions, but labor officers justify their actions with the argument that it is more important to right wrongs and change employer attitudes. In colonies where unions are more advanced and aggressive, their leaders have complained about competition from the labor departments, and labor officers have discontinued their grievance-handling function. Several labor officers told the writer frankly that they took a leading role in shaping union policy under the guise of technical advice, and in collective bargaining under the guise of mediation, but as unions grew strong they retreated to a more proper neutral position.

Labor departments offer to supply mediation and conciliation services, which, in effect, force union recognition upon employers, for mediation starts with the premise that employers should recognize a union and bargain with worker representatives. Employers would be flying in the face of both government authority and public opinion if they did not use the good offices of the labor departments. Just as important is the fact that on a small island almost any strike becomes a "national emergency dispute," and the government requires arbitration of such disputes. The extensive use of compulsory arbitration causes employers to be party to union agreements whether they like it or not. On the one hand, compulsory arbitration of labor disputes aids union recognition and gives union leaders an opportunity they might not otherwise have to plead the workers' case. On the other hand, the arbitration of collective-bargaining issues has been criticized as weakening unions and making genuine collective bargaining impossible.[10] In an economy where every industry is a critical one, the right to strike must be limited; in effect the arbitrator writes the employee-employer agreement.[11] The policies of the labor departments tend to foster British-type trade unionism. Labor departments favor very informal collective bargaining, often without written contracts or formal union recognition as exclusive bargaining agent and without provision for contract termination. In the English tradition, they oppose the use of the check-off and union shop. They oppose any type of legislation providing for representation elections,[12] compulsory collective bargaining, or laws pertaining to unfair labor practices. Labor officers defend this position as fostering a vigorous, honest labor movement. Most interviewed union leaders, however, claim that American-type unionism is better suited to the people and problems of the BWI, and they object to having their labor departments try to impose English-type unionism upon them. With union instability a major threat to both the political and economic health of the BWI, many union leaders argue that the dues check-off, the union shop, and laws requiring representation elections would greatly contribute to needed union stability and thus to the general economic welfare. The World Bank report for Jamaica recommended a voluntary check-off to give Jamaican unions greater financial security and to provide better qualified field representatives for the unions.[13] Several interviewed employers said that greater instability would be created by union shop and check-off, because every ambitious politician would set out to capture a union with assured income and membership. These employers believed that the union shop and check-off brought union stability only when workers elected leaders from their own ranks. Several interviewed union leaders readily acknowledged this but felt that West Indian unions had no future until the union shop with check-off made possible a strike fund and salaries for officers, which would free them from having to seek political office to support themselves. Accordingly, they favor a law permitting the union shop and check-off where the union constitution prohibits outsiders from holding office. The major *industrial* unions of the West Indies have won the union shop and check-off over the opposition of the labor departments.

Most interviewed union leaders favored a "little Wagner Act," believing that representation elections would reduce jurisdictional disputes and that compulsory collective bargaining was necessary in agricultural employments where workers were financially weak and could not enforce collective bargaining through strike. In addition, they believed protection from discrimination was needed against antiunion employers in certain industries. The People's National party of Jamaica is now submitting a "little Wagner Act" to the legislature.[14]

As part of the colonial policy to encourage union development and improve labor conditions, labor advisory boards have been created, representing both employers and unions, to advise colonial administrators on the labor problems in each colony. Through this device prominent employers found themselves discussing policy with labor leaders, and both employers and emergent union leaders learned something about collective bargaining. By becoming members of a government board, leaders of labor gained new status in the colony and among the working classes. The colonial government, however, was not above playing favorites in nominating labor leaders to advisory boards. In some cases labor leaders who were extremely critical of British policies were not appointed to advisory boards even though they had large followings among workers and even union recognition by employers. Other labor leaders, more friendly to the government, were appointed to advisory boards even though their unions were merely paper organizations.[15] In some instances government "favoritism" worked to eliminate irresponsible leaders; in others, government opposition only contributed to the prestige of the union leaders. In other words, the truly irresponsible demagogue was discouraged by this process of government discrimination; but responsible union leaders having anti-British feelings thus gained additional popularity with the disgruntled workers.

Wage boards to establish minimum wage rates were created by law in those industries where unions were weak or nonexistent. Although the desirability of wage boards is debated, they have served to give prestige to union leaders. Once again the issue of government favoritism in the nomination of union leaders to serve on wage boards has arisen.[16] Wage boards exist where no union has won exclusive collective-bargaining rights and where competition exists between rival unions in attempts to win employer recognition. The particular union leader nominated becomes a crucial issue in such cases. As in the case of labor advisory boards, government discrimination sometimes works for the union favored and at other times has just the opposite effect.

Colonial governments also foster union growth through leadership-training courses offering free scholarships to British universities and to the University College of the West Indies. The latter has a tutor in industrial relations who travels through the colonies giving courses in trade unionism and collective bargaining. In awarding scholarships the government has been guilty of playing favorites. The Second Annual Conference of the Caribbean Area Division of ORIT objected to this practice and requested that unions be permitted to select their own candidates for training scholarships.[17]

Following World War II the colonial administration encouraged local legislatures to pass laws affecting sick leave, maternity leave, holiday and vacation pay, severance pay, and workmen's compensation. Although resultant improvements in the welfare of the worker are to be praised, some experts question the wisdom of having these social gains bestowed on workers by an outside authority. It is true that workers in the West Indies want protective labor legislation equal to that of the more advanced industrial countries of the world, but they have received these gains with little or no effort on their part. Accordingly, gratuitous labor legislation has not necessarily contributed to union development but is held by some observers to be a continuation of the benevolent paternalism of previous administrations toward the former slaves.

Finally, in considering the role of the colonial administration, it should be noted that the government is faced with conflicting interests. The first loyalty of the colonial administration is to the Crown, hence the difficulty in distinguishing between labor leaders who are anti-British nationalists and those who are racketeers or Communist agents. Indeed, there is at least one instance where it appears that a pro-British racketeer was favored over an honest but anti-British unionist. Second, the colonial administration has a loyalty to the employers, the most important of whom are representatives of English companies which have political connections in the United Kingdom. The welfare of the colony, of employers, and of English investors is not always the same. Third, the colonial administration must work with the government formed by the majority party in the local legislature. This government is usually the party allied with the labor unions. In Jamaica and in Barbados the labor officer appointed by the colonial officer serves under the minister of labor who is a former local trade unionist in both islands. The relationship is yet to be worked out but a conflict of policy, such as over "little Wagner Acts," could occur.

Employer Attitudes Toward Trade Unionism

One factor contributing to rapid union development in the BWI has been the lack of employer resistance to unions. Despite racial and class issues, West Indian employers have not fought unions in the way they were fought in American trade-union history. There has been no militant antiunion crusade. In part, this lack of employer opposition is the result of government assistance to unions, but just as important is employer fear of large-scale rioting.[18] Strikes in the usual sense of the word would fail in the

BWI because of lack of union discipline and of strike funds, also because of the large number of unemployed workers who are ready to act as strike breakers. Minor strikes, therefore, have a tendency to spread into general ones and take on the character-istics of riots. The unemployed and the self-employed peasantry join with the workers in looting and destruction. Ordinary police protection is inadequate when the majority of the population barricades roads, cuts communication lines, and proceeds to loot, burn estate houses, slaughter cattle, and pilfer estate produce. Commenting on the effect that the riots between 1935 and 1939 had on labor relations, the Jamaica Bureau of Labor Statistics said:

The disturbances had awakened a consciousness in the minds of the laboring classes as to their power as an important factor in the economic system of the country. It also made employers conscious of this awareness. The atmosphere has now considerably eased and the mood was for fuller understanding and better cooperation.[19]

A fear, which is often highly emotional and dates back to the days of slave revolts,[20] that strikes will develop into large-scale rioting attended by rape and murder, causes employers to recog-nize any union leader who has control and the loyalty of the labor force. A union leader in Jamaica told the writer that he exploited employer fears by telling them that the alternative to collective bargaining was not strikes but mau-mau. Most inter-viewed employers were aware of the weakness of existing un-ions but were afraid that some opportunist or (in some islands) Communist organizer would create a rival union and conse-quently were willing to bargain with any responsible union leader who stood for traditional union goals and could maintain control of the workers.

Another reason why employers do not strenuously resist unions is that collective bargaining usually leads to compulsory arbitra-tion.[21] Most industries are considered essential to the economy and therefore are subject by law to compulsory arbitration. In a society so structured that most of the population are workers, with almost no middle class and with few employers, it is almost impossible to secure a qualified arbitrator from among the local population. Anyone who is literate enough to qualify as an arbitrator is inclined to be prejudiced toward the employer viewpoint.[22] Due to the fact that with existing industries in an unfavorable competitive position in world markets and with a reasonable fear that more liberal employment conditions will deter the influx of outside capital and prevent development of pioneer industry, arbitrators usually favor the employers. The result is that union recognition is easy to gain, but little genuine collective bargaining results from the recognition. The employers prefer arbitration because they will win favorable awards, and the unions must submit to arbitration because of laws governing emergency disputes and because they will know that a genuine strike probably would be lost. The secretary of a waterfront-employer association told the writer that his association preferred contract arbitration because the union was too weak to enforce collective-bargaining demands by strike. Breaking a strike would ruin the union and expose employers to uncontrolled rioting and demagoguery. This association was satisfied with the reasonable awards of the arbitrator. However, trade unionists generally are dissatisfied with the awards but feel that, under the circumstances, there is little else they can do but submit.

The fact that employers have not strenuously resisted unions does not mean that satisfactory union-management relations exist everywhere. Only two secretaries of employer associations stated that unions had raised wages to a point higher than they otherwise would be. These employer representatives acknowledged that unions had improved working conditions, established employee rights, ended patronage, standardized wage rates, and forced estate management to improve supervision. Most secretaries of employers' associations expressed identical views, namely, that management was doing all it could for labor considering its low profit margins, that unions accomplished very little for workers and gave management unnecessary trouble. Employers generally took the patronizing view that the union leaders with whom they dealt were reasonable men but, in order to control the rabble, the leaders had to be unreasonable. Accordingly, existing union leadership was tolerated and even encouraged in order to keep the "rabble" under control. Only a few were opposed to the principle of collective bargaining or stooped to victimizing union workers and bribing their leaders.

Where unions were weak and not firmly established, union leaders complained to the writer that victimization was a problem but in general there were few complaints of discrimination against union workers.[23] All employers stressed the point that they themselves, union leaders, politicians, and the colonial administration were victims of an explosive situation created by a population growth exceeding job opportunities. Most of them viewed the situation as utterly hopeless. Although it is true that lack of profit and population pressure are basic limitations to economic improvement of the working class, employers tend to use this as an excuse to absolve themselves of all responsibility for improving employee-employer relations.

As stated in chapter i, white employers, particularly in agriculture, were often frank in expressing their views of the Negro race as inherently inferior. Rottenberg in his study of labor conditions in Grenada suggests that arbitration is favored by employers to avoid the issue of equality at the bargaining table, and adds that union-management relations are complicated by the employers' desire to assume the father role over childlike Negro workers.[24] It is true that paternalism continues in employment relations, particularly in agriculture, and that the employers' attitudes toward workers still alternate between an amusement and exasperation comparable to the behavior of a tolerant mother. Nevertheless, the writer was unable to detect any unwillingness to negotiate with union representatives for reasons of race.

Employers commonly complain that there was union influence in local government. Where the unions' political parties control the government, employers questioned the neutrality of the labor departments in mediating disputes. In Antigua and St. Kitts, employers accused the union of unilateral decisions on working conditions by legislative enactment whenever the union failed to win at collective bargaining. At the time of the interview, West Indian employers in general felt that cards were being stacked against them as increased self-government permitted increased union control of government.

Obstacles to Union Organization

Most workers in the West Indies are engaged in agricultural employment; and as everywhere else in the world, agricultural workers are difficult to organize. Road systems are either poor or nonexistent and communications between union groups are difficult. Workers living in company housing on estates ("compounds"), in the oil fields, lumber camps, and at bauxite mines cannot be reached by union organizers without their trespassing on large areas of private property. The second-largest group of workers in the BWI is that made up of domestic servants, and they, like domestic servants everywhere, are difficult to organize.[25] Low wages and seasonal unemployment make dues collection difficult; besides, workers are simply not accustomed to the idea of paying dues. A large pool of unemployed workers may serve as strikebreakers should workers strike for union recognition. Union development is also handicapped by lack of a clear-cut employee-employer relationship in estate agriculture. As stated in chapter i, an "employee" may also be self-employed, a squatter, a sharecropper, or a landowning peasant. Workers do not fully understand the function of a union, and consequently every kind of dispute is brought to the union for adjudication whether or not it has any bearing on working conditions or employee-employer relations. Successful unions attempt to take care of every problem of their members. Accordingly, Rottenberg raises the question of whether a union can operate on job-oriented lines and survive in a community in which disputes which have no relevance to job relationships are so important.[26]

Union development is also retarded by the "Messiah complex," which tends to keep people lethargic, expecting a God-appointed leader to guide them out of the "wilderness" through supernatural power and with no effort on their part. It has been noted that Messianism is a reaction of the inarticulate and oppressed people the world over seeking a way out of seemingly impossible situations.[27] For instance, there is the popular superstition that white men have special powers not possessed by Negroes; some Negro leaders claim that they have discovered the white man's secrets thereby gaining magic power which qualifies them for leadership.[28] Many working-class West Indians believe that white men have denied Negroes full access to parts of the Bible, especially to the "seventh book of Moses." [29] Some union leaders prey on this superstition by claiming that they are the good shepherds who have learned the secrets of the Bible and can lead their people to the promised land. Sir Alexander Bustamante, a Jamaican union leader, increased his following by publicly placing a curse on Governor Edward Denham who generously and conveniently died a few days later.[30] A rival union leader and critic explained Bustamante's success in spite of alleged corruption, as a "wish fulfillment of a frustrated people." Uriah Butler, a union leader in Trinidad, considers his union made up of God's people fighting the godless.[31] F. W. Dalley, a British union leader who made a study of industrial relations in Trinidad in 1947 and again in 1953, referred to Butler as "a curious phenomenon whose egocentricity and biblical references made him a seventeenth-century man instead of a modern union leader," and concluded that "Butlerism and unionism are incompatible." [32] Butler considered this writer as a messenger sent by God but threatened to put a curse on him if he did not carry the truth to the American people. Edward Joshua, a union leader in St. Vincent, described the economic problems of the colony as a struggle between the supernatural forces of good and evil. E. M. Gairy, a union leader in Grenada, claims to have supernatural powers which he uses against the enemies of the people.

The observation that politics shares many characteristics with religion also applies to trade unionism. Those who tie religion, magic, politics, and unionism together outnumber the more sophisticated. Peasants have always been approached with emotional appeals rather than with reason, and both church and school have taught, "Don't think, just follow me." Speeches are highly emotional; the audience gives responses reminiscent of a revival meeting; the opposition are forces of evil and darkness; and it becomes blasphemous to speak against the leaders.[33]

"Garveyism" is not dead in the BWI, and many of the unsophisticated confuse it with unionism. Marcus Garvey, a Jamaican, led a world-wide organization during the 'twenties to promote Negro nationalism and economic independence. He led the largest mass movement of Negroes in history, imbuing them with a sense of pride, importance, and dignity.[34] Although he served a term in a United States federal penitentiary for financial irregularities connected with his Black Star steamship line, Garvey returned to Jamaica a hero and served as an elected councilman in the city of Kingston. Workers who confuse fantasy with reality do not want unionism to be concerned with collective bargaining and grievance handling but want a unionism which will carry them out of captivity and back to their homeland in Africa —a land of milk and honey. Marcus Garvey died in 1940 but his spirit lives on in the BWI.

The Moyne Report lists pocomania and obeah as obstacles to unionism because of the superstition they foster, the hate and violence they engender, and their high cost to workers. Pocomania is a mixture of Christian and African tribal religions of a revivalist nature involving rites of all-night singing, dancing, and rum drinking. It is a genuine proletarian movement with roots deep in the working-class culture, and its leaders are of the people.[35] As such it is a serious rival to unionism. The greater the unemployment and social disorganization, the greater is pocomania activity for it gives its members a sense of belonging, which is generally lacking in West Indian working-class society. Hence, pocomania has its biggest following in the sugar parishes, where unemployment is greatest, and in the urban slums, where social disorganization is most serious.[36] Obeah, which is illegal, is black magic.[37] The ignorant and superstitious solve their grievances by hiring the obeah man to put a curse on employers and gain "security" through the purchase of magic charms and potions. As workers feel the necessity to protect themselves against the forces of evil, they analyze their day-to-day problems in terms of struggles between supernatural forces. They pay a high price to the obeah man, leaving little of their meager income for the payment of union dues. Consequently, the obeah man is often more influential and affluent than the local union leader. Madeline Kerr observes that reliance on obeah and pocomania are not in themselves pathological, but when tied to an Anglo-American economic system these beliefs and practices become destructive of people trying to compete in a modern world.[38] Escape from reality into the realm of magic undermines the authority of the medical doctors, agricultural advisors, economic planners, and union leaders. Reliance on magic further weakens unionism because magic requires no personal effort and failure is the fault of the magic, not of the individual.[39] Unionism is much more demanding of workers.

Lack of Rank-and-File Leadership

Where the workers are semiliterate, where social distance between worker and employer is great, and where workers, in some colonies, speak a different language or at least a different dialect from that of the employer, it is not surprising that rank-and-file leadership fails to emerge from the depressed masses. A secretary for an employers' association, for example, said that a works-council plan was abandoned because worker representatives became inarticulate when seated across the table from supervisors. The problem is complicated because workers have little respect for leaders from their own group. Workers appear to be unwilling to let anyone from their own ranks act as their spokesmen because they think that as a group they are truly inferior. Since West Indians generally confuse long words and the ability to argue effectively with intelligence and education,[40] barristers and advocates rank high in the West Indian status system, and, where possible, workers will call upon them to act as their national leaders. The Venn Report condemns the theory held by many Guianese workers that the selection of union officers from outside the employee group, and preferably of someone having standing in the community, would promote union growth and improve the union position in collective bargaining. Instead, according to the Venn Report, the result is that unions have become tools of political self-seekers. There is, said the report, a multiplicity of such unions—27 serving the population of 400,000 (in 1948). The movement has been plagued by jurisdictional disputes.[41] Nevertheless, many union leaders from outside the ranks of labor hold office because of a request from a worker delegation to assume leadership of its group. In this manner Bustamante began his union career as leader of the Kingston Dock Workers.[42] Several businessmen in St. Lucia have held union office at the request of worker delegations. F. J. Carasco, for example, was at one time president of the waterfront-workers union and president of the Chamber of Commerce. Quintin O'Conner, the leader of hourly paid government workers in Trinidad was approached by members of the Sugar Workers Union with the request that he become their president. Local union spokesmen for estate workers are often storekeepers. In the racial and class structure the storekeeper is much closer to the workers than he is to the estate owner; he cannot be victimized by the employer; he has above-average intelligence and is literate; and by serving the workers he can obtain a bigger share of the local grocery business. Thus, local union leaders are frequently not themselves workers.

Any worker who does have the ability to become a leader and who can develop a following among workers is so unusual that he stands apart from the group and can no longer be regarded as one of them. Such a man is not content to be a mere rank-and-file leader but demands to be a leader of his own union. Since rank-and-file leaders have doubtful loyalty, top union leaders have good reason not to encourage the development of local leadership.

Madeline Kerr, in a discussion of Jamaican politics, makes observations regarding leadership problems that are also applicable to trade unionism. She notes that the working-class electorate expects the impossible from elected leaders, blames politicians for all its ills, and fails to give sustained loyalty to leaders. The result is that interest is centered on the leader rather than on the party organization; and there are numerous political leaders. Kerr attributes the state of affairs to an ambivalence in the people—desiring a strong leader and at the same time wanting to preserve their independence.[43] A situation therefore emerges in which there are almost as many unions as there are union leaders, with none of the unions having local leadership. This explains in part the great number of weak unions with overlapping jurisdictions. Unions have not developed into established institutions as yet, but rather reflect the personalities and ideologies of particular union leaders. Take the leader away and in many cases there will be no union. Observing the lack of local union leadership in Jamaica and aware of its consequences in lack of representative democracy and stability, the mission of the World Bank recommended as part of its economic-development program a union-training program, salaries for union officers, and the dues check-off.[44]

Sources of Union Leadership

Lower Middle Class.—Since leadership does not ordinarily spring from the rank and file, outsiders often take over unions, frequently for purposes other than those which we consider traditional union goals. One source of union leadership is the self-seeking politicians who form unions as the first step in establishing a political party; and once political success is attained, the politician frequently forgets the union. Commenting on this point in his study of unions in Trinidad, Dalley said:

The difficulties trade unionists and especially their leaders have found in adapting themselves to these circumstances are enhanced by the fact that (1) there are no established political parties in Trinidad (1953); (2) politicians and political aspirants cultivate and sponsor certain trade unions rather to further their own political careers than to assist the union and their members; (3) Trinidad voters on the other hand do not at this stage give substantial support to trade union candidates as such.[45]

Before each political election many unions are formed by ambitious political candidates. Then, if the candidate wins the election he becomes too busy to attend to the union and if he loses the election he has no reason to continue the union. This kind of "union leader" usually comes from the lower middle-class people whose lack of education and darkness of skin bar them from further social and economic advancement. Winning a seat in the legislative council gives such people an income and status not otherwise easily obtainable. For these reasons there may be found among trade-union leaders many former primary-school teachers, shop clerks, and commission merchants. Primary-school teachers seldom receive a secondary education but become school teachers by serving as apprentice teachers in the village primary school. His leadership status among workers and peasants rivals that of the local clergyman. From the role of reader and writer of letters, of advisor, and of "bush lawyer" (many school teachers draw up deeds and wills) the ambitious school teacher will turn to unionism as a stepping stone to politics. A commission merchant is anyone who has a few franchises to sell the goods of a company from an industrial nation. Often a commission merchant has a very small shop, smaller inventory, and little capital. He is merely an order taker. Some commission merchants make little effort to sell anything, and the occupation becomes a respectable form of disguised unemployment. They become self-appointed leaders of labor, hoping through this device to become successful members of the legislature. This group of "union leaders" knows the least about the principles of trade unionism. Frequently they are cynical about the "lower classes," believing themselves to be part of the superior upper class. They do not identify themselves with the working class which they profess to represent and they are frustrated because they are not accepted by the upper classes with which they wish to be identified. Accordingly, they are frequently the most irresponsible type of leader, injecting superstition, antiwhite, and anticolonial feelings into union programs and politics. Even those who honestly identify themselves with the working class are guilty of irresponsible and exaggerated claims as to the responsibility for economic development and as to the evil intentions of British colonialism. Their frustrated ambitions make them emotional nationalists but not very good union leaders. After reviewing the agitated speeches of several union leaders one writer suggests that BWI unions could become models of despotism rather than of democratic control.[46] An example of this situation was the disastrous 1951 strike of the St. Lucia sugar workers engineered by W. G. Brown, commission merchant. Commenting on Brown, the Malone Report said:

Mr. Brown is a remarkable mixture of contradictions; he has a wide knowledge and a wide ignorance of many things; he is incoherent and at the same time expressive; he is fearful yet at the same time plunges into most fearsome situations; he is arrogant, ingratiating, domineering and subservient at one and the same time. In a large country he would probably be no more than the dominating character at the local pub, but in a little country like Saint Lucia he is irritating, incalculable, and at times dangerous.[47]

A U. S. government official, whose duty includes observation of the West Indian labor scene, confirmed a popular allegation that a prominent union leader was guilty of accepting bribes from employers to keep workers under control, of extortion of employers by threatening strikes, and of graft in political office, while at the same time he was posing as a folk hero. Employers were willing to pay bribes because they feared a rival union which appeared to be more militant. In his study of E. M. Gairy's union in Grenada in 1952 Rottenberg concludes that "the union co-exists with its leader and survives only so long as the people pay allegiance to him." [48]

Such a conclusion is applicable to several West Indian unions. Loyalty is to "the chief" rather than to the union. As a consequence, the constitution, conventions, and bylaws are merely paper façades. Union officers are merely lackeys of the leader, and should they forget their subordinate role they are summarily dismissed. Veneration of the leader, rather than dues payment, makes the union strong. To maintain popular support this type of leader resorts to all kinds of showmanship, which Rottenberg describes as the repetitive drama. Through such showmanship he avoids collective bargaining in favor of wild promises and of wildcat strikes. Political issues are confused with bargaining issues. The weakness of this type of "union" is that it exposes the leader to competition from other showmen. Although workers are seeking a Messiah and although the showmen-leaders have won for workers a new sense of dignity and freedom, usually without any tangible gains, the workers are fickle. Either another drama begins or the workers turn to another showman— as happens with native religious sects.

In recent years unions led by lower middle-class "showmen" have suffered a decline, while unions organized along traditional lines and seeking traditional union goals have steadily progressed. Every union in the BWI is exposed to the possibility that another self-appointed Messiah will arise to capture its membership, but this event appears to be merely a stage of West Indian union development which passes as workers come to know the meaning of unionism. In general, unions with more mature and responsible leadership appear to be in the ascendency.

Middle-Class Nationalists.—The other important source of union leadership is the group of middle-class nationalists. Unlike the older middle class, this group is intensely nationalistic and therefore honestly identifies itself with the working class rather than the white upper class. Among these union leaders are former newspaper editors, reporters, barristers, and advocates, usually with a university education. Accordingly, the antiwhite and anti-colonial feelings and the plans for economic development of this group are more realistic and reasonable than are those of the lower middle-class "union leaders." Their intellectualism and reasonableness, however, have been a source of weakness. Since they are less inclined to be rabble rousers, and since they have good middle-class manners, the more Machiavellian leaders of the lower middle class have tended to win control of unions and political offices. The West Indian workers and electorates are not interested in finely reasoned economic analysis supported by statistics but they do enjoy fire and brimstone oratory. Commenting on the state of unionism in British Guiana in 1954, a British trade-union observer stated that the lack of rank-and-file leadership allowed outsiders to take over Guianese unions and, in turn, the middle-class intellectuals lost out to demagogues because "even good middle-class leaders are sissies. Trade unionism is not for gentlemen, and every union leader must know a little demago-guery to keep the extreme demagogues from stealing the show." The success of the uneducated lower middle-class demagogue is probably a temporary situation since the well-mannered colored middle-class nationalists are learning how to campaign under conditions of universal adult suffrage. With their superior education, ability, and honest interest in the welfare of the people, middle-class nationalists appear to be winning the support of the mass of the people.[49]

Other weaknesses of middle-class nationalists as union leaders are their lack of understanding of the problems of the worker and their lack of interest in day-to-day union affairs. Social distances are very great in the BWI, and middle-class leaders are interested in workers more as West Indians than as employees; but the fact that most employers are not West Indians but white obscures this distinction. Middle-class leaders are interested in political affairs for the sake of economic development and political independence, rather than in unions for collective bargaining and grievance handling. For example, an optometrist who was also the president of a union told the writer that he identified himself with the working class because the middle and upper classes were too small to support his business and only a prosperous working class could afford to buy glasses. Nevertheless, union activities were secondary to his interest in politics. A medical doctor who was also a union president explained that he was an East Indian first and member of the middle class second. According to his view the white upper class both oppressed the East Indian workers and socially snubbed the East Indian middle class. Although a vigorous union leader, his primary interest was in politics. Several lawyers who were union leaders and politicians said they realized that they had been young snobs of the colored middle class until a university education had caused them to become nationalists. A newspaper owner who was also secretary of a union explained that he was more interested in politics but someone had to take care of union affairs in order to help his political party.

Summary

The BWI labor movement has its origins in the general riots of 1935–1939. There was no single cause nor were there specific grievances underlying the riots; workers were simply no longer content with their existing way of life. Wartime and postwar economic development, while creating job opportunities, served to whet appetites for further improvement in working conditions and standards of living.

The policy of encouraging union growth subsequently pursued by the colonial government is a major reason for the remarkable development of BWI unions. Problems have arisen in connection with undue government interference in the internal affairs of unions; lack of neutrality in jurisdictional disputes; oppression of legitimate, though anti-British, union leaders; and opposition to the union shop, representative elections, and unfair-labor-practice laws. Nevertheless, the policy of encouraging union growth, which in an underdeveloped colonial area may be a calculated risk, may prove to be basic to emergent self-government and economic development.

BWI employers have not seriously interfered with union growth nor obstructed collective bargaining. Having lost control of the local legislature after the institution of adult suffrage, and with the government supporting the unions, the employer class was in no position to oppose unionism. Moreover, the upper class, constituting a small minority, is fearful of island-wide rioting and was willing to recognize any union leader able to maintain control over the mass of the workers. With but a few exceptions, the writer did not find the attitude of white employers toward race and class an obstacle to collective bargaining.

Several factors retard union development. First, there is the "Messiah" complex and Garveyism. Large numbers of workers believe that leaders with mysterious or God-given powers will arise and lead them to a land of milk and honey. The belief that workers can gain their goals with no effort but through the magic of a leader seriously hampers the development of business unionism concerned with grievances and collective bargaining. Second, pocomania and obeah compete with unionism as a solution to the problems of workers, and for their financial support and loyalty. Workers turn to magic, superstition, and religions of despair as social disorganization increases. To the extent that population pressures and technological unemployment are not offset by economic development, unions will be weakened as social disorganization increases.

Union development also is retarded because of the lack of rank-and-file leaders. Without local leadership, a shop-steward system cannot operate and local union organization is weak. As a result, "outside" leadership dominates BWI unions. "Outside" leaders are of two sorts: the lower-middle-class leaders who use unionism as a stepping stone to political office, and the middle-class nationalists who are more concerned with self-government and economic development than with the day-to-day problems of workers. Lack of rank-and-file leaders causes many unions to be one-man organizations and leaves the union movement vulnerable to infiltration by outsiders whose ideologies and motives may differ from those of the workers.

Chapter III | *Union Development*
in the Larger Colonies

The next two chapters trace briefly the history of union development in each colony in relation to its economic and political background. Readers who are not interested in the details of union
development in each colony may wish to skip these chapters.

JAMAICA

As the largest island, with about half the population of the
British West Indies and exporting more than half the sugar,
citrus, and bananas, and with growing bauxite, gypsum, consumer-goods, and tourist industries, Jamaica is the most important economic unit in the islands.[1] Union development in Jamaica
is equally significant. The first trade union in Jamaica, the Long-
shoremen's Union, was formed in 1918, established two branches,
was active until 1926 despite strong employer opposition, then
failed to develop further. The Jamaican trade-union movement
really began, however, with the spontaneous rioting in May,
1938, which spread from the Kingston waterfront and then developed into general disturbances throughout the island.[2] In the
negotiation of workers' grievances following the disturbances and
in attempts by the trade-union's committee to capitalize on the
unrest by creating a formal organization of unions, it became
clear that there were two rival union movements developing. One
spokesman for the workers was Alexander Bustamante, a money

[1] For notes to chapter iii, see pp. 197–199.

Jamaica, Agricultural Production (1956)

Sugar	396,551	tons
Bananas	10,896,189	stems
Citrus fruit	117,240	boxes
Copra	10,252	tons
Coffee	1,500	tons
Pimento	3,066	tons

Jamaica Industrial Production (1956)

Bauxite	1,700,000	tons
Alumina	438,000	tons[a]
Cement	20,000	tons
Condensed milk	300,000	gallons
Textiles	9,000,000	yards
Shoes	1,500,000	pairs
Gypsum	74,000	tons
Cigars	8,000,000[b]	

SOURCE—*West Indian Yearbook, 1956–57*, Montreal, Thomas Skinner, 1957, pp. 213–219.

[a] To increase 33 per cent by 1960 after the completion of a new alumina plant.

[b] In addition, Jamaica's postwar development includes two knitting mills; 50 garment factories; canneries processing orange, lime, grapefruit, and tomato juice; a paint factory, a match factory, and 15 factories making building materials. A $2,500,000 glass plant is under construction.

lender and writer of political polemics in local newspapers (see chapter ii, p. 59). The other was Norman Manley, a lawyer who had long been a champion of the working class.

The middle-class nationalists associated with Manley followed the example of British trade-union development. They formed unions by craft and industry and federated them into the Jamaica Trade Union Council. The latter was in turn allied with Manley's People's National party, a middle-class nationalist movement formed in 1938 as a rallying ground for self-government. Manley, whose interest was always political, never held union office and looked upon all unions, including the Bustamante Industrial Trade Union, in the early 1940's as allies of his political party. The middle-class leaders of unions federated with the Trade Union Council were also primarily interested in politics and regarded themselves as caretakers of the union movement until a rank-and-file leadership developed. Because of the scarcity of leadership, a small group—Florizel Glasspole, Noel Nethersole, Will Isaacs, Ken Hill, and Richard Hart—found themselves holding office in all the unions. Membership in the fourteen unions of the council was made up primarily of workers whose economic status and job security gave them middle-class aspirations and caused them to be identified with the People's National party platform. The strength of the Trade Union Council developed in the small factories in Kingston, among railroad, public-works, and other government employees, and white-collar workers.

Shortly after his release from jail in 1938, Bustamante formed the Bustamante Industrial Trade Union, a blanket-type union. The Bustamante Industrial Trade Union's constitution makes Bustamante president for life and makes him a standing committee of one in control of finances.[3] As the name of the union implies, the organization was built on his personal magnetism and unbounded egotism. The union's original strength lay with the waterfront workers and the unemployed of Kingston but membership grew with "the chief's" popularity, particularly in the country districts and the sugar parishes. His imprisonment in 1938 and "internment" from September 1940 to February 1942 added to "the chief's" stature as a popular hero. During his internment Manley negotiated the Sugar Agreement and waterfront agreement for 1941 for Bustamante's union. The Bustamante Industrial Trade Union soon became the largest union in the BWI and by 1944 had 54,000 members or more than 80 per cent of the total union membership in Jamaica. From time to time Bustamante was associated with the Trade Union Council, with Manley assisting him in negotiations and in legal difficulties, but Bustamante always returned to an independent position.

In some respects Bustamante was a follower rather than a leader, for, according to the temper and custom of the times, the workers struck first and Bustamante negotiated in their behalf after the strike had taken place. In 1938 riots began when the waterfront workers rejected a compromise agreement worked out by Bustamante. Little serious effort was made to establish branch organizations with the Bustamante Industrial Trade Union or to develop local leadership. Union-management relations were summarized in the slogan "Telegraph Duke Street," the union headquarters. Workers struck, telegraphed Duke Street, and Bustamante or his able assistant, Hugh Shearer, came out to negotiate a settlement.

In 1944, just before the granting of universal adult suffrage, Bustamante formed the Jamaica Labour party.[4] At this point labor disputes and union competition for membership became a struggle for political power. For several years pitched battles were fought between rival gangs for the right to organize and the right to hold street-corner political rallies. The crisis and turning point in this struggle came during the Mental Hospital riot, when Bustamante led the waterfront workers against the striking Trade Union Council hospital employees. Several people were killed, many injured, and Bustamante was indicted for murder, though acquitted.[5] (Fighting between rival political groups resulted in the death of one man during the political campaigning of 1958.) Denouncing Manley's self-government platform which, according to Bustamante "would replace a white man by a brown man on the backs of black men," the Jamaican Labour party won the majority of legislative seats in 1944 because of Bustamante's personal popularity. By 1948 self-government had become a popular cause and Bustamante adopted it as his platform. The Labour party won again in 1948 when Bustamante poked fun at the People's National party's Socialist planners and promised "just a little more bread." In both elections the Manley party had an organization and a platform while the Labour party had neither. The Labour party, however, had Bustamante's personality.[6] The People's National party was handicapped by a Socialist platform, Communist fellow travelers, and an economic program that the voters did not comprehend. Although Bustamante did not win many tangible gains in union agreements or in legislation he gave the Negro masses a new sense of dignity and self-respect. The Trade Union Council and the People's National party, on the other hand, were not in touch with the mass of workers. With their visionary talk they frightened the more respectable members of the upper and middle classes, causing them to become supporters of the Jamaica Labour party. The white upper classes supported Bustamante as a man with whom they could do business.[7]

The second split in the Jamaican labor movement came in 1952 when the People's National party expelled the Hill brothers and Richard Hart from the party for Communist connections and specifically for their refusal to withdraw their unions from the Communist-dominated World Federation of Trade Unions. Leaders of the People's National party then formed the National Workers Union (NWU) as the union arm of its party. The Trade

Union Council soon discovered that it had lost its union membership to the new union. In 1953 the Hill brothers expelled Hart from the Trade Union Council. Hart in turn joined Ferdinand Smith, recently deported from the United States and expelled from the National Maritime Union for Communist activities, to form the Jamaica Federation of Labor. Both the council and the federation remained paper organizations with small followings. Each hoped to capitalize on any mistakes made by the National Workers Union or the Bustamante Industrial Trade Union. In 1956 the Hill brothers, who by then were active in the Moral Rearmament movement, affiliated their union with the World Federation of Christian Trade Unions.

The original strength of the National Workers Union was with the skilled workers who could identify themselves with the middle-class ambitions of the People's National party. Rapid postwar industrial development in Jamaica created a new type of industrial worker who gave additional strength to the union. Also, with the development of the bauxite industry by three American aluminum companies in 1951, the United Steelworkers of America, AFL-CIO, gave financial aid to the National Workers Union for the organization of the bauxite workers. Kenneth Sterling, formerly an organizer of the People's National party, was employed by the steelworkers and did an outstanding job in the organization of bauxite workers and the development of a union along traditional lines. In this task he was helped by the technical assistance of the Steelworkers Union; by the bauxite companies who wanted a shop-steward system for the orderly processing of grievances; and by the fact that the cream of the Jamaican labor force, many with union experience in the United States, had been hired by the aluminum companies. The bauxite-workers division became the backbone of the union, and Sterling became its general secretary.

With funds contributed by the Cuban Sugar Workers Union, the National Workers Union undertook an organizing drive of the sugar estates in 1954. Although the Bustamante union still controls most of the estate workers, it is important to note that the National Workers Union won over estate workers by stressing the need for a union organization that would attend to day-to-day grievances promptly. Bustamante called an unsuccessful strike on seven of the island's twenty-one sugar estates in January, 1957, apparently for political reasons. This failure was a blow to his prestige in both politics and unionism.[8] With sixty-eight branches, the National Workers Union, with 200 collective-bargaining agreements, controls most of the industries (resort hotels, mining), and also the government services; and it has joint bargaining right on the waterfront and in agriculture. It claims to be the largest union in the BWI with 64,000 registered members (1957) and is beginning to assume the character of a federation of industrial unions.[9] Union leadership is separating from political leadership; pure trade-union issues are given careful attention; the organization is democratic and is building local leadership in branches which are based on industrial rather than geographical units. The National Workers Union may well become the model union in the West Indies.

The Bustamante Industrial Trade Union has been steadily losing membership in recent years to its rival the National Workers Union, for several reasons. First, the leaders of the Bustamante Industrial Trade Union became so tied up with politics as to neglect their union. (See chapter vi, pp. 136–137 f.) Second, the union is built around a few men at the top with almost no local organization or leadership. Application for membership in the Caribbean Area Division of ORIT was denied the Bustamante Industrial Trade Union on the ground that it was undemocratic.[10] Finally, there has been a growing belief or suspicion among workers that Bustamante has sold out to the employers.[11]

Bustamante's success in the first federal elections in March 1958 (see chapter vii) has renewed the strength of both his party and his union, and large-scale transfer of membership from the National Workers Union to the Bustamante Industrial Trade Union is reported to have taken place in April and May of 1958. The People's National party won the 1955 election and Manley became first minister. The decline of the Jamaica Labour party resulted from a series of scandals in government and from the lack of a constructive program. The People's National party gained strength from its Communist purge and by dropping excess Socialist ideological baggage.

Union-management relations during the Jamaican labor movement's brief history present a confusing picture. In 1941 the

Bustamante Industrial Trade Union succeeded in winning the first collective-bargaining agreement in Jamaica in a union contract with the Sugar Manufacturers Association which covered more than 35,000 field hands and 6,000 factory workers. The union's negotiations with employers were for general wage increases and failed to establish the foundations for industrial government. Confusion also arose, because unions had little control over the workers, who called for union help in contract negotiations and grievance settlement only after they had already struck. Workers lacking in union loyalty played off rival unions and political parties against each other, expecting free union service in return for political votes. Third, the Labor Department held representation elections on the waterfront and in the sugar industry to end union jurisdictional rivalry. Instead of exclusive bargaining rights, however, proportional representation according to the percentage of votes cast was awarded. As a result the Bustamante Industrial Trade Union, the National Workers Union, and the Trade Union Council jointly represent the workers. The consequence is the injection of politics into labor disputes, continued rivalry for membership, and an undermining of the worker's cause by lack of coördination of bargaining strategy. (See chapter ii, pp. 63–67 f.) Fourth, there is a tendency to take all disputes to arbitration, and as a result there is little genuine collective bargaining. (See chapter ii, p. 56.) The emergence of the National Workers Union as the dominant labor union which has separated itself from politics and follows traditional trade-union lines, and the example of the bauxite companies which expect the traditional collective bargaining relationship, indicate a trend toward the type of union-management relations found in more advanced industrial countries. Whereas contract negotiations used to be concerned solely with the size of a general wage increase, labor agreements are now, under National Workers Union leadership, concerned with every detail of the employment relationship.

During the 1940's there was despair in Jamaica, because the only alternatives were a union-political party led by a "demagogue" and a union-political party headed by "dangerous radicals and impractical dreamers." At present the People's National party offers efficient government and practical economic planning. The National Workers Union, now a separate institution allied with the

People's National party, follows traditional union objectives. Given a period of stability, these organizations may entrench themselves, but the Communist-tinged Jamaica Federation of Labor, the opportunistic Trade Union Council, and the revitalized Jamaica Labour party-Bustamante Industrial Trade Union stand by to capitalize on any misstep on their part.

TRINIDAD

Trinidad (1,862 square miles) and its dependency to the northeast, Tobago (116 square miles), lie just off the coast of Venezuela; their rapidly expanding populations now total 720,800. Petroleum is the number-one revenue producer of Trinidad, accounting for three-fourths of the colony's exports and directly providing more than one-third of the government's revenue. Annual production is about twenty-five million barrels a year. Sugar is the principal agricultural export with an annual production of 160,000 tons. The sugar industry is dominated by nine estates controlling 80,000 acres. Two companies own 62 per cent of the sugar-producing land and manufacture 69 per cent of the sugar output.[12]

EMPLOYMENT AND WAGES IN TRINIDAD SUGAR AND OIL INDUSTRIES

Industry	Number Employed	Annual Wage Bill
Oil	20,000	$30,000,000
Sugar	19,000 in crop (12,000 out of crop)	3,000,000

SOURCE—*CAD-ORIT Information Bulletin* (December, 1956), p. 21.

Other crops are cocoa, copra, citrus fruits, bananas, rice, and coffee. Total agricultural employment is 76,000 and yields $95,-000,000 worth of commodities in contrast to the $212,000,000 oil industry. Bauxite from Dutch Guiana and British Guiana is transshipped in Trinidad from shallow-draft river boats to ocean-going vessels from the United States and Canada. Manufacturing of light consumer goods for domestic and West Indian consumption is increasingly important. The island's strategic location on north-south air and sea routes has resulted in a tourist trade catering to both North and South America. The petroleum industry, together with the growth of light manufacturing industries, has made the problem of unemployment less acute in Trinidad than in other West Indian colonies. Negroes constitute about half of the population; they man the oil fields, docks, public works, and sugar factories, and follow industrial occupations. Two-fifths of the population are descended from indentured servants recruited in India between 1845 and 1917; these people furnish the field labor for the sugar estates. Approximately 20 per cent of the East Indians are Mohammedans and the remainder Hindus. Since World War II the East Indians have made rapid strides in business and the professions, and as independent farmers growing fruits, vegetables, and rice. There are also several thousand Chinese and a number of Syrians, Lebanese, and Portuguese, all of whom earn their livings in commercial enterprises. The colored middle class is composed of the Spanish Creoles, descendants of the original Spanish settlers and their slaves; French Creoles, who fled Haiti during the slave uprising; and the more recent mixture of English and Negro. Although race relations are peaceful and all kinds of racial relationships may be observed, in general there is little social intermingling between groups.[13]

Trade unionism in Trinidad dates back to 1890 with the formation of the Trinidad Working Men's Association, which collapsed after the disastrous waterfront strike of 1902. The association was revived again in 1919 by a Captain Cipriani as a political party and protest movement. Its platform included demands for self-government, universal adult suffrage, equal job opportunities regardless of race, and federation of the BWI. Cipriani advised against the formation of unions because of the oppressive trade-union laws but one branch of the association, made up of stevedores and railroad employees, operated as a labor union. As champion of the "barefoot man," Cipriani had a following of 120,-000 workers in Trinidad and was influential throughout the BWI as a middle-class political agitator. The Trinidad Workingmen's Association was essentially a one-man show, and Cipriani was not a man of outstanding ability. The organization collapsed in 1933.[14]

Modern labor relations in Trinidad begin with the 1937 general riots, which started in the oil fields, touched off by Uriah Butler whose "speeches and literature were of a violent character." [15]

Butler lacked the leadership abilities of a Bustamante, however, and failed to capitalize on the situation. He precipitated the rioting and a general strike, but other leaders formed the unions and won the collective-bargaining agreements.

As background facts in their study of the "disturbances" the Forster Commission enumerated the following:[16]

An industrial court for the settling of industrial disputes was established in 1920 but never functioned.

A trade-union ordinance was passed in 1932 but permitted no peaceful picketing and allowed unions to be sued. On the advice of the British Trade Union Congress branches of the Trinidad Workingmen's Association refused to register as a union because of the nature of the law.

An International Labor Office (ILO) Convention of 1928 adopted rules on minimum wages, which were ratified by the United Kingdom in 1929; a minimum-wage ordinance was passed in Trinidad in 1935. A minimum-wage board was established in 1936, and nothing more was ever done.

The workmen's-compensation law, also in violation of the International Labor Office Convention treaty, did not cover agricultural workers.

The secretary of state for the colonies in 1935 asked that a Department of Labor be set up. No action was taken in Trinidad.

The governor claimed that he was negotiating wages in the oil field dispute before the riots but there are no records of such negotiations.

The Forster Commission listed the underlying causes of the "disturbances" as follows (Italics mine):[17]

General dissatisfaction for which there was no adequate means of articulation through recognized machinery of collective bargaining.

Little regard of the employers for employee welfare.

Rise of the oil industry, creating a social ferment in an agricultural society.

Minor grievances such as favoritism in job opportunities and lack of ambulance service.

A general restlessness caused by the influence of radio, cinema, and labor disputes in the United States.

Racial issues and self-government issues were not part of the causes of the disturbances.

In his summary of Trinidad union history, F. W. Dalley describes the unions which grew out of the 1937 riots as youthful,

exuberant, impatient, desiring drastic action, having some irresponsible leaders, and looking upon strikes as the only form of
union action.[18] There was considerable overlapping of unions and
competition for membership, with half of the unions claiming
jurisdiction over all workers. Six different unions, for example,
claimed jurisdiction over civil-service employees. By 1938 there
were sixteen registered unions, the most important of which were
the Oil Field Workers Union, the Federated Workers Union, the
Seamen and Waterfront Trade Union, and the All-Trinidad Sugar
Estates and Factory Workers Union. The Trinidad and Tobago
Trade Union Council, formed in 1938, represented the major
unions but was ineffective in resolving jurisdictional disputes.
At the suggestion of the British Trade Union Congress and the
Trinidad government, the Trade Union Council joined the newly
formed World Federation of Trade Unions in 1946. The Trinidad
government financed the trips of union leaders to the first convention of the World Federation of Trade Unions. When British
and American unions broke with the World Federation of Trade
Unions to form the anti-Communist International Confederation
of Free Trade Unions, leaders of the Trinidad and Tobago Trade
Union Council refused to follow. Although they never paid dues
to the World Federation of Trade Unions they said that they were
not at the beck and call of British unions or the colonial government. Although the great majority of unions were not Communist-
dominated, the Trinidad Trade Union Council was controlled by
John Rojas and Quinton O'Conner, who were sympathetic to the
Russian point of view. As a result the Trinidad labor movement
was considered Communist-dominated. With the leadership of
the waterfront-workers union, six small unions representing
13,000 workers split off from the Trinidad and Tobago Trade
Union Council to form the Trinidad and Tobago Federation of
Trade Unions which affiliated with the International Confederation of Free Trade Unions in 1951.[19] Under the pressure from
employers, the government, and their own unions, O'Conner and
Rojas withdrew from the World Federation of Trade Unions but
stated that their sympathies remained with it.[20] In December,
1957, the two rival federations united to form the Trinidad and
Tobago National Trade Union Congress, representing 40,000
workers and all major unions.[21]

The Trinidad Oil Field Workers Union

Although the oil-field workers had come under the spell of Uriah Butler, who led them in the riots of 1937 and again in 1947, Butler's lack of ability as an administrator caused his union to lose membership, and his inability as a negotiator resulted in ineffectiveness in dealing with management. One of the strongest (12,000 members), best organized, and financially soundest unions in the West Indies is the Trinidad Oil Field Workers Union founded in 1937.[22] With company encouragement, because of management's fear of Butler, and with excellent leadership of rank-and-file origin, the Oil Field Workers union follows traditional union principles. It is a democratic union with local branches led by rank-and-file leadership which concentrate on collective bargaining and grievance settlements. The union has no political affiliation, and its executive board asked Rojas to resign from the pro-Communist West Indian Independence party.[23] Although Rojas has been associated with left-wing political groups in Trinidad and has made trips behind the Iron Curtain he has scrupulously avoided involving his union in his own personal political affairs. The union is made up of skilled and semiskilled workers who enjoy job tenure and above-average pay. Their problems are those normally associated with modern industry. The progressive management follows modern personnel practices. A peaceful and harmonious collective-bargaining relationship has existed between the union and the Oil Field Employers Association since their first contract in 1938. Their constructive collective-bargaining relationship has been marred only by the Butler-led riots of 1947.

The Federated Workers Union

The Federated Workers Union of Trinidad, founded in 1937, is made up primarily of government railroad employees and government public-works employees. It is an industrial union with a nucleus of skilled craftsmen who provide rank-and-file leadership. Union strength is based, in part, on the fact that these workers have job tenure and regular income permitting lower middle-class standards. Since as the government is committed to the principle of collective bargaining, the union did not have to fight an antiunion employer. The Federated Workers Union strength in government departments has been limited by jurisdictional disputes with six rival unions of government workers. Negotiations for the amalgamation of government unions continue, but to no avail.[24] The Federated Workers Union's ability to expand into private enterprise has likewise been limited by the union's inability to give adequate service to new branches. Its leader and general secretary, Quinton O'Conner, is regarded as one of the ablest leaders in Trinidad, but, lacking in rank-and-file leadership assistance, there are only so many branches of his union that he can service.

Although the union has always been nonpolitical and has concentrated on collective-bargaining and grievance issues, and although O'Conner withdrew from the World Federation of Trade Unions and the West Indian Independence party, his continued association with Communist groups has caused a decline in membership and defection of some branches.[25] The recent unification of the union movement together with the ending of the Communist-influence issue should strengthen the Federated Workers Union.

Trinidad Seamen and Waterfront Workers Union

The Trinidad Seamen and Waterfront Workers Union, founded in 1937, is one of the most conservative, "pure and simple" unions in the BWI. Its founder and long-time president, Cecil Alexander (who died in 1956), was a longshoreman. It is a democratic union with rank-and-file leadership. Once again we note that union membership is predicated upon workers enjoying year-round employment and above-average wages. Occupying a strategic position in an island economy dependent on both imports and exports, this union concentrates on collective bargaining and grievance handling.

Speaking of the excellent relationships on the waterfront, Fred Dalley said:

The labor relations in the port industry on the whole may be said to be very good, and credit for this is rightly shared between the shipping association and the management of the port services department (of the government) and the Seamen and Waterfront Workers Union which caters to the majority of the employees. . . . It is generally recognized that the collective agreements in this industry are of high standard and there is little doubt in my mind that future managers will carry on in the best tradition of their predecessors.[26]

The union has had a good bargaining relationship with the Shipping Association ever since its first contract in 1938. It enjoys a closed shop and check-off and coöperates with the employers' association in the operation of a hiring hall. The government port authority, by tradition, follows the agreement with the employers' association in the government's dealings with the union.

Cecil Alexander was an exception to the rule in the West Indies in that he had no political ambition nor even an ambition to become leader of all Trinidad workers. The Waterfront Union took no part in the political oratory on the need for self-government, and its political interests are limited to issues which touch directly on the problems of the waterfront workers. Instead of taking part in local politics the union manages its political problems through its affiliation with the British Transport Workers Union, which in turn takes the problems up directly with the British Parliament. The union gives aid to the unorganized through the Trade Union Federation, which it was instrumental in forming. The unwillingness of the waterfront workers to support other workers in their bid for union recognition explains in part the limited extent of union organization in Trinidad. On the other hand, by concentrating on job-centered goals the Seamen and Waterfront Workers Union has become one of the most stable, financially strong, and successful unions in the BWI.

Unions in the Sugar Industry

The sugar industry is the major employer of labor, maintaining 12,000 field hands (19,000 during crop season) and 6,000 factory workers. Field hands are East Indians, and factory workers are Negros. Working conditions on sugar estates may be summarized as follows:[27]

Most workers live in villages apart from estate property, and therefore are not subject to the complete authority of estate managers. Loss of employment does not mean loss of home. Casual employment and lack of job tenure, however, create insecurity.

Housing is poor but rapidly improving. The law requires the pulling down of the "barracks" type of dwelling and the sugar welfare fund is used entirely for housing development. Nevertheless, there is need for improvement in housing, water supply, sanitation, and social services.

Supervision is generally poor, resulting in payroll padding, kickbacks, and favoritism in job assignments.

The wage structure is chaotic between regions, between estates, and even on the same estate.

Employers have been opposed to unions and discriminate against union members.

Estate workers are generally discontent and have serious grievances.

Union organization in the sugar industry has been "confusion-compounded," to use a West Indian expression, in part because East Indians tend to be aloof and are uninterested in unionism. Before every political election new sugar unions are formed by ambitious politicians only to be abandoned if the candidate fails in the election, or to decline from neglect if the candidate wins. Among the three more enduring unions there have been serious jurisdictional disputes and rivalry, resulting from the political ambitions of the union leaders. Taking advantage of the unstable situation, Uriah Butler undermines the strength of existing unions and leads irresponsible strikes to create further confusion. Finally, there are three rival associations of small cane farmers, organizations of self-employed workers who lease land from the big estates and sell cane to the estate factories. These organizations have also been used by the politically ambitious, and the inability of the rival organizations to coöperate minimizes their effectiveness.[28]

The All-Trinidad Sugar Workers Union formed in 1938 is the oldest union in the sugar industry. From 1945 to 1948 the Sugar Manufacturer's Association recognized the union even though it did not have a majority membership, but the collective-bargaining relationship was not satisfactory. During this period Uriah Butler attempted to break up the sugar union by intimidation and violence. Although failing in his objective of winning recognition for his British Empire Workers, Peasants, and Rate Payers Union he did cause the employers' association to withdraw recognition from the All-Trinidad Sugar Workers Union. Under the leadership of MacDonald Moses, the All-Trinidad Sugar Workers Union began to grow and prosper again, but he quit the union when the sugar workers failed to support his candidacy for the Legislative Council, and the union again began to decline. A struggle then ensued between two men, Oli Mohammed and Lionel Seukeran, for control of the union. Mohammed gained the secretaryship of the union, and on a technicality removed Seukeran from office and invited Quinton O'Conner of the Federated Workers Union to become president. O'Conner, although president of the All-Trinidad Sugar Workers Union, failed to assume leadership of the union. Seukeran retaliated by forming the Sugar Workers Union —a union weak in membership but influential because of the friendliness of the government toward Seukeran.

Meanwhile Mitra Sinanan, a member of the Legislative Council, invited Osman Ali Mohammed, a former officer of the Seamen and Waterfront Workers Union, to organize the sugar workers, and they formed the Sugar Industry Workers Union. The Federated Workers Union and the British Colonial Citizens' Taxpayers and All-Workers Union, each of which claimed membership on some sugar estates, agreed to withdraw from the sugar industry in 1954. In 1953, the All-Trinidad Sugar Workers Union and the Sugar Industry Workers Union agreed to federate under the presidency of Bhadase Maraj, a businessman who is alleged to have made a fortune under questionable circumstances dealing in United States war-surplus goods. He formed a quasireligious political party and was elected to the legislature in 1952. Commenting on Maraj as a union leader, Fred Dalley said:

Another member of the Legislative Council, the honorable Bhadase Maraj then appeared on the scene and having made himself popular in several ways the two registered unions agreed to federate under his presidency. . . . I feel constrained to point out that I had no evidence of Mr. Maraj's qualification as a trade union leader. I particularly disapprove of any idea of members' contributions being paid for them [Maraj's services] as has been suggested.[29]

Prominent Trinidadians interviewed by the writer went further to accuse Maraj of bringing Chicago-style racketeering methods to Trinidad and feared that he would succeed in joining together in Al Capone manner politics, business, trade unionism, and religion.

The friendly advice to trade unionists offered by Fred Dalley coupled with the public opinion generated by the release of his report, succeeded in partially undermining Maraj's status as a union leader. With the aid of the Caribbean Area Division of ORIT and the British Trade Union Congress the All-Trinidad Sugar Estate and Factories Workers Union was amalgamated with the smaller Cane Farmers Union to form the Federated Unions of Cane Farmers and Sugar Workers. The All-Trinidad Sugar Workers Union severed connections with the Sugar Workers Union. The new federation called a successful strike on sugar estates in 1955 and won collective bargaining rights from the Sugar Manufacturers Association.[30] Failure of collective-bargaining negotiations with the employers' association precipitated a strike in 1956 which failed and ended the brief bargaining relationship. Officials of the Caribbean Area Division of Inter-American Regional Organization of Workers diagnosed the failure to organize the sugar industry as one involving personal rivalries, political ambitions, and the failure of established unions to assist the workers of the sugar industry.[31] The British Trade Union Congress sent Martin Pounder to Trinidad in 1957 to assist in the reorganization of the unions in the sugar industry.[32] Under Pounder's guidance the All-Trinidad Sugar Estates and Factory Workers Union once again won recognition from the employers' association in March 1958 with the signing of a two-year agreement which provides, among other things, for the check-off of union dues.

British Empire Workers and Rate Payers Union

The British Empire Workers and Rate Payers Union has no union agreements and no members but nevertheless is a force to be reckoned with. Its leader, Uriah Butler, described by Fred Dalley as a "curious phenomenon," led the riots of 1937 and 1947 (see chapter ii, p. 59). In the absence of strong, stable unions he could precipitate further rioting. Although a persuasive orator, his failure lies in his inability as organizer and administrator. Regarding the Butler union Fred Dalley said:

He still attempts to run the union as a political organization to promote his own Messianic career, regardless of the trade union ordinance. The irresponsible and violent type of worker seems to be attracted and fostered by his union—the secession of short-period secretaries of the organization may be noted as indicative of his autocratic methods—and a very unsatisfactory state of affairs as regards the union funds has once more been revealed by the auditors of the books.[33]

In addition to the described major lines of union demarcation there are a multitude of small, weak unions in government departments, quasipublic utilities, and small businesses. Some are the instruments of personal and political ambition and others are isolated by disgust with and distrust of the over-all union situation in Trinidad. Some thrive because of the benevolence of a friendly employer and others are handicapped by antiunion employers. As observed by Fred Dalley, effective unionism requires that these splinter groups be amalgamated into a few unions along rational, jurisdictional lines and supported by a unified trade-union council.[34] After twenty years of turmoil it appears that the Trinidad union movement is now moving in this direction.

Politics

In addition to union weakness stemming from the rivalry between two union federations; the inability of East Indians to organize themselves; strong antiunion employer opposition in the sugar industry; and the disruptive influences of Uriah Butler, weaknesses in the union movement also arise from the lack of established political parties. Despite the fact that there were four political parties, the banner under which a candidate was elected was not a reliable guide to the stand he would take on issues of the day or the groups with which he would align himself in the council.[35]

Although its political parties present few conflicting issues, Trinidad's democratic development has been handicapped by claims of individual politicians all of whom pose as friends of the working man. In addition, a political split developed between East Indian and Negro sectors of the community and, more recently, between Moslems and Hindus, creating divisions along racial-ethnic lines rather than political differences over economic policy. Butler's Home Rule party adds to the confusion. It was able to win a majority of the legislative seats in the 1953 elections and, in parliamentary tradition, he should therefore have been recognized as the leader of the legislature and the executive council. The governor refused to recognize him, and his majority disappeared as elective legislative members deserted his party. The fact that Butler could be elected indicates his popular following and the possibility that he could undermine established unions. The election of such a man provides another reason why Great Britain must proceed cautiously in establishing self-government in her colonies.

Finally, because of lack of unity among middle-class Creoles, Portuguese, Chinese, and East Indians, a nationalist party comparable to Jamaica's People's National party was slow to emerge.[36] In a labor movement riddled with ideological, racial, and personal differences, and without a middle-class nationalist movement to rally about, Trinidadian politics has been a confusion of personal rivalries. The People's National Movement, established in 1955 and winning control of the legislature in 1956, may be the beginning of politics based upon parties and issues. The People's National Movement is led by Dr. Eric Williams, an Oxford graduate, former professor of political science at Howard University, director of research for the Caribbean Commission (a regional research group financed by the British, American, Dutch, and French governments), and economic adviser to the Caribbean Area Division of the Inter-American Regional Organization of Workers. The People's National Movement has succeeded in politics by stressing economic development and national unity of all racial-ethnic groups as West Indians. Williams is not a Socialist, and his economic program won popular favor by calling for vigorous action in economic development.[37] The nationalistic appeal of the People's National Movement has united the middle class and the trade unionist in political action for the first time in Trinidad. If Williams's party succeeds in consolidating its rapid advances, it should contribute to union development and stability: (a) by discouraging self-seeking politicians from forming unions just to win political office; and (b) by offering unionists a legitimate and autonomous political party with which to affiliate.

On the other hand, it should be noted that although the People's National Movement won thirteen of twenty-two seats and the remaining seats were split among three other parties, a coalition of rival parties could threaten the now dominant party. Four parties won no seats at all, but received 18,000 votes, and if these votes went to a coalition party they could be decisive. Accordingly, the trade-union and political picture appears to be clearing, but it could change overnight. Williams's defeat in the federal elections (see p. 152), especially since he campaigned on local issues, indicates the fluidity of the political situation.

BRITISH GUIANA

Economic Background

British Guiana's 83,000 square miles make this colony by far the largest British possession in the Caribbean. The interior is a vast rain forest, lacking fertile soil or mineral resources, and hence virtually without population. The coastal strip is an alluvial plain, some 270 miles long and 8 to 10 miles wide. Here is concentrated the population and the sugar industry of British Guiana.

Below sea level at high tide, the coastal strip depends on a vast system of dikes and canals built by the Dutch more than two hundred years ago to keep out the sea in front and the swamp floods "aback." High cost of maintenance caused the abandonment of many estates, which allowed the land to "go to bush" and made possible the amalgamation of the remaining estates. At present there are twenty-one estates cultivating 155,000 acres of land. The firm Booker Brothers, McConnell and Company, operates fourteen estates and eleven sugar factories, together with chain retail stores, ship lines, and allied enterprises. This large concern has inspired the catch phrase, "Booker's Guiana." Two other companies operate the remaining sugar estates. The sugar industry is the principal source of employment, providing 25,000 of the colony's 61,000 jobs, but is second as a producer of revenue. The bauxite industry is the major source of revenue producing two and a half million tons of ore in 1956 but providing fewer than 3,000 jobs. The major bauxite mines (an ALCOA of Canada subsidiary) are situated about 70 miles up the Demmera River and are somewhat cut off from the rest of the life of the colony. Rice is becoming an important crop (89,000 tons in 1956) with a surplus for export. Although a poor second to sugar as a revenue producer, it is a source of employment for 15,000 farmers. East

Indians have developed rice cultivation from peasant holdings to sizable farms, and the government is experimenting in large-scale operations. Since the rain forest does not yield much merchantable timber (5,000,000 cubic feet per year), lumber operations are of minor importance, providing only 1,200 jobs. There are no other important agricultural crops, and the colony's mineral potential is thought to be very small. In 1957, an American firm secured a 37,000-acre lease to mine manganese; and large-scale ore shipments are expected by 1960. Unlike Jamaica and Trinidad, Guiana had little development of light manufacturing and consumer-goods-processing industries.

The population is made up of 230,000 East Indians, 171,000 Negroes, 55,260 persons of mixed decent, 19,000 American Indians, 8,070 Portuguese, 3,320 Chinese, and 4,130 Europeans. As in Trinidad, Pakistanian and Indian nationalism are creating disharmony where heretofore peaceful isolation between racial groups existed. With effective malaria control since World War II, British Guiana's population of 491,000 is rapidly expanding. Although the population ratio per square mile is very low, the density along the productive coastal strip is high, creating serious employment problems. The Venn Report estimated that current population trends would require the creation of 30 per cent more jobs in the next 12 years, at the very time that the sugar industry was to reduce employment opportunities through technological change.[38] The World Bank mission recommended the reclaiming of abandoned coastal areas with modern earth-moving equipment as the only reasonable solution to the growing specter of unemployment created by population pressure.[39]

Working Conditions

Until recently, conditions on the big absentee-controlled estates of British Guiana were the worst in the BWI. East Indian workers and their families were housed rent-free in "ranges" (barracks-type multiple-dwelling units) which by today's standards were not fit for human habitation. Water, sanitary facilities, school buildings, social and recreational facilities, and medical care, which also were supplied free of charge by the estate, were grossly inadequate. Unfortunately, the contrast between the huge estate slums (worker compounds) and the quarters of the estate manager and overseers (management compounds), with green lawns, white cottages, club houses, tennis courts, and (in some instances) swimming pools, was glaringly obvious. This contrast was emphasized by strict observance of the color bar in the job hierarchy.[40] Anyone born on an estate had a right to live there and share in the job opportunities. This population pressure made the slum conditions and unemployment even worse. The Venn Report estimated that 20 per cent of those living on estates had no connection with the sugar industry but took advantage of free-rent housing and services—such as they were. Negroes living off the estates in their own villages where housing amenities were only slightly better, supplied factory labor and cane cutters during crop seasons.

Although the Venn Report is mild in its criticism of estate supervision,[41] this writer, after field trips to the estates and interviews with labor leaders, labor-department officials, and management representatives, has come to the conclusion that it deserves severe criticism for abuse of authority. Supervision and conditions of employment, as described in chapter i, were at their worst in British Guiana. The Communist threat to British Guiana which precipitated the suspension of the constitution in 1953 set into motion a major reform program. Workers and their families are now being moved off the estates to be settled in autonomous villages with community services supplied by the government. Credit is extended to permit home ownership by workers. A campaign is being waged to teach workers the art of collective action in everything from Boy Scout work to village government. The theory is that workers freed from the autocratic paternalism of the estate and made home owners and participating members of the local community, will develop new dignity, a stake in the established order, and ways of helping themselves in the solution of their own problems. Unfortunately, the program has been slow to make itself felt on the way of life of most East Indian estate workers, and discontent remains high. It is too soon to evaluate the results of this large-scale social experiment but if the consequences of more than a century of neglect can be overcome within a few years, the program will be significant for underdeveloped areas everywhere. (This program is being carried out with the aid of specialists from the University of Maryland, the technical assistance being financed under the Point Four program.)

The 1953 disturbances also created an acute awareness of the need for improved personnel practices, but, even under near-revolution, estate management continues to resist change. Government, union leaders, and the top management of the sugar companies know the need for reform, but the problem of just how to convince estate managers, overseers, headmen, and drivers almost defies solution. The new personnel policies that companies wish to follow are obstructed by estate managers, and the companies are in no position to replace the entire line organization of twenty-one estates and of fifteen factories with new supervisory staffs. Eventually the steady pressure from top management and from an effective union will bring about the changes in attitudes of line management necessary to changes in personnel policy. In bauxite mining, a high-profit operation with progressive management, working conditions are good. Located in the jungle and accessible only by river boat, the company of necessity has had to supply housing and all amenities. Even superior facilities and premium pay, however, are not enough to offset the lure of civilized living conditions on the coast, making labor turnover a problem. Unlike the situation on the sugar estates, personnel practices in the bauxite mines are good. The company makes every effort to avoid paternalism, and encourages workers to organize themselves for self-government in the conduct of village affairs. It has won the approval of the people of British Guiana, especially of the colored middle class, through its strict policy of nondiscrimination.[42]

Union Development

The first union in British Guiana was the British Guiana Labour Union formed in 1919 by Hubert Critchlow. Critchlow, a popular hero as a champion cricketer, was discharged for making demands on behalf of fellow workers for an eight-hour day that they might have time for cricket. Although his union was weakened by his contention that the appointment of officers outside the worker group would help union growth, status, and negotiation ability, the B. G. Labour Union was the only one formed during World War I in the BWI that has had a continuous existence. Its main strength has always been among the waterfront workers.[43] A review of recent union development may be divided into three periods: that between the 1938 riots and the rise of Communist influence; that of Communist dominance; and that following the decline of Communist dominance. As elsewhere in the BWI, the general riots of 1938 mark the beginning of union development in British Guiana. Following these riots a multitude of small unions, with overlapping jurisdictions, officered by leaders from outside the ranks of workers, and often created to support the personal ambitions of the union founder, were born. Every annual report of the British Guiana Department of Labor from 1938 to 1952 remarks on the abundance of unions, the lack of dues-paying members, the jurisdictional disputes, the tendency of fragmentation of existing unions, and the need for rank-and-file leadership. The British Guiana Trade Union Council, formed in 1941, attempted without success to work out jurisdictions among fifteen of the colony's twenty-eight unions which joined the council. During this period the major unions were the B. G. Labour Union; the Manpower Citizens Association (a blanket union whose strength was among the East Indian sugar workers); the Transport Workers Union (made up of government railroad and ferry service employees); and the Federation of Government Workers Union.

The second phase of union development begins with the formation of the People's Progressive party led by Cheddi Jagan. Originally a discussion group led by a Communist clique,[44] it won the support of colored, East Indian and Chinese middle-class nationalists. Leaders of the People's Progressive party also gained the support of most union leaders, infiltrated other unions, and in 1945 gained control of the Trade Union Council. Although elected treasurer of the Manpower Citizens Association in 1945, Jagan was unable to control this largest and strategically most important union in the colony. Consequently, Amos Rengela—another Manpower Citizens Association officer who was also vice-president of the British Guiana East India Association, which sometimes acted as a labor union—and J. P. Latchmansingh, a medical doctor, formed the Guianese Industrial Workers Union. Jurisdictional rivalry between the Manpower Citizens Association and the Guianese Industrial Workers Union resulted in strikes (in which workers were killed as a consequence of police ineptness) in 1948, 1951, 1952, and 1953. The People's Progressive party and the Guianese Industrial Workers Union succeeded in completely undermining worker confidence in the Manpower Citizens Association but the Sugar Producers Association and the government resisted efforts of Jagan's union to win recognition.[45]

The B. G. Trade Union Council joined the World Federation of Trade Unions in 1948 with the encouragement of the colonial government and broke with it in 1950 at the same time as the British Trade Union Congress withdrew. The B. G. Trade Union Council did not respond to the anti-Communist International Confederation of Free Trade Unions invitation for affiliation, but Jagan of the Guianese Industrial Workers, Jackson of the Government Workers Union, and Blackman of the Sawmill Workers Union took prominent parts in the Communist World Federation of Trade Unions activities as "observers" between 1951 and 1953.[46] The Manpower Citizens Association and the Bauxite Miners Union affiliated with the International Confederation of Free Trade Unions. In a move of questionable legality, the anti-Jagan, non-Communist elements of the Trade Union Council voted, while supporters of the People's Progressive Party were out of the country, to dissolve the B. G. Trade Union Council.

In the first general election of April, 1953, under universal adult suffrage and a new liberalized constitution, the People's Progressive party gained 51 per cent of the popular votes and 18 out of 24 seats. This majority gave the People's Progressive party six ministerial posts and 6 out of 10 seats in the executive council. Its first move was to seek recognition from the Sugar Producers Association for Jagan's Guianese Industrial Workers Union. A general strike was called in which union leaders who were also ministers of the government urged worker participation in the strike in the name of the government. By this time, membership in the Guianese Industrial Workers Union outnumbered that of the Manpower Citizens Association, but even so, the response to the strike was not wholehearted. The Sugar Producers Association's offer of joint recognition to the two unions was rejected by the Guianese Industrial Workers. The Jagan government then railroaded a "little Wagner act" through the legislature using mob intimidation which would force employer recognition of the

Guianese Industrial Workers Union as a matter of law.[47] At this point the governor suspended the constitution, British troops were landed, and an interim provisional government was established. In the white paper justifying this extreme action of the British government, the following examples of ministerial misconduct leading to the collapse of the British Guiana government were enumerated:[48] Fomenting strikes for political ends; attempting to oust established trade unions by legislative action; removal of the ban on the entry of West Indian Communists; introduction of a bill to repeal the undesirable-publications ordinance and the flooding of the territory with Communist literature; misuse of the rights of appointed boards and committees; the spreading of racial hatred; planning to secularize church schools and to rewrite textbooks to give them a political bias; neglect of their administrative duties; undermining the loyalty of the police; attempting to gain control of the public service; threats of violence.

In the more recent stages of British Guiana union development, unions reorganized and regrouped after the collapse of the People's Progressive party. The British Trade Union Congress has given money and assistance to the reorganization of the unions. George Woodcock, assistant secretary of the British Trade Union Congress, and Andrew Dalgleish, retired secretary of the metal and engineering group of the Transport and General Workers Union, have been active since 1954 in reorganizing non-Communist unions. In 1955 the People's Progressive party split, and L. F. S. Burnham, lawyer-leader of the B. G. Labour Union, and Dr. Latchmansingh, leader of the Guianese Industrial Workers Union, withdrew their unions from the Jagan group. Jagan has been left alone without formal union organization but with a large popular following among East Indian sugar workers. In 1956 the British Guiana Trade Union Council was re-formed with 28 non-Communist unions and affiliated with the International Confederation of Free Trade Unions. Unfortunately, the trade-union council suffers from the attacks made by Jagan on its general secretary, Rupert Tello. Tello, former Manpower Citizens Association president and leader of the government rice-workers branch of the union, is an able union leader, but he served as a member of the interim government appointed by the governor and is now an appointed member of the legislature. His outstanding work in government service leaves him open to the charge of being a stooge for British authorities. The Manpower Citizens Association became an industrial union and agreed to limit its jurisdiction to the sugar industry. The Guianese Industrial Workers Union has applied for affiliation with the B. G. Trade Union Council and is seeking a rapprochement with the Manpower Citizens Association.[49] The Communist threat to trade unionism is now in abeyance, but East Indian nationalism, the enormous amount of social and economic reform necessary in the face of serious population pressures, and the recalcitrant attitudes of estate management make the union future uncertain.

When representative government was restored by the general elections of 1957, Jagan again won the majority of legislative seats. The remaining legislative seats were split among Negro candidates supported by Negro groups in the Georgetown (the capital city) area. Without union and middle-class support, the People's Progressive party won with the votes of East Indian sugar workers. East Indian nationalism rather than communism was the issue. In its effort to disentangle itself from politics, the B. G. Trade Union Council endorsed no political candidate, but individual union leaders ran as independents or with Burnham's Peoples National Congress. It appears that the B. G. Negro population is now united for union action but not for political action. The non-Communist East Indian leaders are unable to win the support of the East Indian population, and this leadership is divided. Most East Indians do not support the union that represents them and in politics continue to support Cheddi Jagan.[50]

British Guiana Labour Union

The British Guiana Labour Union, an industrial union made up of waterfront workers, was founded by Hubert Critchlow in 1919 and is the oldest union in the BWI. Critchlow is now honored as one of the founding fathers of West Indian trade unionism, but he was never a strong leader. Having invited middle-class leaders to become officers of it, the union has been exploited by a succession of political opportunists. Although it had 12,000 members in 1922, it suffered many ups and downs arising from alleged corruption of union leaders and burdensome debts. The union's collective-bargaining relations have been weak because of internal dissension and preoccupation of its leadership with politics. In recent years, the B. G. Labour Union had been led by Burnham, who was once second-in-command of the Communist-dominated People's Progressive party and is now leader of the non-Communist but anti-British People's National Congress. The union is now affiliated with the reformed B. G. Trade Union Council, and bargaining relationships with the Shipping Association have been reëstablished.

Union Development in the Sugar Industry

The British Guiana Workers League, formed in 1931, had a small following among Negro sugar mill workers; was never an aggressive militant union; never won employer recognition; and, finally, faded out of the picture in 1951. The Manpower Citizens Association, formed in 1937 by Ayube Edun, editor of the *Guiana Review*, a journal catering to East Indians, gained strength among East Indian sugar workers during the riots of 1938. After a bitter two-year struggle the union won recognition from the newly formed Sugar Producers Association in 1939. This meant little, however, for the union lacked local organization and leadership, and estate managers were not disposed to change their traditional pattern of labor relations.[51] Also, worker confidence in the union received a set back from which it never fully recovered when it was learned that Edun was in the employ of the Sugar Producers Association as a "industrial advisor." A weak, poorly led union, an antiunion employers' association, reactionary estate management, and dissatisfied workers made the wartime era a confused one in the sugar industry. Spontaneous local strikes, continual union-employer dissension, and the failure of the union to establish effective relations at the estate level caused the Department of Labor in 1945 virtually to impose the Joint Estate Council system on the sugar industry. The Joint Estate Council plan called for the election of seven worker representatives from the entire work force, regardless of union membership, to meet regularly with estate management. Workers did not understand the operation of the plan; elected representatives were weak and ineffective; and estate management made unwilling and unenthusiastic participants who, in general, refused to act on the points brought up in discussion. Only the efforts of the Labor Department officers, who often stepped out of their neutral roles as observers to speak on behalf of the workers, kept the councils functioning. Finally, the rival Guianese Industrial Workers Union had no difficulty in convincing workers that the ineffective Joint Estate Council representatives were stooges of the government and of the employers.[52]

Leaders of the Manpower Citizens Association seek to absolve themselves from responsibility for the collapse of their union by pointing to the ignorance of the workers, the opposition of management, and communication difficulties created by the great distances over difficult roads that officers had to travel in order to hold their union together. (British Guiana has 260 miles of roads, 74 miles of which are hard-surfaced.) Nevertheless the Guianese Industrial Workers Union leaders did manage to travel, without financial aid from the International Confederation of Free Trade Unions, and to contact workers despite government and employer opposition. It is true that the Guianese Industrial Workers Union created false issues (for example, the "cut-and-load" controversy)[53] but it was successful in reaching the workers. The government, the Sugar Producers Association, and the Manpower Citizens Association could not convince workers of the value of the Joint Estate councils or of the truth of the cut-and-load controversy. As the Guianese Industrial Workers Union grew in strength the Sugar Producers Association and the Labour Department of the government moved to support the Manpower Citizens Association, thus confirming the suspicions of the workers that the Manpower Citizens Association was the tool of Booker Brothers.

Union development in the sugar industry was further complicated by three small craft unions: the drivers', the estate clerks', and the sugar boilers' unions, all of which received recognition from the employers in 1948. These unions represented the skilled groups of estate workers who could have given an industrial union of sugar workers local leadership, but for reasons of status and political intrigue instead went their separate ways. Their small size and middle-class political leadership also has made them ineffectual.

At the time of the suspension of the constitution in 1953, the Manpower Citizens Association had virtually no membership, because the mass of East Indian estate workers were supporters of the People's Progressive party and the Guianese Industrial Workers Union. In 1954 the union elected Richard Ishmael, former New York University dental student, principal of the Indian Trust College (High School) and president of the Sugar Boilers' Union, as its president. Although Ishmael has definite political ambitions, he has given the Manpower Citizens Association effective leadership. He has won back the loyalty of key groups of workers, rejuvenated the Joint Estate councils, won a new and improved collective agreement with a check-off from the Sugar Producers Association, and is now working to revise the wage structure and incentive system on estates. George Woodcock, labor member of the commission to study the suspension of the constitution, has given invaluable aid in rebuilding the union. The rebuilding also has been assisted by a £3,000 grant from the British Trade Union Congress. A jurisdictional problem with the Guianese Industrial Workers Union, the popular support given Jagan by East Indian workers, and the reactionary attitudes of estate managers remain to be resolved before satisfactory union-management relations can be developed.

The future of unionism in the sugar industry is not promising. Living conditions are slow to improve in spite of the government's $44,000,000 development program. The operating management of estates is slow to change its reactionary ways. Any improvement in living or working conditions is acclaimed by Jagan as a personal victory. The past record of the Manpower Citizens Association, its affiliation with Negro unions, its aid from British unionists, and even recognition by the employers association is regarded with suspicion by East Indian sugar workers. The defection of Dr. Latchmansingh's Guianese Industrial Workers Union has neither hurt Jagan's position nor helped the Manpower Citizens Association. An impasse will continue as long as Jagan remains unacceptable to the employers and colonial government as spokesman for East Indian sugar workers or until the sugar workers accept some other East Indian leader as their spokesman.

The Transportation Workers Union

The Transportation Workers Union, founded in 1938, is an industrial union made up of government railroad and ferry-service employees. It is a strong, democratic, rank-and-file-led union catering to skilled workers with steady jobs and above-average wages. The union won the closed shop by strike even though the employer—the government—is opposed to the union shop in principle. Assured dues payment makes it financially the strongest union in British Guiana. The Transport Workers Union has not become embroiled in politics, the People's Progressive party was unable to infiltrate it, and consequently it has the strength and stability to give its members effective representation.

British Guiana Bauxite Miners Union

The B. G. Bauxite Miners Union attempted unsuccessfully to win employer recognition by strike several times during the early 1940's and finally won recognition after a four-week strike in 1947. This union has rank-and-file leadership and is democratic and nonpolitical. It disaffiliated itself from the Manpower Citizens Association in 1950 because its leadership considered the latter to be weak and corrupt. Cut off from the rest of British Guiana by almost a hundred miles of trackless jungle, the bauxite miners at MacKenzie were able to resist Communist penetration; they never became embroiled in the Communist-dominated People's Progressive party; and the political district of its area was the only one that did not elect a supporter of Jagan to the legislature in 1953. Upon recognizing the union, the company changed its personnel policy to one of genuine acceptance of the union, and an era of harmonious relations followed. However, union membership declined; employees became suspicious of the integrity of union leadership; and the leadership became too dependent on the wisdom and guidance of the company. Although it was not a company-dominated union, company officers feared infiltration by Jagan's followers unless the union leadership showed more independence and militancy. The bauxite miners' affiliation with the Caribbean Federation of Aluminum and Allied Workers in 1956 should give it strength through coördination of collective-bargaining activities and through the technical services of the United Steel Workers of America. For example, the steelworkers' and the bauxite miners' federation is determined to wipe out the differential between the 58 cents an hour minimum wage for Guianese miners and the 94 cents an hour minimum wage for

Jamaican miners (1957). The Bauxite Miners Union has also affiliated with the revitalized British Guiana Trade Union Council.

British Guiana Timber, Saw Mill, and Quarry Workers Union

The Timber Workers Union is a small industrial union which is weakened by the limitations of its potential membership. Timber and quarry operations are carried out in the jungle, where the only means of transportation is by river boat, making communications between union members and officers particularly difficult. Workers do not stay with one employer but tend to drift from job to job. Most employers are antiunion, and the union is in no position to fight discrimination against union members. The British Guiana Timber Company, a joint government and Booker Brothers operation, is the largest employer in the industry. It offers above-average working conditions and union recognition but, when the writer visited its operations in 1954, an antiunion policy was followed by the operating management despite a stated policy of the Georgetown office of the company to the contrary. The union was further weakened by the involvement of its leadership in the People's Progressive party. Its leadership was among the first to disassociate itself from the party following the suspension of the constitution, but was suspended from the Trade Union Council for supporting Jagan in the 1957 elections.

Chapter IV	Union Development in the Smaller Colonies

BRITISH HONDURAS

British Honduras, in Central America, has an area of 8,600 square miles and a population of 81,000. Logging and milling of mahogany is the principal source of employment and provides 63 per cent of the colony's revenue. In tropical rain forests, virtually without roads, logging is a high-cost operation. On the one hand, the demand for mahogany is declining, while at the same time timber reserves are near exhaustion. Mahogany exports have been declining steadily since World War II. With a growing population and an estimated seventy years needed to rehabilitate the mahogany industry, British Honduras faces serious economic problems. Chicle, the gum of the wild sapodilla tree and the base for chewing gum, is the second important source of employment and provides 12 per cent of the colony's revenue. With the development of synthetic chicle, exports and prices have declined.[1] The problems of the Stan Creek citrus development, the third important industry, are described in chapter i. Aside from citrus growing, agriculture is virtually nonexistent, because, according to a popular explanation "loggers are not interested in farming." Other reasons are: The Belize Estate and Produce Company owns nearly 20 per cent of the land and is not willing to develop the potential of the land nor will it permit others to do so; laws permitting homesteading of crown land need improvement; the government has been backward in soil and crop re-

---

[1] For notes to chapter iv, see pp. 199–200.

search; and roads and farm credit necessary to agricultural development are lacking. Recent experiments in production of rice, sugar, beef, sisal, and raising of dairy cattle, appear to be promising.

Unemployment created by the decline of the two major industries is further complicated by seasonal layoffs. Timber operations can be carried out only during the dry season of five to seven months, while chicle is available only during the wet season of five to seven months. Negroes are the loggers and Mayan Indians are the chicleros; one group is unemployed while the other group works. Should the companies attempt to combine jobs, one group in the labor force would be permanently unemployed. Seasonal unemployment and jungle operations create poor working conditions. Both loggers and chicleros return from months in the jungle for sprees in Belize, the capital city. Soon without funds, they ask for advances from their employers on next season's wages. Chronically in debt to their employers and subject to imprisonment for failure to carry out a season's contract, the employees are in a poor bargaining position. Nevertheless, employers who refused to advance wage payments would be without labor, and if they did not rely upon the law they would be without both labor and the wages advanced. Legislation regulating the size of the wage advance and union opposition to any advances have had small effect. Loggers must live in temporary quarters and depend on the company commissary. Conditions in logging camps were severely criticized in both the Moyne and the Orde Browne reports, and regulatory legislation has been enacted.[2] Labor officers, however, complain of the difficulties of inspection and enforcement when roads are lacking. Moreover, permanent camps are not subject to regulation. Chicleros are self-employed contractors working for brokers who in turn rent harvesting rights from the government. Union officers claim that chicleros are in an inferior bargaining position and favor a coöperative marketing arrangement; the brokers, on the other hand, claim that they are squeezed by both the chicle companies and the chicleros. In any event, the Mayan chicleros, who generally look upon chicle merely as a source of liquor money, appear to be interested in neither unions nor coöperatives.

The General Workers Union was formed in 1938 but did not

become a significant force until it was taken over by a group of young Catholic radicals in 1951. Their brand of trade unionism is based on an interpretation of Catholic doctrine which calls for just prices—which in this case means higher prices for mahogany exports and lower prices for manufactured imports; and just wages—which they define as minimum standards of health and decency which are much higher than the existing wage levels. The union's strong ideological base gives its leadership a missionary zeal that makes its officers effective organizers. As it is a blanket union, its membership includes mahogany, citrus, banana, waterfront workers, retail clerks, and government public-works employees. The union is rank-and-file led and democratic, and in spite of communication problems in trackless jungles its leadership keeps in close touch with its membership.[3]

In 1952 union leaders formed the People's United party and began a vigorous anticolonial campaign. They charged the government and lumber companies with a conspiracy to exploit the colony by keeping it a private lumber camp instead of developing it into a country. The facts that reforestation has been neglected, agriculture ignored, a part of the country left unexplored, and harbor facilities and roads lacking lend support to the charge of the People's United party. Interpretation of Catholic teaching and politics, namely, the need for individual dignity and for a minimum living standard essential to the salvation of the soul, was presented in a platform calling for independence outside the British Empire, nationalization of the mahogany industry, and an elaborate system of consumer and producer coöperatives. The attack of the People's United party on the colonial government together with alleged connections with Guatemalan Communists caused the government to discourage and harass the union. Leaders of the People's United party and General Workers Union lost their seats in the Belize City Council for refusal to give allegiance to the queen; their public speeches caused them to be jailed for sedition; and the public-works department refused to deal with their union. A stalemate in collective bargaining, closely related to these political issues, led to a disastrous general strike in 1953. On the eve of the 1954 general elections, the first under universal adult suffrage, a commission of inquiry cleared the union-political party leaders of charges of Communist conspiracy.[4]

No middle-class nationalist leadership of unions or political parties developed in British Honduras, because the colored middle class tends to identify itself with England and the West Indies, whereas the working class tends to be against the West Indies (among other things fearing a labor migration from Jamaica and Barbados) and considers itself Latin American. Accordingly, middle-class politicians, who have been poorly organized, do not appeal to the working-class electorate, and the People's United party talks of the problems of the Central American republics rather than those of the West Indies.

Having won the majority of seats in the legislative council in the elections of 1954 and 1956, leaders of the People's United party dropped their extreme anti-British views and gave allegiance to the queen. Coöperation between the elected leaders and the colonial government in a program for economic reform followed. The General Workers Union, recovering from the 1953 general strike, likewise prospered and progressed. It had a total membership of some 11,000 workers, an impressive figure when compared with a population of only 81,000,[5] at the time of the union-party split over personal rivalries in 1956. Nick Pollard, a former president of the General Workers Union formed the Christian Democratic union and political party, and the strength of his union rose as the Christian Democrats won several legislative seats away from the People's United party leaders in the general elections of 1957.[6] ORIT-ICFTU representative Harry Pollak has sought to mediate the dispute, but little progress has been made. While the General Workers Union and People's United party, under the leadership of George Price, continues to dominate in the union and political affairs of British Honduras, they are weakened by the split.

ST. KITTS-NEVIS

St. Kitts-Nevis Trades and Labour Union

St. Kitts and Nevis are two adjoining islands with a combined population of 53,000 and an area of 152 square miles. Nevis serves as the rather badly organized supplier of local food produce while St. Kitts is entirely engaged in sugar production. The sugar estates of St. Kitts are small and some are absentee-controlled but they are efficiently managed as a single unit by one operating company. The estate owners also hold 50 per cent of the stock in the island's only sugar factory. Although the sugar industry is far from prosperous, the extreme disparities in income between those of the small minority of white employers and the masses of unskilled, underemployed Negroes are a source of tension. A political party formed in 1931 preceded the formation of a labor union. Since 1938 the Labour League has held seats in the legislature even under limited franchise and agitated for improved working conditions without actually attempting collective bargaining. After the riots of 1939 the union was formally organized and has enjoyed steady growth without serious employer opposition.[7] The union is rank-and-file led, democratic, militant, and stresses grievance handling. Since St. Kitts is small and has a good road system, union representatives are in close touch with the workers. The union and its political party, the leadership of both being virtually identical, have no opposition and have controlled the government since 1940. It is generally agreed that the union has done a good job in improving working conditions and the political party has excelled in social-welfare work.

In union-management relations the major issue concerns the profits of the sugar mill. The union claims they are excessive; employers refuse to "show their books" and will negotiate wages only as related to costs of living and price of sugar. The union threatens to nationalize the mill, thereby gaining through political action what it is unable to do in collective bargaining. In politics the major issue is housing and efficient land use. Before labor's rise to power, workers were settled in "guts"—deeply cut, tree-shaded gullies that drained the hillsides—and were resentful of what they considered to be inferior housing sites. The labor government has appropriated flat, level, treeless cane land for housing developments—a move which pleases the worker electorate but which reduces the already limited acreage available for money crops. While dues-paying membership (8,177 in 1956) has fallen off in recent years, no one doubts worker loyalty to the union and its political party. Lack of collective-bargaining gains and preoccupation with political issues are reasons given by local observers for the decline in financial support. Two reasons given for union success in organizing agricultural laborers are the autocratic attitudes of estate management before 1939 and the hard-working union leadership which remains in close contact with the worker and his on-the-job problems.

Antigua Trades and Labour Union

Antigua is an island of 170 square miles with a population of 51,000. Although 500,000 pounds of Sea Islands cotton were produced in 1957 as a peasant crop, 90 per cent of the labor force is dependent on the sugar industry. Low average annual rainfall together with frequent droughts result in low crop yields and contribute to the poverty of Antigua. Most sugar estates have been amalgamated into a syndicate that efficiently operates the island's cane land and sugar factory. The Antigua Trades and Labour Union was founded in 1939 after an island-wide spontaneous strike. This union, formed with the aid and advice of Sir Walter Citrine, has a blanket structure with forty-four branches divided into industry, trade, and geographical units. All branches have elected officers and effective leadership. With 12,175 dues-paying members (1956), branch units have been able to purchase their own buildings. Membership includes all wage earners —domestic servants, tradesmen, shopowners, teachers, civil servants, and independent peasant farmers. The union is rank-and-file led, prohibits nonresidents from holding office, and is distrustful of all outsiders, "particularly lawyers." Antigua is the only BWI colony that has no union affiliated with the International Confederation of Free Trade Unions. Officers of the Trades and Labour Union told the writer they felt that subsidies from abroad would tend to make them soft and weak and they were too poor to offer financial assistance to other unions.

Over the years the union has secured contracts with all employers of labor in sugar, shipping, stores, civil service, building trades, public works, and for domestic servants. The Federated Employers' Association, formed in 1950, brought together major employers for joint negotiations. As a result, there is now a master contract on an island-wide basis. In dealing with employers the union is militant. All grievances are given prompt and careful attention and wildcat strikes are not uncommon to support workers' claims. In 1951 employers attempted a showdown with the union and lost. In 1946 the union leaders formed the Antigua Labour party and with the advent of universal adult suffrage won all the seats in the legislature.[8] As a political party, the leadership has fought vigorously and successfully for economic development and increased aid from the United Kingdom, and is active in self-help projects, coöperatives, education, and recreation programs. The party is particularly pleased with its program of creating an independent peasantry. Urging the syndicate to sell marginal lands, which were either idle or rented, the labor government supplied credit for land purchase and improvement, and has followed up with a technical-assistance program.[9] The result has been more acreage in production and better yields in marginal land, giving the peasants the dignity accruing from land ownership.

In evaluating the facts making unionism in Antigua so strong, local observers make two points:

First, before 1939 estate management was autocratic even by West Indian standards; since 1939 and until 1951 estate management has resisted unions to a greater degree than elsewhere, which led to greater union militancy.

Second, the leadership works as a team and is close to the workers. The integrity and sincerity of the leadership has won the loyalty of the workers. Any person who attempts to act as spokesman for workers is severely attacked and criticized by the union and political-party leadership.

BARBADOS

Unlike the other West Indian islands, Barbados is of coral and limestone rather than of volcanic origin. Consequently, the land is relatively flat and well drained, making it ideal for sugar cane. The entire economy is based on the sugar industry; there are no commercial tree crops, and most food supplies are imported. Although the fine beaches of Barbados have created a thriving tourist trade, 94 per cent of the island's income is derived from sugar products. The sugar industry offers direct employment to 3,000 sugar-mill workers, 23,000 field hands during crop, and 30,000 peasant farmers who own ten acres or less.[10] Seasonal unemployment is between 6,000 (government estimate) and 12,000 (union estimate). General unemployment is widespread, but no statistics are available.

With 230,000 persons occupying 166 square miles of land, Barbados is one of the most densely populated agricultural areas in the world.[11] "Bajuns" (Barbadians) are acutely aware that their population increase of 36,000 a year not only creates further unemployment, and increases the cost of community services; but takes valuable cane land out of production to make room for more people. For this reason Barbados is more concerned with the population problem than any other West Indian colony. The government subsidizes the Family Planning Association and has created a revolving fund to aid workers who wish to migrate to jobs abroad. The brightest prospect for Barbados, which is relatively poorer per capita than other islands, is the relaxation by other BWI colonies of immigration bars, after federation.

Sugar estates are relatively small, and family-owned and -operated. Unlike most West Indian whites, "Bajun" planters are proud of their 300-year history and identify themselves with their native island rather than with England. In interviews with the writer they expressed concern for the welfare of the island and a sense of personal stake in its future. As a result, labor relations on estates have not been marked with the bitterness found on the large, corporate-owned, absentee-managed estates.

Barbados has the most extensive color bar in the BWI. Only recently a law was passed prohibiting discrimination in hotels—prompted as part of an unsuccessful bid by Barbados to become the capital of the Federation of the British West Indies. Manual workers do not like the color bar, but accept it because they lack the education for white-collar jobs and the money for admittance in the better clubs and hotels. The colored middle class is vocal in its displeasure but, perhaps because it is small even by BWI standards, it has not succeeded in lowering the color bar to the extent found in other islands. Without speculating on why the color bar continues to be so strong in Barbados, the writer can only observe that the color bar is not an issue in union-management relations.

The period of the late 1930's and the early 1940's was one of intense bitterness and strife between the white employer class and the Negro working class led by middle-class nationalists. Describing the conditions leading to the 1937 riots one writer called the employer class one of the most conservative oligarchies in the West Indies.[12] The Barbados Progressive League, led by Grantley Adams, a lawyer and Oxford graduate, was formed in the early 1930's as a middle-class nationalist movement attacking "the dictatorship of land owners." [13] As the movement grew, the league formed two units, the Barbados Labour party and the Barbados Workers Union. Since 1948, when sufferage was broadened, the Labour party has controlled the legislature. (Unlike in other BWI colonies, however, in Barbados white men run for office and are elected in Negro constituencies. Mrs. Florence Daysh, Barbados National party, was the only white person elected to the first legislature of the Federation of the West Indies.) Adams was made prime minister in 1954, knighted in 1957 in recognition for his excellent administration, and given the power to form a cabinet in January, 1958. (Barbados proudly boasts of having the third-oldest parliament in the world and having had greater freedom at the time of the American Revolution than the thirteen colonies of North America.) This parliamentary tradition together with the high degree of political stability that has followed universal adult suffrage has permitted Barbados to push ahead of other colonies in gaining a greater measure of independence. Adams and the Labour party profess to be Socialist, but as there is little to socialize the ideology has been expressed in progressive taxation for improved community services. After years of bitterness, relations with the white employer class are good on economic and political policy matters. Barbadians offered the writer many theories to explain the era of good feeling, but none of them explained why Barbados is politically more advanced than other colonies. For example, one employer reasoned that Barbados was too poor for the Labour party to dare to be too radical or for employers to become too conservative. "Cold reality forces us to be reasonable and work together," he said. Unfortunately, reality is just as brutal in other colonies, but without the salutary political effects.

Latent political conflict exists in the middle class. The "Young Turks" feel that they have not had a large enough voice in the Labour party; that Adams and his generation have become too conservative and too compromising with the upper class. Dissident elements within the Barbados Labour party formed the Democratic Labour party in 1955. Since 1955 they have held a few seats in the legislature and have some support in the union. The "Young Turks" have unsuccessfully sought union office, but should they succeed in winning control of the union they could use their position to embarrass the present government. While Adams and his Labour party control 15 of 24 seats in the legislature, and have the support of the bulk of the middle class and working class, the younger, more aggressive middle-class group stands ready to exploit any dissatisfaction within the electorate. Although union and political development are far advanced in Barbados, the union finds itself in a position where it may become the victim of a power struggle between rival middle-class groups contending for the working-class vote.

The Barbados Workers Union grew directly out of the 1937 riots. Following the advice of Sir Walter Citrine the union became a separate unit within the Progressive League. Although a blanket union in structure, the Barbados Workers Union has twenty-two industrial branches and negotiates eight basic agreements including the areas of trucking, shipping, retail stores, bakeries, telephones, electric utilities, sugar, and the tobacco factory. The union has its center of power primarily in the waterfront workers and secondly among the manual workers of Bridgetown. Each branch of the union elects its own officers and manages its own affairs; the central executive council is elected by the annual delegate conference. Although the union has a collective-bargaining agreement with the Sugar Producers Association and the sugar industry is the principal employer of labor, few estate workers actually belong to the union. Little attempt is made to organize branches among sugar workers or to settle their day-to-day grievances.

There have been no rival unions nor jurisdictional squabbles in Barbados. Every person interviewed had a different and sometimes conflicting explanation for the excellence of union organization. As a tentative explanation subject to further research, the writer suggests that the smallness of the island, ease of communications, homogeneity of the labor force, and quality of leadership are basic reasons for the stability and growth of the Barbados Labour Union. Upon gaining political power the middle-class nationalists of the Progressive League withdrew from the union, which is now led by rank-and-file leaders. Unlike Bustamante, Adams resigned from union office when he became majority leader of the government in 1953. Frank Wolcott, long-time general secretary of the union is recognized as one of the ablest union leaders in the BWI. At the present time it appears that the union is becoming independent of middle-class leadership, concentrating on collective-bargaining issues although affiliated to a political party led by middle-class nationalists. Union leaders play secondary roles in party councils and when elected to the legislature do not gain ministerial posts. Although union and party development in Barbados may be regarded as a model for other colonies to follow, it may be well to remember that some union leaders would like a bigger role in politics[14] and some middle-class radicals would like a bigger voice in union affairs. A coalition of these groups could split the union and embroil it in political factionalism. The strength shown by Bustamante in the first federal elections has increased the possibility that the Democratic Labour party will form a rival trade union.

Union-management relations (as in politics) have changed during the years from strife to harmony. The 1957 sugar-industries agreement, for example, was the first in the BWI to be concluded without strike or compulsory arbitration.[15] Many theories were offered the writer as to why union-management relations in Barbados were superior to those of the BWI in general but they remain only speculation. It is a fact, that Barbados, based on sugar economy, has a democratic, stable union and satisfactory relations with the principal employers. A short strike of sugar workers to support union demands in March, 1958, ended when the governor appointed a board of enquiry—illustrating the problem of collective bargaining in a small island economy. The governor stated that the crop was already endangered by drought and a strike could not be tolerated.

GRENADA

Trade Unionism in Grenada

Grenada is a mountainous island of 133 square miles and a population of 82,000. Its major source of revenue is tree crops—cocoa, nutmeg, and bananas. Estates are small and family-managed, and peasant proprietors form a high percentage of the work force. Although underemployment and low income are serious problems, in comparison with the rest of the BWI, Grenada is described as "the rich man of the poor house." [16] The Grenada Manual and Mental Workers Union was formed in 1951 by the Honorable E. J. Gairy, a former school teacher and former Aruban oil worker, who claims supernatural powers. He led a successful general strike of near-riot proportions in 1951 but could not consolidate his gains. Unable to organize and delegate authority or to handle ordinary union business, Gairy had a huge personal following but a chaotic union organization. With political success following universal adult suffrage in 1951, his inability to hold the union together, and scandals developing over misappropriation of union funds, his union was allowed to disintegrate.[17] In 1954 Gairy called a general strike without the benefit of a union organization and without making collective-bargaining demands. Although the initial response to the strike call was good, men gradually drifted back to work when police effectively prevented looting of estates. Later, when a wage increase was unilaterally granted by employers, Gairy was acclaimed a hero who had won a wage increase for the workers. His political party also lacks formal organization and is more a coalition of politicians who find his popularity useful to their own political careers. Although he represents the majority of the elected legislators, he has no political program and has not made positive contributions to the legislative process. "Uncle Gairy" remains a popular hero who has no difficulty in winning political elections although his union and his political party have no program to offer.

The Grenada Workers Union, affiliated with the International Confederation of Free Trade Unions, is a rival of Gairy's union led by a group of lower middle-class politicians who are more concerned with their own political careers than with union organization. With only fifty financially contributing members, mostly retail clerks, the union suffers from weak and ineffectual leadership.[18] The Waterfront Workers Union, also an affiliate of the International Confederation of Free Trade Unions, is the third union in Grenada. As its leader is a successful small businessman and harbor pilot; as it is not very aggressive; and as it refuses to strike in sympathy with other work groups, it is regarded by some workers and politicians as company-dominated. Despite its good relations with employers and lack of aggressiveness, however, it has the support of waterfront workers; and its membership did not desert to Gairy. The Waterfront Workers Union has split with the Grenada Workers Union over the latter's preoccupation with politics and refuses to form a trade-union council until the General Workers Union concentrates on unionism.[19]

St. Vincent

St. Vincent is an island of 150 square miles and a population of 75,000. Its major crop is arrowroot, and Sea Islands cotton is a poor second. The economy is dominated by five families who control the biggest estates and whose conservative views have not contributed to the island's progress. Even by BWI standards, working conditions are poor, and population pressure together with growing discontent of the work force make for an explosive situation that defies solution. There are three blanket unions in St. Vincent, each claiming complete jurisdiction over all workers. The St. Vincent Working Men's Association formed in 1934 is the oldest and weakest union, led by elderly men with liberal middle-class views. Following the advice of Captain Cipriani, the leaders of this union did not attempt collective bargaining with employers but sought to influence the small middle-class electorate in favor of social legislation. The United Workers Union, affiliated with the International Confederation of Free Trade Unions, completely undermined the old Working Men's Association in 1951 when George Charles, a former Butlerite, returned from Trinidad with promises of a genuine trade-union movement. The United Workers Union was in turn undermined by the Federated Industrial Workers Union when Ebenezer Joshua, another Butlerite, returned from Trinidad to "save the people" later in the same year, 1951. His union is affiliated with the World Federation of Trade Unions. The Honorable Ebenezer Joshua does not appear to be a Communist or even a fellow traveler, but rather a confused opportunist. No one of the three unions has been able to win a collective-bargaining agreement, although there is some worker support for the United Workers Union and the Federated Workers Union. Charges and countercharges of graft, corruption, and sell-out to the employers and to the colonial administration leave the workers confused. Officials in all three unions are leaders of rival political parties who concentrate on politics, and as members of the legislature they fight each other in the political arena.[20] Unionism in St. Vincent is basically weak because the waterfront workers were never organized. Jim Bury, assistant secretary of the Inter-American Regional Labor Organization, Washington, D. C., organized the waterfront workers in 1957, but recognition of the union by the Shippers Association remained in doubt in August, 1958, because of a deadlock over the hiring hall issue.[21]

St. Lucia

Unions in St. Lucia

With a population of 90,000 and occupying 233 square miles of land, St. Lucia is not overpopulated by BWI standards. It is one place in the BWI where tillable land goes uncultivated; but heavy rainfall, malaria, plant diseases, and lack of an adequate system of roads are factors holding back development. Another reason for failure to exploit resources more fully is St. Lucia's repeated strokes of good fortune such as the establishment of two United States Army bases there during World War II which are still there and attract labor away from the land. Abundance of land also permits subsistence living by peasants and squatters, which dulls the biting edge of poverty. Major sources of employment and revenue are sugar, coconuts, and bananas. Failure to develop agriculture has resulted in a lower than BWI average per-capita income.

The St. Lucia Cooperative Workers Union claims jurisdiction over all the island's workers except those of the waterfront, but, in fact, represents only the manual laborers in government service. The union has a middle-class nationalist leadership which is primarily interested in politics. It once represented the workers of the sugar industry, the dominant industry of the island, without having them organized. The instability of blanket unions was well illustrated when a commission merchant, the Honorable W. G. Brown, campaigned for a seat in the legislature on the platform that he would win wage increases for sugar workers. Brown considered all voters in his constituency automatically union members (see chapter ii, p. 64). His effective oratory won the election, and he thereupon called a strike in the three sugar valleys without benefit of a union or union members. The workers struck to win the wage increase promised them. The result was a government investigation, and recommendations for a profit-sharing scheme that caused the three sugar estate owners to close down. The owners' refusal to abide by the findings of the Commission of Inquiries and the recommendations of the government led to serious unemployment and the disruption of the entire economy. Brown was deported on a technicality. To save the island's economy the government bought and is now operating two of the three estates.

In March 1957 a spontaneous, unorganized, five-week strike of sugar workers took place. Leaders of the Cooperative Workers Union became the spokesmen for the sugar workers. A board of inquiry, appointed by the governor, condemned the practice of members of the legislature serving as union leaders, recommended a wage increase when it was learned that the wage rate was from $0.74 to $1.56 for a ten-hour day, and awarded bargaining rights to the Cooperative Workers Union. The International Confederation of Free Trade Unions contributed to the workers victory in that Harry Pollok, formerly of the UAW (AFL-CIO) assisted in the preparation of the union's case before the Board of Inquiry.[22] The one remaining privately owned sugar factory closed its operations rather than submit to the union.

The St. Lucia Workers Union is a splinter group of dissident politicians formerly associated with the St. Lucia Cooperative Workers Union. It has no membership or bargaining rights and exists solely to further the political ambitions of its leaders.

The Seamen and Waterfront Trade Union of St. Lucia, affiliated with the International Confederation of Free Trade Unions, is a strong and democratic industrial union that has collective bargaining agreements with the shipping association and the Cable and Wireless Company. The workers do not attempt to select leadership from their own ranks but rather ask prominent businessmen to become heads of their union. At one time their president was also president of the St. Lucia Cooperative Workers Union and at the same time president of the Chamber of Commerce. The former president, F. J. Carasco, who resigned his positions to assume management of the government sugar estates, explained to the writer that there was no conflict of interest between workers and small businessmen and that they have a common interest in fighting the big employers that dominate the island's economy. The waterfront workers are not dominated by the outsiders they select as leaders, however, and when one small businessman-politician attempted to create a union issue to further his own political career the union membership voted him out of office.

In summary, union strength in St. Lucia is found with the waterfront workers and the public-works employees. The Cooperative Workers Union has some support in the sugar valleys but no attempt has been made to organize workers on the coconut and banana estates. Personal and political rivalries among the middle-class union leadership have handicapped union development.

| Chapter V | Survey of BWI Trade Unionism |

Extent of Union Organization

Although unions have become a significant force in the political and economic life of the BWI, the majority of workers remain unorganized. Workers in the sugar industry, which is the largest single source of employment, are poorly organized. In Jamaica the confusion arising from dual unionism, conflicting personalities, political issues, and charges of union graft and corruption have hampered effective unionization of the sugar industry. In Trinidad, where unionization of the sugar industry is weakest, the organization of sugar workers has been impeded by political intrigue, employer opposition, "Butlerism," personality issues, jurisdictional disputes, lack of harmony between East Indian field hands and Negro factory workers, and the failure of the Trinidad union movement to support the sugar unions. Unionization of the sugar industry of British Guiana has suffered from friction between East Indian and Negro workers, employer opposition at the estate management level, ineffective leadership, and the Communist issue. In Barbados the dominant union represents the sugar workers in collective bargaining, but does not have the workers organized. Only in St. Kitts and in Antigua are sugar workers effectively organized.

Cocoa, banana, arrowroot, nutmeg, and coconut estates are second only to sugar estates in providing employment opportunities, but union organization on these estates is even weaker than in the sugar industry. Planters explain this lack of unionization as due to the smaller size of these estates, management by owner instead of by absentee corporation, steadier employment, better living conditions, and the higher status accorded work in crops other than sugar. In addition, workers on these estates are often part-time self-employed peasants whose wage-earner status is less clearly defined. Unionization of the nonsugar sector of BWI agriculture is undeveloped also because most of these estates are in the Windward Islands where union development in general is the weakest. Some authorities interviewed by the writer attributed the instability of agricultural-workers unions in the Windward Islands and Trinidad to the islands' French and Spanish history and to the fact that British rule is relatively recent. The Leeward Islands and Barbados, on the other hand, have a long uninterrupted history of British rule and have the strongest, most stable unions. However, the existence of a causal relationship in such a correlation would be difficult to prove.

Unionization of BWI workers is lacking also because so many workers are engaged in jobs which do not lend themselves to unionism. The peasant and the share cropper may be underemployed and available for work, but they are only briefly engaged in wage employment. A large sector of the BWI work force is unemployed at various times, has no regular employment, and works at odd jobs from time to time. Such a condition encourages casual employment and reduces the number of regularly employed workers—the type who would be interested in unionism. Finally, union officers state that most BWI workers, and especially agricultural workers, are yet to be convinced of the benefits of unionism.[1] As noted in chapter i, a high percentage of the BWI work force is in domestic service, which frequently is a form of disguised unemployment, and domestics, anywhere, are difficult to organize. The extent of underemployment is indicated by the high proportion of the labor force engaged in clerical work in retail stores and offices. White-collar workers the world over are notoriously difficult to organize, but in the BWI the problem is complicated by the insecurity of the clerical class. In general, clerks are on the lower fringes of the brown-skinned, middle-class group whose members are darker in pigmentation and of uncertain family background. Accordingly, clerical workers

---

[1] For notes to chapter v, see p. 200.

are afraid to be identified with the Negro working-class movement for fear that their insecure middle-class status will be undermined. Moreover, the supply of colored clerks far exceeds the
demand; wages are extremely low; and victimization of union
clerks is general.

To summarize: the BWI lacks the economic base for strong
unionism. Unemployment, underemployment, casual labor, seasonal employment, and disguised unemployment limit organizing
opportunities. The lack of a clear-cut wage-earner status for many
agricultural workers is also an obstacle to unionization.

Paper Unions

Analysis of union development in the BWI is confused by the
creation of unions on paper which are in fact not unions in the
ordinary sense of the word. For example, a politician running for
office as an independent and without benefit of party organization will form a "union" on the eve of an election campaign. (See
chapter ii, pp. 63–64.) His union will hold no business meetings,
elect no officers, and sign up no workers as dues-paying members. His union has a vague jurisdictional boundary which in effect
covers all voters in the constituency and no collective-bargaining
goals are intended. The politician then holds street-corner meetings, posing as a union leader, denouncing all other politicians
and union leaders as scoundrels, and claiming to be the true
friend of the worker. As election day draws near it becomes clear
that the solution to the problems of the worker is to vote for the
politician rather than follow traditional union methods. If the
politician loses the election, he closes his union operation for it
has no further use to him, and if he wins, he abandons it because
it has served its purpose. Accordingly, there is an increase in the
number of unions registered with departments of labor before
each political election.

Another type of union is formed by the underemployed commission merchant partly because of the notion of eventual political benefits for business reasons and for ego satisfaction; or because of his sincere hope of helping workers with their problems.
As lower-middle-class businessmen, commission merchants are
both close to the working class and respected by workers for
their ability and learning. Workers frequently bring their troubles

to a commission merchant for consultation and advice, and it is not unnatural that they should bring their grievances to him. While commission merchants have become effective leaders of legitimate unions, others have only created paper unions. Once again labor-department statistics record an increase in the number of unions because a commission merchant has registered a "union." Such a union may have officers, but its membership consists of regular customers of the store. Grievances are handled to win customer good will, but no attempt is made to bargain collectively, much less win exclusive bargaining rights. In effect, the commission merchant becomes the employee's agent in individual bargaining. Lacking the compelling force of a strike, the success of the commission merchant as worker representative is limited to his powers of persuasion.

Finally, there are unions formed by small groups of workers which never become functioning unions in the true sense of the word. Such groups exist because workers do not understand unionism; they are distrustful of the larger, more firmly established unions; and because some local leader prefers to have his personal following without being subservient to a larger organization. Some of these unions are large enough to win plant-wide bargaining in small shops, but most of them are more in the nature of social clubs.

To summarize: There are many "unions" listed on the rolls of the departments of labor in the BWI that are not really unions. In Trinidad and British Guiana, at the time of the writer's visit, there were registered unions whose leaders' mailing addresses or even whose continued existence was not known for certain by labor officers. These paper unions lack organization and their membership consists of the small personal following of a local leader. In general, the leadership has only the haziest notion of the functions of a union or the nature of collective bargaining. The significance of paper unions lies in the confusion they generate in the minds of workers as to the nature and function of unionism, and as a force retarding the development of legitimate trade unionism. Visiting labor experts have criticized the multitude of small unions with overlapping jurisdictions. Labor officers advise against the proliferation of unions, but their duty is to register unions rather than serve as a jurisdiction-allocating agency. Paper unions probably represent a stage in union development. As political parties become stabilized the opportunities for independent candidates will be reduced, and, hence, there will be fewer unions created before each election. As workers become more sophisticated about the meaning of trade unionism they will be less gullible. Finally, as job-oriented unions become more firmly established they will appeal to a widening circle of workers.

Jurisdictional Rivalry and the "Parcellation" of Unions

Unions not plagued by jurisdictional rivalry are the exceptions to the rule in the BWI. Only St. Kitts, Antigua, and Barbados have one union covering the entire colony, without rivals. Besides, there are industrial unions in British Guiana and Trinidad which have securely established themselves in their industrial jurisdictions. Everywhere else in the BWI there are rivalries between genuine unions professing interest in collective bargaining. Jamaica is split by two dominant unions—the Bustamante Industrial Trade Union and the National Workers Unions—based upon differing union philosophies, conflicting personalities, and affiliations with rival political parties. In addition, there are smaller unions competing for the same membership. Aside from the unions in the oil industry and on the waterfront, unionism in Trinidad is a confusion of overlapping jurisdictions. The British Guiana union movement is in the process of rebuilding following the Communist debacle of 1953. The People's Progressive Party has lost control of unions but still has a large following among East Indian workers. The non-Communist wing of the People's Progressive party formed the Peoples National Congress party and has taken its unions into the reconstituted Trades Union Council, but the jurisdictions between two rival sugar unions remain to be settled. In St. Lucia, St. Vincent, and Grenada several unions claim island-wide jurisdiction; none of them have large memberships. The General Workers Union of British Honduras is the dominant union and has a large percentage of the work force organized, but it has been confronted with small rival unions and the defection of some of its leaders.

Jurisdictional rivalry is complicated by what the CAD-ORIT officials describe as a "tendency to parcellation." By parcellation they mean that BWI unions lack a binding force to hold them together, and the slightest discord causes unions to split. Union leaders fall out over personal ambitions within their union, political ambitions, ideologies, and suspicion of corruption. Since unions are held together by membership loyalty to the leader rather than to the union, it is fairly easy for disgruntled leaders to take their followings into new unions. Unions lack the power of the purse string to discipline their branches, because few unions collect dues in appreciable amounts.

Union Structure

The structure of the BWI unions is adapted to special environmental problems. There are no craft unions because there are no crafts. Small island economies do not permit specialization in production or in trade skills. Visitors to the West Indies often marvel at the wide range in abilities of the average West Indian worker, each of whom may be a combination carpenter, plumber, mason, auto mechanic, shoemaker, and piano tuner as the occasion demands. No wonder, visitors also marvel at the crude workmanship generally prevalent in the BWI. Without apprenticeship training, without pride in workmanship, and with casual employment in several trades, the worker lacks the community of interests with other workers on which craft unionism is built. Industrial unions exist where a measure of modern technology makes them possible—in bauxite mining, in railroads, in the oil fields, in ferry service, on the waterfront, and in government public works. Workers in these industries are of above average ability; they enjoy job tenure and earn above-average wages. They have an income and status which enable them to break from the peasant and field-hand society to establish a lower-middle-class way of life. It is not surprising, therefore, that industrial unions are more stable, more democratic, more likely to be rank-and-file led, stronger financially, more oriented to collective-bargaining goals, and less directly identified with political parties than other West Indian unions. There are not many industrial unions in the BWI because there are not many industries, but postwar economic development has encouraged the growth of this type of unionism, and at the same time has encouraged greater union stability.

Other unions have what is described as a "blanket" structure; that is, all workers are in one big union. Blanket unions are a logical development where industrial units are too small in membership and finances to permit autonomous existence. On the smaller islands and among agricultural workers where income is low, the work seasonal, and the workers usually casual laborers, the blanket-type structure appears to be most workable. As noted in chapter ii, there is a shortage of union leadership in the BWI; since this is particularly true in occupations covered by blanket unions, the blanket structure enables varied groups of workers to use the services of the same leadership. The industrial branches of the blanket union tend to be the strongest and best organized, the agricultural branches tend to be the weakest. Frequently the nucleus of a blanket union is the waterfront workers, and where agricultural workers do not receive the support of the waterfront workers, as in British Guiana, Trinidad, and the Windward Islands, blanket unions of agricultural workers are the weakest. The dominance of blanket-type unions in Jamaica, one of the largest and economically most advanced of the colonies, is a historical accident. The small industrial unions of the Jamaica Trade Union Council found that they could not stand up against the big, loosely organized union of agricultural and waterfront workers controlled by Bustamante. Moreover, they found that a small group of middle-class leaders were elected as representatives of each of the industrial unions. Accordingly, it made sense to make the industrial unions branches of a blanket union—the National Workers' Union. With the postwar economic growth of Jamaica, particularly in bauxite mining, the National Workers Union has developed a strong base of industrial branches from which it has invaded the agricultural and waterfront jurisdiction of the Bustamante Industrial Trade Union. The National Workers Union of Jamaica, presently the largest union in the BWI, may be more accurately described as a federation of industrial unions.

In degree of organization and type of orientation, blanket unions range from those bordering on paper unions to those resembling a federation of industrial unions. At one extreme are those that are loosely organized, without branch officers, dominated by one leader, undemocratic, weak in grievance handling, and more interested in politics than in collective bargaining. This type of blanket union differs from paper unions in that it has the loyalty of large numbers of workers, can call strikes in critical industries, and is a political power. At the other extreme there are blanket unions with dues-paying members, rank-and-file leadership in branch subdivisions, democratic, and more oriented to grievance handling and collective bargaining than to politics. In general, however, blanket unions tend to be financially weaker, more dependent on outside leadership, and more closely tied to a political party than the industrial unions.

Statistics of Union Growth and Organization

CAD-ORIT lists over 150 unions and federations in the BWI, but because of the tendency to "parcellation" mere numbers are misleading. There were (in 1956) 60 unions and three federations in Trinidad with a total membership of 41,000; 38 unions in British Guiana with 15,000 members; 14 unions in Jamaica with 100,000 members. In some of the smaller islands there are as many as six unions claiming jurisdiction over all workers, with none of them having significant membership. On the other hand, a few unions hold the bulk of the membership in Jamaica and Trinidad; one union dominates all others in Barbados, Dominica, and British Honduras; and there is but one union representing all workers in St. Kitts and Antigua.[2] While the complaint of CAD-ORIT officials that the BWI suffers from too many unions and not enough union members is justified, it is also true that membership is gradually becoming concentrated in a few significant unions.

An analysis of unions in 1954 by type of organization and orientation leads to the following grouping:

Four industrial unions that are rank-and-file led, democratic, and completely nonpolitical.

Five well-organized blanket unions that are rank-and-file led, but are either affiliated with a middle-class nationalist political party or the union leaders themselves are also leaders of a political party advocating a greater measure of self-government and economic reform.

Four unions, one industrial and three blanket, that have middle-class nationalist leadership; in one the middle-class leaders are withdrawing in favor of rank-and-file leadership, in another, political rivalry among leaders destroys the effectiveness of the union, and in the other two the radical political views of the middle-class leadership has hurt their unions.

Sixteen blanket unions that are led by officers of middle-class origin who stress politics to the neglect of collective-bargaining goals. Their political parties are as haphazardly organized as their unions. They are neither nationalists nor reformers, and their political platforms consist of the vaguest generalities. Leaders of such unions are suspected of being opportunists.

Four blanket unions are led by demagogues. These leaders do not even attempt to develop formal union organization, but are content to call strikes as an election maneuver.

In addition to these 33 unions, which are significant either as going concerns or because the leadership can call an effective strike, there are more than a hundred smaller unions of the paper variety.

Caribbean Federation of Labor

The first attempt to form a federation of BWI unions was made in 1926 when a convention was called for that purpose by the British Guiana Labour Union. Because that union was the only genuine labor union in existence at that time, the meeting was attended by middle-class nationalists who combined their anti-colonialism with a concern for the problems of the working man. The British Guiana and West Indian Trade Union Congress, formed at the 1926 convention, proved to be a paper organization. The Caribbean Trade Union Congress was formed in 1944 at a conference in British Guiana, met again in Barbados in 1945, but fell apart after the 1947 meeting in Jamaica. Although the Congress included almost all BWI unions, it was dominated by unions led by Socialists and Communists. Coöperation between these parties grew out of the unity between Russia and Great Britain during World War II, and coöperation ceased as the "cold war" developed. Communist sympathizers, who were influential in Jamaican, Trinidadian, and Guianan unions in 1947, dominated the 1947 convention of the Caribbean Trade Union Congress, and as a consequence other union leaders quietly withdrew their support.[3] The Caribbean Area Division of the Inter-American Regional Division of the International Confederation of Free Trade Unions (CAD-ORIT-ICFTU), which was created in 1954 to serve the non-Spanish-speaking areas of the Caribbean, acts as the coördinator of union activities in the BWI. In practice CAD-ORIT is made up of the major unions of the BWI and the unions of Dutch Guiana (Surinam).[4] Some BWI union leaders feel that BWI unions should be federated for greater coöperation now that the BWI is a nation, but CAD-ORIT officials argue that their organization can better serve the function of a federation and that a BWI Trade Union Congress would be needless duplication. Instead, CAD-ORIT stresses the need for closer coöperation among Caribbean unions along industrial lines.[5]

Summary

Union development on a significant scale followed the general riots of 1935–1939. As might be expected of a young labor movement, many unions had a meteoric growth only to decline rapidly, many were formed but never developed, and still others remain unions only on paper. There are many unions in proportion to total population, few members in proportion to the total work force, and overlapping jurisdictions. Union birth rate and mortality are high. The degree to which unions pursue traditional union goals of collective bargaining and grievance handling varies, but most BWI unions are not job-oriented. In making such an over-all summary of BWI unionism it should be remembered that the union movement is only twenty years old and had no union traditions upon which to build. For this reason it is not proper to compare BWI unionism, in its present stage of development, with British or American unionism. Moreover, although most BWI unions are the despair of orthodox unionists, taken together they have wrought a revolution in employee-employer relations, a revolution which does not appear in formal agreements. Workers now know that they have the power of the strike, which can hurt employers. This knowledge gives them dignity and status, makes them less submissive. Employers know that even the poorest organized union can, under certain circumstances, call an effective strike and, therefore, collective bargaining is not necessary to bring about a subtle but important shift in employer attitudes toward workers.

In spite of the confusion apparent in the over-all view of BWI unionism, a closer analysis shows that a few unions have the bulk of union membership, have had the longest continuous existence (in spite of many ups and downs), and are continuing to grow. These few unions are, in general, characterized by development of internal organization and leadership and a growing emphasis on collective bargaining. Although confusion and instability have marked the past twenty years of unionism, they appear to be passing stages in the maturing labor movement.

Many reasons are given for the lack of organization among BWI workers: underemployment, dominance of agriculture, transportation difficulties, and the down-trodden condition of workers. But analysis shows that certain unions have overcome these obstacles. Antigua and St. Kitts, for example, are entirely without mining and manufacturing industry, but unions in these islands have effectively organized their sugar industry. Indeed, the Antigua Labour Union has also organized shop clerks, civil servants, school teachers, and independent peasant farmers. Although the Barbados Workers' Union does not have the sugar-estate workers organized, no one questions the loyalty of the sugar workers to the union, and all other wage earners are organized. In the face of a hostile government and employers, and in a colony almost without roads, the General Workers' Union of British Honduras was able to organize most of the colony's wage earners. Communications in British Guiana are even more difficult, and government and employer opposition even greater, but the Guianese Industrial Workers' Union (then Communist dominated) was able to undermine the employer-recognized Manpower Citizens' Association and win the support of most sugar workers. Although these unions differ in ideology, type of leadership, and politics, their success in organizing agricultural workers and workers in the back country gives them one thing in common—hard work and close contact with workers. There is more to organizing workers than holding mass meetings and printing leaflets, and too many BWI unionists attempt to organize workers from behind their desks. Agricultural workers can be organized by unionists willing to get out with the workers and "talk union."

Chapter VI	*External*
	Factors
	Influencing
	Union Development

Union development in the BWI is not only a product of the particular environment but also of external factors—the Harlem West Indians, United States Caribbean military bases, employment opportunities in the United States, communism, socialism, Catholic radicalism in British Honduras, unions in the United States, and the British Trade Union Congress.

The Harlem Influence

The influence of American Negroes has always been important in the West Indies. At the outset, the work of Booker T. Washington, the National Association for the Advancement of Colored People, and the race riots of 1917 in St. Louis and in Chicago in 1919 made West Indian Negroes aware of the similarities and differences of their various problems. Most important in BWI affairs, however, is the influence of West Indians now residing in Harlem who have become American citizens. West Indian immigrants are very "British" in Harlem, but become "Yankees" when they visit the West Indies, advocating the "American way" as the solution to the problems of the islands. These Harlem West Indians, who have organized and financed many BWI political parties, became interested in collective action when they formed the West Indian Defense Committee to defend those arrested during the riots of 1936–1939.[1] The Jamaica Progressive League

---

[1] For notes to chapter vi, see pp. 201–202.

formed by Harlem Jamaicans in 1935 was influential in the organization and financing of the People's National Party and its allied unions. PNP leader Norman Manley, makes an annual tour of the United States to raise funds for his political party. Wilfred A. Domingo returned to Jamaica after twenty-seven years in Harlem to spend two years advocating socialism. Nevis-born Hope Stevens, a Harlem lawyer, spent a year touring the West Indies assisting in the formation of unions and of the Barbados Progressive League. Garveyite William H. Seale returned to Barbados to help in the organization of the Progressive League. Harlem groups aided in the financing of the Caribbean Labour Congress in 1945 and 1947, and Harlem Communists attempted to infiltrate the organization. The American Committee for West Indian Federation not only promotes West Indian federation, political parties, and labor unions but its officers serve as connecting links between the islands themselves through their regular trips throughout the Caribbean.

The Influence of American Military Bases

American military bases built in the West Indies during World War II were an important external influence in changing the attitude of labor and influencing union development. As a result of a trade of overaged destroyers for Caribbean military bases made between the United Kingdom and the United States, thousands of West Indians found employment on American bases in Jamaica, Antigua, St. Lucia, Trinidad, and British Guiana. The bases, besides providing employment, afforded new experiences and new ideas. American construction methods were new to the workers; they were amazed to see roads rapidly cut through what had heretofore been called impenetrable jungles and through difficult mountain terrain. The people of British Guiana were startled to learn that a modern city sporting the only swimming pool in the colony had been built in the jungle interior. Inhabitants of St. Lucia were surprised to see Americans move a mountain to one side, fill in a swamp, and change the course of a river to build an air strip. Residents of Trinidad enjoyed some of their fine beaches for the first time because Americans built roads over difficult mountains opening up almost one-half of the island for new development. From such experience West Indians have come to view economic development in terms of what a bulldozer, instead of a cutlass and hoe, can do.

In accordance with modern personnel practices, American treatment of employees was different from the almost feudal treatment by West Indian employers. West Indian workers learned that one could do manual labor and still maintain dignity; when interviewed by the writer they were enthusiastic over the idea of a foreman working with his men instead of ordering them about. For the first time West Indians saw white men as manual laborers. The writer interviewed several union organizers who said that their goal was not to gain the American standard of living but to get for the workers the kind of treatment from West Indian employers that they enjoyed on American military bases. West Indian employers who complained about the "occupation" by American troops also complained to the writer that the Yankees had pampered and spoiled the workers. As a consequence, the once happy, carefree workers had now become "surly." Summarizing the findings of interviews with estate owners the writer found that surliness meant two things: first, that workers demanded to be treated with dignity and respect instead of as wayward children or as "Uncle Tom's." Secondly, that workers were no longer content with the work relationship established by custom and the good will of the employer. Instead, the worker wanted to know how much work was expected of him and just exactly what he was going to get for it. For example, one estate owner explained to the writer why improved telephone facilities were necessary. He said that in the old days he could call on one of his workers at any time to run a message for him. Nowadays the worker demands the use of the estate owner's car and wants overtime pay for these errands. The estate owner explained that workers have suffered from their unreasonable demands, because the owner is no longer so generous in making loans to faithful workers as he was in former days.

The lower middle class was also impressed by the economic by-products of American bases such as improved roads, harbor facilities, water supply, sewage disposal, and malaria control. Equally important was the middle-class shopkeeper's discovery that steady purchasing power in the hands of workers meant middle-class prosperity. The owner of a bicycle shop in British

Guiana, for example, explained that upper classes do not buy or rent bicycles, but when employment was high on American bases his business prospered. It is true that these advantageous develop-- ments were, in part, offset by incidents of racial discrimination that occurred on U. S. bases. They antagonized the local population but, as Eric Williams observed:

The rank and file of American troops have fitted into local society. Barred from officers clubs, looked down upon by white and colored aristocracy, the enlisted men have gravitated toward the people of their own social milieu, the colored middle-class and the lower classes. Left alone, white soldiers and colored population can and will work out an adjustment of their own.[2]

This writer gained the same impression from interviews with West Indian workers and members of the middle class. It is, of course, possible that West Indians said what they thought a visiting Yankee would like to hear, but the information was volunteered by all who were connected with U. S. bases. Questions on this point were not part of the regular interview schedule. It is also possible that the presence of a visiting Yankee may have recalled the balmy days of war-bred prosperity. All those interviewed, whether working-class and lower-middle-class members associated with U. S. bases, stressed the influence of the Americans on the West Indians' aspirations for a higher standard of living, more dignified treatment, and better tools with which to work.[3]

United States Farm Labor Recruitment Program

The United States farm-labor recruitment program which brings thousands of West Indian workers to Wisconsin, Connecticut, Maryland, and Florida for three-year periods reënforces the ex- perience on American bases in the Caribbean. During World War II the War Manpower Commission and the War Food Administra- tion recruited 15,000 West Indian workers in 1943, and 23,000 in 1944; in 1945 there were 40,000 West Indian workers employed in 36 states and sending home an estimated $12,000,000 an- nually.[4] Under the postwar farm-labor recruitment program the number of West Indian workers employed in the United States averages 9,000 workers.[5]

The importation of Mexican and Japanese farm labor has been

protested by American unions, but the West Indian farm-labor program has received the blessings of the American labor movement. Carefully supervised by BWI labor departments, West Indian workers in the United States have better working conditions and a higher rate of pay than native American farm labor; there is rigid inspection and enforcement of standards; workers are encouraged to join local unions, to refuse to serve as strike breakers, and to quit work when there is a strike in the area. The supply of West Indian labor is correlated with deficits in labor needs and the availability of American farm labor. Under these conditions, American unionists approve of the opportunity of West Indians to strengthen their economy and, in turn, help to promote hemispheric defense through their employment in the United States.[6] Colonial administrators and union leaders, in interviews with the writer, agreed that farm laborers returning from the United States have new levels of aspiration, new attitudes toward marriage, diet, work methods, and employee-employer relations. The returning workers are even demanding that shopkeepers bestir themselves from their lethargy to order new and greater varieties of merchandise for their shelves.

Union leaders and colonial administrators disagreed, however, on the effects of the farm-labor recruitment program on labor relations. Colonial administrators generally took the view that (as a result of careful selection of farm labor), the worker returning from the U. S. would use his accumulated savings to buy a plot of land, and his new knowledge to become a successful small-scale farmer. Most labor leaders disagreed, believing that the high price of land in the West Indies would make such a goal unattainable. Union leaders generally believed that returning farm laborers would be so discontented as to become rank-and-file leaders in labor unions and political parties. Although the writer was unable to interview a statistically significant group of returning farm laborers, those whom he did interview were unanimous in their enthusiasm over most of their experiences in the United States and generally dissatisfied with the life they had returned to. Considering the shortage of rank-and-file leadership in the West Indies it is significant that several rank-and-file interviewed leaders were motivated to engage in union activity by their experiences as farm laborers in the United States. For example, the writer interviewed a National Workers Union organizer of hotel employees in the Montego Bay Area of Jamaica, who is also a peasant farmer. When asked why a peasant farmer allied himself with wage workers and contributed free time to organizational activities, he explained that he had learned about trade unionism while a farm laborer in the United States. His relatives in America were active members of the Hotel and Restaurant Workers Union, and he became thoroughly indoctrinated in trade unionism. Such a man makes an ideal rank-and-file leader for he has no ambitions to become a paid officer of the union nor does he have political ambitions. Dedicated men such as these are closer to the working classes both sociologically and geographically in a country where travel is difficult and social distances are great.

The Influence of Communism

Communist activity and influence are at a low ebb in the BWI, having lost out in Jamaica, British Guiana (despite Jagan's 1957 election victory) and Trinidad. The Communists lost influence in Jamaica in 1952 when the People's Progressive Party purged itself of Communists and created the National Workers Union. The Communist Jamaica Federation of Labor led by Richard Hart and Ferdinand Smith is at present only a paper organization.[7] Communist influence in British Guiana has declined since the suspension of the constitution in 1953, the split within the People's Progressive party in 1955, the loss of middle-class support, and the rebuilding of the union movement with the aid of the British Trade Union Congress and the International Confederation of Free Trade Unions.[8] The allegedly Communist-dominated West Indian Independence party of Trinidad has a meager following.[9] Reports of Communist activity in British Honduras are without foundation although the General Workers Union and its political ally, the People's United Party, are outspoken in their criticism of almost everything British. A Commission of Enquiry was unable to establish a conspiracy between the leaders of the People's United Party-General Workers Union and the Guatemalan Communists.[10] Edward Joshua of St. Vincent is also affiliated with the World Federation of Trade Unions and has associated with Communists in the Caribbean. When interviewed he was annoyed because the International Confederation of Free Trade Unions had denied his petition for membership; he claimed that he was not a Communist and saw no reason why he could not belong to two international federations. In the opinion of this writer, Joshua is not a Communist but he is likely to support anyone who will give him assistance.

Communist influence in British West Indian unions reached a peak when it threatened to dominate the West Indian Federation of Labor in its conventions of 1945 and 1947. Hart, Smith, and Jagan have attempted, without success, to revive the West Indian Federation of Labor, having been blocked by the Caribbean Area Division of ORIT. Elsewhere in the BWI, authorities worry over "liberals" who were close to Communist circles while at universities in England and who may cause trouble when the time is ripe. In evaluating the possible resurgence of Communist influence, several factors need to be weighed. First, the general economic and social conditions in the BWI lend themselves to Marxian doctrine without too much distortion of fact. The lower middle class, educated, ambitious, and with nowhere to go, is susceptible to Communist reasoning. On the other hand, much is being done to remove the causes of discontent. Second, union instability leaves the door open for Communist penetration; however, the International Confederation of Free Trade Unions has done a fine job in promoting union stability and exposing Communist influence. Third, in the see-saw struggle for the friendship of colonial peoples, Russia has not fared well in recent years in the BWI, but with the present fluid situation in international relations, attitudes in the BWI could suddenly change.

Socialist Influence

In Barbados and Jamaica socialism is an important ideology brought to the colonies by middle-class West Indians returning from English universities. Generally, this brand of socialism is mild and intellectual with an emphasis on anticolonialism, and the need for self-government and economic planning. Lip service is paid to Socialist theories but it is generally recognized that socialism is not a practicable approach to the problems of small-island agricultural economics. However, as an ideology it is important in supplying missionary zeal and contributing to the honesty of leaders where many of them tend to be dishonest.

In Antigua and St. Kitts, rank-and-file leaders claim to be Socialists but admit that their socialism may be more correctly called liberal idealism. Trade-union leaders told the writer they called themselves Socialists only because capitalism has such a bad reputation in a colonial area. Union leaders emerging from the rank and file in these two colonies have had little contact with official international socialism, and their ideology is one of protest against the poor economic, social, and political conditions in their colonies. Capitalism is synonymous with lethargy and the status quo, and is, therefore, unacceptable to many West Indians. Similarly, socialism does not mean nationalization of industry and redistribution of wealth, but rather an enthusiastic determination to improve social, economic, and political conditions. As one trade-union leader explained, "One cannot be a radical on a small island, a poor island—an island that has suffered two droughts and two hurricanes in four years." Although "socialism" may be an inappropriate description for nationalists who are more interested in attracting foreign capital than in nationalizing existing industry, imported Socialist ideology is meaningful in that economic development must be initiated by the state. In the absence of private capital and entrepreneurs the government must assume capitalist functions.

Catholic Influence

It is not surprising that the economic and political programs of the General Workers Union and the People's United Party are expressed in terms of Catholic doctrine, because more than 60 per cent of the population is Catholic, as a result of Central American Spanish influence. Unlike the Irish and French priests in other parts of the BWI who tend to be easy-going, the American Jesuit priests of British Honduras are unusually well-trained, dedicated men. The Jesuits work tirelessly at their own technical assistance program: Improving agriculture, developing coöperatives, assisting in self-help housing, and conducting trade-union education classes. Leaders of the General Workers Union-People's United Party received high-school education from the Jesuits and now attend Jesuit union-education classes. The union-party program therefore reflects the philosophy of the American Jesuit priests. (See chapter iv, p. 103.)

British Trade Union Influence

The influence of British unions began with the aid and advice given to BWI unions by Sir Walter Citrine as a member of the Moyne Commission. The British Trade Union Congress finances scholarships to Ruskin Labor College for BWI union leaders and offers correspondence-school courses in unionism. F. W. Dalley's visits to Trinidad in 1947 and 1954 were influential in shaping the course of union development. The British Guiana crisis of 1953 renewed British Trade Union Congress interest in the British West Indies. Two organizers were sent to British Guiana to aid in reëstablishing the union movement and 6,000 pounds were given to BWI unions.[11] A British Trade Union Congress organizer was sent to Trinidad in 1956 to attempt to straighten out the confusion among unions in the sugar industry.[12] The British Trade Union Congress gave 120,000 pounds to the International Confederation of Free Trade Unions to aid unions in underdeveloped areas, 75,000 pounds of which were allocated to Commonwealth countries.[13]

American Union Influence

To protect labor standards in the bauxite and aluminum industries in North America, the United Steelworkers of America, AFL-CIO, has given financial and technical assistance in the organizing and bargaining activities of unions of the bauxite industry in Jamaica. The Steelworkers Union placed Kenneth Sterling, formerly an organizer of the People's National party, on its payroll to organize Jamaican bauxite workers.[14] (See chapter iii, pp. 73–74.) In addition to representing the bauxite workers, Sterling is acting secretary of the National Workers Union, secretary-treasurer of the Caribbean Aluminum and Allied Workers Federation, secretary of the Caribbean Area Division of ORIT, and leader of the movement for federation of Caribbean Plantation Workers Unions and Waterfront Workers Union. Advocating the philosophy of the United Steelworkers, he has demonstrated that strong unions can be built in the West Indies by stressing dues payment, local organization, a shop-steward system, attention to grievances, and emphasis on collective bargaining.

The influence of the Steelworkers Union is illustrated in a statement made by one of its representatives to Jamaican bauxite miners that they need not be so pleased with their new prosperity that bought bicycles, for North American bauxite workers received wages that bought automobiles. "A bicycle is a child's toy," he said. This remark led the Jamaican government to protest to the United States State Department over American union influence in local labor affairs. Since the time of this incident the Steelworkers have sent Canadian Steelworker representatives to the West Indies. A government official, alarmed by such inflammatory talk, reported to the writer that it was only a few years ago that workers could not afford to buy shoes, much less bicycles, and that putting the idea of owning automobiles into the minds of workers was dangerous. Bauxite miners now receive wages sufficient to permit them to buy second-hand cars.

In 1958 the United Steelworkers bought a car for the National Workers Union of Jamaica, paid the salary of an organizer for the British Guiana Miners Union and supplied him with a boat, and gave technical aid to the Surinam Miners Union.[15] In addition to the major assistance given by the Steelworkers, the Oil, Chemical and Atomic Workers International Union, AFL-CIO, has assisted the Oilfield Workers Union of Trinidad; and the Communication Workers of America, AFL-CIO, have assisted the telephone and telegraph unions of Barbados, Trinidad, and British Guiana.

The International Confederation of Free Trade Unions

The most important external stabilizing force is the Inter-American Regional Organization of the International Confederation of Free Trade Unions (ORIT-ICFTU).[16] Unions admitted to the confederation enjoy a stamp of legitimacy as democratic, non-Communist unions seeking traditional union objectives. Affiliated unions are given advice and training in union administration and collective bargaining through the Caribbean Area Division of ORIT-ICFTU (Trinidad) and through regular conference visits of Serafino Romualdi and Harry Pollak, Latin American representatives of the AFL-CIO. CAD-ORIT officers, by mediating jurisdictional disputes, encouraging amalgamation of unions, and seeking the establishment of colony-wide federations, are deterring the splintering of the West Indian labor movement. Working through the ICFTU, member unions are given financial assistance by British and American unions in the form of office equipment and cars for organizers. In some areas the writer could not help wondering whether union leaders were in business to organize workers or merely to enjoy the subsidy offered by the ICFTU. A car, a public-address system, typewriters, and mimeographing machinery are status symbols of great value to ambitious leaders from the lower middle class, and sometimes the writer surmised that the equipment was used more for furthering the commission-merchant business and the political ambitions of the "trade-union leader" than for organizing workers. Officers of the ICFTU are well aware of the problem and told the writer that this same situation exists in unions in other underdeveloped areas of the world. They went on to point out, however, that in most instances the material aid and technical assistance supplied by the ICFTU has made possible a start toward business unionism based on the principles of collective bargaining.

Summary

Trade-union development in the BWI is not entirely a product of its particular environment because the country is becoming progressively less isolated from the rest of the world. From the outset, the British colonial administration has fostered the development of British-type trade unionism through the labor departments and labor laws of each colony. English unionists have given aid and advice to BWI unions and have sponsored an education program. Middle-class nationalists learned their principles of trade unionism along with Fabian socialism at English universities. Their contribution to stable, job-oriented trade unionism has been great. In many respects, however, American influence on the working class and on unions has been even greater. The activities of the Harlem West Indians, the impact of the U. S. military bases, the U. S. farm recruitment program, and the support of the United Steelworkers of America have been powerful influences in arousing worker interest in unionism and in furthering job-oriented unionism. Moreover, the activities of the ICFTU, which promotes non-Communist, job-oriented unionism, have in large part been led and financed by American unionists. Consequently, some English and BWI employers complain that American influence in West Indian unionism is too great. While national pride may have been offended, American influence has neither dominated BWI unions nor been subversive. On the contrary, the influence of American unionism, like that of the English, has been instrumental in combatting the mystics, rabble rousers, racketeers, and subversives, all of whom threaten the young labor movement.

Socialist influence in BWI trade-union development stems from the close ties between the middle-class nationalist political parties and the unions. As nationalists and West Indians these leaders identify themselves with workers, and as Socialists they considered themselves the enemies of worker oppression by colonial capitalists. Realistically, workers needed the Socialist-nationalist leadership because they lacked rank-and-file leaders, and the Socialist-nationalists needed unions to buttress their political parties. The weakness of the Socialist-nationalist leadership has been in its emphasis on politics to the neglect of union goals, while its contribution has been in providing responsible and inspiring leadership. Despite Socialist preoccupation with politics, Socialist-led unions are more job-oriented than those by lower middle-class opportunists.

Communist influence reached its height during the late 1940's but has since declined. The rise and fall of Communist influence in BWI unions coincides with international events. Communism gained from the war-time alliance between Russia and the Western powers and from the creation of the World Federation of Trade Unions immediately following the war, but lost influence in the cold war and with the creation of the International Confederation of Free Trade Unions. The BWI and its unions are part of the world battlefield in the Communist fight for power, and the BWI environment, together with the instability of its young labor movement, provides a fertile field for Communist infiltration. Nevertheless, the policies of the colonial government, the efforts of the ICFTU, and the postwar disenchantment of Socialist-nationalists with communism have effectively blocked Communist influence.

Trade unionism in British Honduras is influenced by Catholic radicalism as a result of the effective work of American Jesuits. To be sure, the environment was receptive, but it was Jesuit dedication to their tasks that spelled success. Communist, Socialist,

Catholic-radical, and job-oriented union leaders have developed successful unions in the BWI, and workers have accepted their various ideological frameworks to the extent that the unions have met the needs of the workers. We may conclude therefore that although the ideology may motivate the union leader, workers will accept the ideology of the union which meets their day-to-day, on-the-job needs.

Chapter VII | *Unions*
and Political Parties

Reasons for Union Emphasis on Political Action

As indicated in the preceding section, industrial unions place
political action second to collective bargaining but nearly all
blanket unions are wedded to political parties. Unions and parties
must be closely allied when some 90 per cent of the voters are of
the working class. In the smaller colonies, where there is no mining or manufacturing, these voters are made up almost entirely
of estate laborers. The middle class of independent peasant
farmers, shopkeepers, and professional people is extremely small
and cannot be depended upon to be a stabilizing influence in
voting. Moreover, the middle class, unlike that of the United
States, is sympathetic to the worker rather than to the employer
viewpoint for reasons of race, nationalism, and economic self-
interest. It follows that whoever controls the worker vote in the
West Indian colonies controls the politics. It is only logical that
union leaders would seize upon the political power which is within
their grasp.

A second reason for the close relationship between unions and
political parties is the fact that union development and adult
suffrage developed almost simultaneously in the BWI. There were
almost no unions in the West Indies before 1939, and few political
parties before 1946. Before World War II half of the colonial
legislators were appointed by the governor and the other half
elected under limited franchise which permitted only the small
upper and middle class to vote. In every colonial legislature, how-

ever, there were one or two middle-class radicals who were the self-appointed spokesmen for the disenfranchised working class. Middle-class leaders in the fight for representative government included such men as Captain Arthur Cipriani of Trinidad, Albert Marryshow of Grenada, and Cecil Rawle of Dominica. Following the advice of Captain Cipriani these leaders did not attempt to organize unions, because of union liability for torts under existing laws. Instead they were able to win enough votes from dissident elements in the middle class to be elected to the legislature. Always critics of the upper classes and the colonial government, they spoke in behalf of labor but the relationship was somewhat distant.[1]

With the union growth after the riots of 1935–1939 these middle-class liberals did not participate directly in union activities but continued their role as friends and spokesmen for the working class under a political system of limited franchise. During World War II the British government began to extend universal suffrage to the colonies of the West Indies. Labor leaders quickly formed political parties, and ambitious politicians and opportunists with equal rapidity set up unions as bases for political parties. Many old-line, colored, middle-class liberals were swept out of office along with white upper-class representatives. During this period only the People's National Party of Jamaica and the Barbados Progressive League made any serious attempt to distinguish between political parties and trade unions—modeling themselves along the lines of the British Labour party in its relationship with the British Trade Union Congress.[2] As indicated in chapters iii and iv many "unions" are merely instruments of hopeful politicians.

A third reason for the close association of unions and political parties is that, under the conditions existing in the BWI, politics is a more attractive goal than collective bargaining. Union administration requires hard work with little monetary reward and no contribution to social status. Using the union as an instrument for winning elections is much more rewarding in terms of gaining social status and steady income.[3] Union leaders who are middle-class nationalists are primarily concerned with economic development and self-government. They are sincere in their belief that

---

[1] For notes to chapter vii, see p. 202.

political action along these lines will mean more to the worker than collective bargaining. Middle-class nationalists frankly admit that they are politicians first and trade unionists second but claim that they find it necessary to assume union leadership to keep unions out of the hands of demagogues, since there is a serious lack of rank-and-file leadership. Many of these told the writer that they looked forward to the emergence of a rank-and-file leadership and a more clear-cut separation between politics and unionism.

Some unionists argue that political action is more fruitful than collective bargaining, because it is easier to legislate gains for workers when labor is assured control of the government than it is to overcome employer opposition in collective-bargaining sessions. True as this may be, it also leads workers to conclude that the union is of little value if wage increases and fringe benefits come only through legislation. The emphasis on political action to the neglect of union action leads to a situation in which any demagogue can campaign on a platform claiming that he can legislate even more generous benefits if elected to office. Finally, there is a close relationship between unions and political parties because most workers understand neither the principles of unionism nor the objectives of political parties. On this point the Labor Advocate of British Guiana stated:

Unfortunately in British Guiana workers continue to link politics with trade union objectives. We do not claim that these two can be entirely divorced from each other but we are of the opinion that they are too closely intermarried.[4]

Workers tend to support those leaders who make the biggest promises and to vote for the noisiest, most flamboyant, and colorful leader, hoping that he will raise the most rumpus in both unions and in politics, thereby gaining more subsidies from the British government. Colin Hughes observes that "the demagogue has long been the most outstanding figure on the West Indian scene . . . interminable oratory, obscurantism, ponderous language, eccentricity."[5] Workers reward union leaders by giving them votes to send them to the legislature instead of by paying dues to the union. In return for his vote the worker expects the union leader to settle grievances, negotiate wage increases, and win further gains for the workers in the legislature. Union leaders interested in the relative security of political office and in winning political objectives are willing to perform union services in return for political votes.

As a result of this close tie between blanket unions and political parties it is difficult to say that these unions have a "membership." Rather, it would be more nearly correct to say that workers have an allegiance toward a union. They express their allegiance by going on strike when told to do so and by voting in political elections for union leaders. Blanket unions are financially insecure because workers and union leaders consider political votes more valuable than dues payment. Unions have a necessarily loose organizational structure when a union leader will attempt to handle complaints of any group of workers, not because they are paying members of his union, but because they may vote for him if he wins their case. Thus the grievance settlement stands alone, not becoming part of a body of industrial common law. Union organization is neither improved nor furthered, but the leader hopes that he has won a few votes for the coming election.

Under such circumstances it is not surprising that an ambitious politician forms a paper union and campaigns among workers promising greater benefits in working conditions and in social legislation. Also, if he is an effective leader he can call the strike which, in effect, means the workers have repudiated their former bargaining agent. If the strike is successful the new leader will be elected to political office and employers will recognize him as the spokesman for the workers. In other words, close union-political ties without real union organization invites both union and political instability. Jurisdictional disputes, ill-timed collective-bargaining demands preceding political elections, and personal leadership rivalries are directly attributable to close union ties with political parties. In its Second Annual Report, 1955, the Caribbean Area Division of ORIT lists specific disputes in British Guiana, Trinidad, Grenada, St. Vincent, St. Lucia, and Monserrat in which its affiliated unions suffered because these disputes were directly related to political ambitions of rival union leaders.[6]

Commenting on the disintegration of unions as a factor contributing to Communist success in British Guiana, the Constitutional Commission studying the situation leading up to the suspension of the constitution said: "If trade unionism in British

Guiana is to climb out of the rut in which they now find it, two things are needed: Firstly, for trade unionists to develop a healthy mistrust of motives behind patronage of personally ambitious politicians and secondly, for union executives to pursue their industrial objectives by industrial and not by political means." [7] A United Kingdom Board of Inquiry study of labor relations in the Trinidad sugar industry, in January, 1955, deplored the fact that union organization of the sugar industry has been diverted from its main function by political associations "mainly concerned with promoting the careers of individual politicians." [8] Thus while close union ties with political parties are inevitable under conditions found in the BWI, the nature of these alliances found in many colonies is a source of weakness to both unions and political parties.

Reasons for Separation of Unions and Political Parties

Although the close relationship between unions and political parties has led to instability in both, given time there may be greater separation between the two. First, the interest between a branch of a blanket union and that of the total economy may not always be the same and may lead to a break between the union and the political party. This was demonstrated in the telephone and the gasoline-tank-wagon-drivers' strikes of 1953 in Jamaica. Bustamante as first minister of the government made speeches in which he stated he would not permit the interest of the strikers to be above national interest, that he had to protect the welfare of the people as a whole. Then, changing hats, Bustamante as president of the Bustamante Industrial Trade Union in other speeches encouraged the strikers and denounced the employers. The union members were not happy with this standoffish attitude when Bustamante maintained an arms-length relationship with striking branches. The strikers practically blackmailed him into giving them assistance; furthermore, the rest of the community was annoyed by his attempt to act as leader of the union and head of the government simultaneously. Bustamante found himself in this difficulty also in 1953 when the telephone workers struck.

The People's Progressive party ministers used their government positions to further the objectives of their unions, thus providing an immediate reason for the suspension of the constitution, an action which has been an object lesson to West Indian unionists and politicians.[9] The National Workers Union of Jamaica has been disappointed by the failure of the government under its political ally, the People's National party, to raise the wages of government workers.[10] Eric Williams of Trinidad has also found that union interest and party interest are not always identical. When the Postal and Telegraph Workers asked Joseph E. Dunne, international representative of the Communication Workers of America AFL-CIO, to represent them in collective bargaining, the government telegraph agency refused to negotiate with an "outsider." Williams was condemned by union leaders for his refusal to intercede and the issue precipitated a strike.[11] As another example, CAD-ORIT secretary Kenneth Sterling in welcoming the goodwill visit of the U.S.S. *Ranger*—with seven American union leaders aboard—took the occasion to criticize Williams for his attempt to make the U. S. naval base at Chaguarsmus a national issue.[12]

All politicians have to resist the demands of waterfront workers who, being in a position to extract large benefits from employers and in turn from the economy as a whole, have a stranglehold on the island economies. The union leader who is also a politician knows that if he supports the waterfront workers he loses the support of the community, and if he supports the community, he loses the support of the waterfront workers. The same problem exists with respect to civil-service and public-works employees who are generally loyal unionists and party supporters. The objectives of middle-class liberal nationalists for over-all economic development cannot help but conflict with particular interests of groups within the union. An outstanding example of the gradual separation of a blanket union and its political party is that of the Barbados Progressive League and the Barbados Workers Union (see chapter iv).

Another example of the growing separation between unions and political parties is found in the relationship between the People's National Party of Jamaica and the National Workers Union. More than any other politician in the West Indies, Norman Manley has kept his distance from unionism, serving unions only as legal adviser and maintaining as his principal role that of leadership of a party seeking self-government and economic reform in Jamaica. Many leaders of his party, however, were also union leaders because the union could not provide its own leadership. As the National Workers Union has progressed in successful organization and has succeeded in collective bargaining it has been able to develop its own leadership, and with this leadership has gained greater independence from the People's National party. This development came about largely through the efforts of two able leaders—Kenneth Sterling and Michael Manley, son of Norman Manley. (Michael Manley, who interestingly enough studied under Harold Laski at the London School of Economics, has thus far refused to assume an active role in his father's political party, claiming that Jamaica and the People's National party need a strong independent labor movement.) When the People's National party won control of the government in the elections of 1955, the middle-class leaders who still held positions in the union resigned to assume ministerial posts in the government. This has further widened the gap between the union and the political party.

The success of Eric Williams's People's National Movement in the elections of 1956 may serve to clarify both union and political alliances in Trinidad. The People's National Movement has managed to form an alliance of middle-class groups of all races and gain the support of major unions. This development tends to keep ambitious politicians from forming new unions and equally ambitious union leaders from forming new political parties. The groundwork has thus been laid for a working relationship between middle-class nationalists and union leaders which should contribute to the stability of both unions and political parties.

Only in British Guiana does continued political confusion obstruct union development. Under the guidance and advice of representatives of the British Trade Union Congress and the International Confederation of Free Trade Unions, unions of British Guiana are now emphasizing collective bargaining and are placing politics in a secondary role. Unions of Negro workers may be expected to consolidate their position by concentrating on collective-bargaining gains. The issue remains in doubt as to whether business unionism can succeed among East Indian sugar workers so long as political and racial issues remain muddled. Forbes Burnham, leader of the waterfront workers and the

People's National Congress flatly states that political action must precede union development because unions cannot survive until political reform raises the economic level to a point where unions can function.[13] In St. Kitts and Antigua the distinction between political parties and unions is not sharp, but in these colonies there has been no political rivalry that would undermine unions.

Another reason for anticipating greater cleavage between political parties and unions is the possible development of a stronger middle class. Even though the middle class must be a small minority and cannot contribute much in total votes, its financial resources, leadership ability, and educational level makes it important. Rabble-rousing demagogues have seldom become successful administrators in BWI, and once the novelty of political campaigns and elections has worn off we may expect the mass of voters to turn to a more responsible political leadership. The middle class will assume a more important role in politics now that the issues of universal suffrage and self-government are resolved. There is no longer a split between those of the middle class who think that continued colonial rule is advisable and those who wish for immediate self-government. The issue now is whether good self-government can be had. Under the limited franchise the middle class tended to be amateurish and only half serious about politics and was caught unprepared for the kind of electioneering necessary under universal adult suffrage. It has now learned the art of electioneering, and as middle-class nationalist feeling grows we may expect the return of middle-class leadership in politics.

Also we may expect greater separation between unions and politics as middle-class professional groups and peasant-farmer groups develop and prosper. Ironically enough, political programs sponsored by unions for land reform, economic development, and greater purchasing power for workers lead to the development of a stronger and larger middle class. This middle class will have different political objectives from those of the working class because of its differing economic interests. An example of this type of development is found in Antigua where the union-political party created a peasant class through appropriation of estate land and supplied technical and financial assistance to the newly created peasant proprietors. Now as a result the peasants, although belonging to the union and its party, have divergent interests. We may also expect greater separation between unions and political parties as unions emerge as stable organizations with dues-paying membership and able leadership. Moreover, economic development creates industries which in turn provide jobs at higher rates of pay, with job tenure permitting the development of unions emphasizing collective bargaining. Leaders of these unions are finding it wise not to compete for political office, but instead to remain content with the income and increasing social status which their position in a powerful union offers. Although it may be a pious hope rather than a statement of policy, the report of the CAD-ORIT officers stated that free trade unionism was impossible as long as unions remained subservient to political parties, and concluded that "CAD-ORIT should take immediate steps to pursue a programme of development of unions on a nonpolitical basis, with established working understandings with progressive political organizations." [14]

Attitudes Toward Federation of the West Indies and Dominion Status

Since 1944 the BWI have moved steadily toward greater self-government with universal adult suffrage, increasing power of the elected branch of the colonial legislature, and the development of ministerial systems. In 1958 these colonies were federated and, within five years, are to be given dominion status and independence. British Honduras and British Guiana refused to join the federation but the way is left open for them and the British Virgin Islands to join at a later date. Although the governor general (Lord Hails), appointed by the queen, has control of foreign policy, appoints the 19-member Senate, and may veto finance bills, the federation is on its way toward becoming a self-governing democracy.[15] The 45-member House of Representatives was elected in the first federal elections in March, 1958, and the first parliament convened in April, 1958.

Nationalists and labor leaders beginning with Critchlow and Cipriani have agitated for federation and independence. All union leaders have gone on record as favoring federation and dominion status, yet nearly all of those interviewed privately opposed or at least feared federation.[16] First, they fear that it will be harder for each colony to get its "fair share" of the British subsidy through the dominion legislature than directly from the British Colonial Office. Also, they fear that the real intent of the British in forcing federation on West Indian politicians, who were dragging their feet on the issue, is to remove the subsidy entirely. Unionists in the relatively rich islands of Jamaica and Trinidad fear the consequences of unrestricted immigration from the smaller and poorer islands, while unionists on the smaller islands demand unrestricted emigration as a condition of federation. As matters now stand it is legally more difficult for West Indians to move from one island to another than it is for them to travel to England. Freedom of movement is one of the major issues facing the federation even though West Indian leaders at the London Conference on Federation, 1956, agreed in principle to "the greatest possible freedom of movement."

All islands have some protected industries. There is fear therefore that pre-federation tariff barriers will eventually fall and the unrestricted flow of commerce will wreck sheltered industries. At the London conference it was agreed to integrate trade policy and form a customs union as quickly as possible. This problem is especially acute in Trinidad and Jamaica where, with the assistance of tariff barriers, new industries have been successful. At the present time, the agreement on federation includes a provision permitting the continuation of existing tariff barriers. Critics claim that this is technical rather than organic federation. Also, under the present arrangement each politician can become a "prime minister" of his own small island; few are willing to permit a reduction in number or prestige of local offices. Some argue that federation will not reduce the number of necessary officers and civil-service employees in local government, and that the federated government cannot provide any real services to local government. It is claimed therefore that in the West Indian tradition one bureaucracy will be piled upon another, which poor countries cannot afford. The relatively richer islands fear that they will have to subsidize the poorer islands through federal taxation, while at the same time the smaller and poorer islands fear complete domination by Trinidad and Jamaica. Also, much of the postwar economic stability of the BWI has been created by the long-term bulk-purchase agreements of the British government covering sugar, bananas, and citrus. Doubting the motives of the British, many union leaders fear that along with dominion status will also come the end of these bulk-purchase agreements. To sell tropical produce on a "free" market, which is really a residual market because of extensive purchasing agreements between nations, would lead to economic catastrophe.

Finally there are those who argue in all sincerity that the West Indies are not ready for self-government. Without the restraining hand of the British Colonial Office, it is feared, the rabble-rousing elements may take over the entire BWI. Haiti and the Central American republics are pointed to as examples of the type of self-government that the West Indies could best do without. In a CAD-ORIT editorial, for example, the general secretary of CAD-ORIT stated that too many politicians are still fighting colonialism and overlook native exploiters. The labor movement is not assured safety with independence, he said, and observed that in two colonies within the past ten years it was "colonialism" that saved the labor movement from destruction.[17]

The reasons given for favoring federation and dominion status are: First, that all colonies suffer from lack of specialization in the growing and processing of consumer goods. Substantial economies with a higher standard of living could be achieved if different islands specialized in different fruits, dairy, and meat products for consumption by other members of the federation. Next, it is generally accepted that the British cannot as a matter of pride permit the United States to give technical assistance to their colonies. And it is believed that the British have opposed and tended to undermine plans for private capital from the United States to enter Caribbean colonies. Were the BWI a dominion, however, the British government would find no objection to both private and public aid from the United States, no more than it objects to Canada's joining with the United States in the St. Lawrence seaway development. Many West Indians and even some English colonial administrators believe that the West Indies are in the American sphere of influence and should become an American responsibility. Federation and dominion status may be of major significance as a means of paving the way for closer ties with the United States. Finally, it is held that national pride arising from West Indian Federation is necessary to economic development.

Political Stability

Other new nations have been more divided in color, race, religion, politics, and geographical distance than the Federation of the British West Indies. Likewise, other nations have faced the problem of a semiliterate, superstitious working-class electorate with little political experience.[18] There is speculation, nevertheless, as to whether the scramble for federal political power will not lead to conditions similar to those immediately following universal adult suffrage. During the period 1953–1957 the major unions made progress as collective-bargaining institutions allied to nationalist political parties, and this contributed to the stability of unions and parties. The question arises as to future progress toward union and political stability now that federal politics have become an issue.

The middle-class nationalist group led by Manley, Adams, and Williams formed the Federal Labour party in 1957, to which most CAD-ORIT unions are allied. A rival coalition led by Bustamante, Albert Gomes (Trinidad politician and one-time labor leader) and Maraj formed the Democratic Labour party. In the first federal elections, March 1958, the Federal Labour party won 24 seats, the Democratic Labour party 20, and the Barbados National party one seat (it will vote with the Federal Labour party). Political observers are not sure whether the narrow majority indicates a healthy rivalry or instability. The emphasis on local issues in the campaign, the light vote, and the difficulty in getting leading citizens to accept ministerial posts does indicate an apathy toward federation.

The strength of the Democratic Labour party is more significant that its 20 seats indicate because it represents 6 of 10 seats from Trinidad and 12 of 20 seats from Jamaica, and because Williams and Manley were defeated in the federal elections. It appears that the strength of the Democratic Labour party lies in its championing of local sovereignty and its antagonism against the small islands. The strength of the Federal Labour party, on the other hand, is in Barbados, the Leeward and Windward Islands. As stated in the preceding section, the electorate of Jamaica and Trinidad have good economic reasons to place local autonomy over West Indian nationalism. It is possible that the federal government will be torn by a split between the big and small islands.[19]

It is too early to guess what the outcome of the first federal election portends for the labor movement. The strength of the Democratic Labour party may be construed as worker repudiation of CAD-ORIT unions in Jamaica and Trinidad, and an improvement in the position of the unions led by Bustamante and Maraj, or it may be considered a victory for local autonomy with no significance to unionism. It is possible that unions will become even more deeply concerned with politics to protect themselves from rival union-party coalitions while politicians become further concerned with unionism to strengthen their parties. On the other hand, the economic issues of federal politics may be such as to insulate unions from the fortunes of federal political parties. It appears that local politics will dominate the political scene for some time to come; the relationship of unions to local politics has already been reviewed.

Summary

BWI unions and political parties are closely allied. Such an alliance is understandable when the majority of the electorate consists of workers; when both unions and political parties are new to the West Indian scene; when leadership is scarce; and when workers do not fully understand the function of unions or political parties. Unity of union and political party is harmful to both unions and parties when used by political opportunists for personal objectives; when union goals and the day-to-day problems of workers are neglected for political ends; and when rivalry between opposing union parties creates jurisdictional disputes and ill-timed collective-bargaining demands. There are indications that union alliances with political parties will be placed on a sounder basis as middle-class nationalists gain the ascendency in politics and as rank-and-file union leadership emerges and bars both opportunists and nationalist politicians from union office.

The BWI was federated in 1958 and will be granted dominion

status. Many BWI leaders privately oppose federation because of the multitude of problems raised, but, as nationalists, they cannot officially oppose it. In the unsettled, fluid situation which will exist in the first years of federation, some demagogues could capitalize on the confusion. There is a possibility that ambitious self-seekers in their scramble for high office will seize on the difficult problems posed by federation to create general turmoil in both unions and in politics. Machiavellian leaders may possibly infiltrate the existing unions or create rival unions with which to launch into politics in order to gain control of the new nation. The field is open for Communist agents and for those seeking personal gain. Union stability, therefore, can hold the key to the future of this newest of nations. The physical proximity of the new federation to the United States and to the approaches to the Panama Canal, as well as its importance as a source of bauxite, may cause a quickening of U. S. interest in BWI unionism.

| Chapter VIII | Union-Management Relations |

Grievance Procedures

As might be expected, BWI industrial workers have the same types of grievances as found everywhere in modern industry. An important function of industrial unions in the BWI, as elsewhere, is the adjusting of complaints. Rank-and-file leadership and a shop-steward system operates successfully in industrial unions, perhaps because workers selected for skilled and semiskilled jobs are of higher caliber. In addition, managements in these concerns have had experience with grievance handling in the United States and Great Britain and assist in the establishment of grievance procedures. Unions and management work to educate local foremen to observe the contract and process grievances properly.[1] Blanket unions, in general, don't have the organization, leaders, or interest to be concerned with day-to-day grievances. Leaders are scarce; prefer the comforts of the capital city to the hardships of the back country; and are more interested in politics than in union routine. Usually there are no local union officers or shop-steward systems. Serious grievances result in wildcat strikes, which bring out a union officer from the capital city.

Those interviewed disagreed on the importance of grievances in estate employment. Most estate owners and many union leaders claimed that estate work is so unskilled, supervision so lax, and the work method governed by custom so clearly understood, that there are no grievances. Estate managers in British

---

[1] For notes to chapter viii, see pp. 202–203.

Guiana denied the existence of serious grievances, attributing acute labor trouble to Communists and the "cussedness" of East Indians. Inadequate housing and water supply were admitted to be sources of discontent, but not considered grievances in relation to working conditions. In colonies where unions were weak, estate managers explained that (a) estates were small and management was close to the workers; and (b) the drivers came from the working class and knew how to deal with the workers. Therefore, formal union grievance machinery was unnecessary, they said. In these same colonies union officials appeared to have little knowledge of day-to-day worker problems; they concluded that workers had few grievances; and they were primarily interested in broad issues such as employer "exploitation" and "economic development." Some union leaders, particularly successful ones, disputed the view that estate workers had no grievances. Unions in St. Kitts and Antigua handled many grievances and claimed that anyone willing to send representatives to the estates would find the grievances. The secretary of the St. Kitts Sugar Producers Association stated that grievances did occur on sugar estates and that he preferred to deal with the union representative rather than with a gang of twenty irate, incoherent workers. The National Workers Union of Jamaica made headway against the Bustamante Industrial Trade Union on sugar estates by stressing the importance of effective grievance handling— even thought it acknowledged that at the time no further wage increases could be won. The Guianese Industrial Workers Union, although misrepresenting issues, gained the workers' support on sugar estates by concentrating on grievances rather than on Communist ideology. The top management of Booker Brothers estates felt that failure to resolve worker grievances was a major cause of labor unrest. The Joint Estate Council plan, which broke down for lack of effective union leadership and because of the obstinacy of estate managers, could have reduced Communist influence among workers if it had functioned properly.

Collective Bargaining

As stated in chapter ii, union-management relations are influenced by government encouragement of collective bargaining; the necessity to arbitrate collective-bargaining issues in essential industries;

the willingness of employers to negotiate with unions; and the fact that union leaders emphasize legislative control of employment conditions over control by collective bargaining. Patterns of collective bargaining in the BWI vary considerably. At one extreme are those of modern corporations dealing with an industrial union over such contractual matters as are found in any typical labor agreement. As in grievance handling, union leaders and management take their cues on contract clauses from the United States and the United Kingdom. For example, there are the unions asking for shift differentials, while companies are adamant in their stand that plant guards shall not be in the same bargaining unit as production workers. These provisions are gradually finding their way into other contracts and finally into agreements covering agricultural workers. At the other extreme are loose associations of estate owners, whose decisions are not binding upon members, dealing with a blanket union whose right to represent the worker is open to doubt. In this relationship there is no formal recognition of the union as exclusive bargaining agent, nor is there a written agreement. Employers make unilateral decisions concerning conditions of employment if the situation demands it, while the union raises any issue at any time if workers become aroused or if political elections are imminent. There is no "management prerogative" issue, and "year-round" collective bargaining is accepted. Management authority is not threatened, however, because union leaders do not make extravagant demands. Instead, bargaining is limited to demands for general wage increases.

Between these extremes are the more typical union-management relationships. As in the evolution of union-management relations everywhere, the first agreements were rudimentary. The psychological effect on workers, who gained a new sense of power and importance, was more important than any contract clause. After the labor disturbances of the late 1930's, even without the benefit of union organization, contracts, or grievance procedures, employers treated employees with new respect. Wildcat strikes followed by a visit from a union official supported the worker point of view without the necessity for stated contractual rights. Influenced by contracts with industrial corporations and under the tutelage of the International Confederation of Free Trade Unions' officers, however, union-management relations in estate agriculture are becoming more formal and contracts more detailed. As a check on union influence, especially American, the British Overseas Employers Federation is now attempting to coördinate relations between BWI unions and employers. This development should also further a movement away from the casual and vague union-management relations. Since estates traditionally supply a variety of community services as part of the wage payment, it is surprising that union leaders generally did not consider such items as estate housing, medical care, water supply, and recreational facilities as proper subjects for collective bargaining. Although the extent and quality of these services varied greatly from one estate to another, most unionists felt that they should be left to legislative regulation. While a trend is developing in which employee-employer relationships are more carefully defined, wage bargaining predominates over all other issues.

Wage Determination in Marginal Agriculture

As emphasized in chapter i, West Indian estates are high-cost marginal producers competing in world markets. Under these circumstances, wage increases cannot be passed on to the consumer by higher prices. Responsible union leaders appreciate the fact that estate agriculture is the principal source of revenue and employment, and that wage demands are limited by world prices over which no one in the Caribbean has control. The problem is further complicated by the widely fluctuating prices paid for tropical produce. Historically, wages have remained steady while profits from estate agriculture have varied from extreme losses to very high profits according to the vagaries of world prices. Workers and union leaders are tempted to point to the periods of high profits and ask why the workers cannot share in the estate owner's good fortune. Planters interviewed by the writer claimed that in averaging out the periods of losses with those of high profits estates earned about 10 per cent, which was inadequate considering the size of the risk. Although there has been talk of profit-sharing schemes, there is at present no such scheme in the BWI. Instead, production bonuses have been negotiated in most agricultural labor agreements. In some respect these production bonuses work as profit-sharing schemes. A good crop is not due entirely to the efforts of management or labor, but to the fortunes of weather, disease, and hurricanes. Production bonuses then amount to sharing of profits on production over and above the break-even point. Estate owners like the production-bonus system because the wages vary with their ability to pay and because they tie the bonus in with a plan to reduce absenteeism and turnover. Workers like the production-bonus plan because it rewards them according to the size of the crop rather than serving as an incentive to greater individual effort. Their production bonus is paid to them in the off-crop season when money is scarce.

From 1833, when slaves were freed, until 1939, when unions were formed, wages in estate agriculture were virtually static.[2] Since 1939—and especially since World War II—wages have moved rapidly upward. Many estate owners attribute the rise in wages to the postwar inflation. Union leaders, on the other hand, argue that workers would not have held their own against inflation if it had not been for the unions. They suggest that wages would have remained low as they had for the past hundred years because there was no change in the demand for or supply of labor— if anything, there has been an increase in supply of labor. Several union leaders and many estate owners worried what would happen when wage increases could no longer be financed through continued world-wide inflation. If wage increases were not forthcoming, estate workers, who have little union loyalty and who are easily swayed by rabble rousers, might shift their allegiance to less responsible union leaders. Estate owners and colonial administrators expressed fear that falling prices or a drought might necessitate wage cuts; they believed that even the strongest and best-established union could not submit to this and survive. As the secretary of one sugar producer's association put it: "The union leaders are responsible enough fellows but they have to be irresponsible and unreasonable to maintain control of their unions." Union leaders, estate owners, and colonial administrators alike pointed to the falling off in union membership and lagging interest in union activities where wage increases were not forthcoming.

Employers in colonies having stable unions and established collective-bargaining relationships expressed fear that the unions had run out of major collective-bargaining issues. Marginal industry can offer only so much and no more. Dues-paying membership has declined, these employers believe, because new gains have not been won, and unions in several colonies were accused of calling strikes for no other purpose than to arouse the membership. These employers were sympathetic to the union's dilemma for they also feared that the restless memberships might switch loyalties to more irresponsible leaders.

Wages and the Supply of Labor

In wage negotiations in agriculture, estate owners correctly argue that higher wages restrict the supply of labor. As agricultural employment is considered undignified and since most estate workers continue a strategy of passivity in the face of difficult economic odds, they limit their economic wants and maximize leisure time. Accordingly, it is true that wage increases have resulted in shorter work days and weeks. With a higher wage it takes fewer task-work assignments to earn the minimum money wage to support the estate worker's standard of living. Although unemployment and underemployment are among the most serious problems in the West Indies, the negative sloping supply curve of labor enables estate owners to oppose higher wages. On the other hand, there are signs that the old pattern is crumbling and that as estate workers demand a higher standard of living the arguments of estate owners will no longer hold true. An American sawmill operator in British Honduras analyzed the problem as follows:

When workers become 'hooked' by the desire for manufactured goods they will drop their cloak of laziness and become as ambitious as workers in industrial nations. When wives come to consider lipstick and nylon panties as necessities, the men will work.

The sawmill operator explained that he had observed that this process of becoming "hooked" took place in Panama, and he was sure that it occurred in every underdeveloped area. Union leaders and observers of the West Indian scene in general assured the writer that the problem of an adequate supply of disciplined labor was in large part a merchandising problem. They criticized West Indian merchants for their lack of vigor in exploiting working-class consumer markets. Only one colonial administrator interviewed by the writer held the opinion that West Indian workers would continue to restrict the supply of labor. His conclusion, which expressed the planter point of view, was that West Indian workers would get their higher standard of living through higher prices for tropical produce and not through harder work on their part.

West Indian workers have demonstrated their willingness to work an eight-hour day, forty-hour week, without absenteeism, tardiness, or labor turnover in nonagricultural employments in the United States and in the BWI. This leads to the general conclusion held by West Indians that they prefer manufacturing employment to agriculture. The real difference in attitude toward work may be explained by a wage differential which enables workers to assume a lower-middle-class way of life; to have superior supervision and a type of work that is not of the beast-of-burden variety. If such employment conditions prevailed in agriculture, perhaps West Indians would find estate work more attractive. Also there is a difference of opinion as to why West Indian workers perform well as agricultural workers in the United States. West Indian estate owners argue that the very high wages, the short duration of the assignment (three years), and the fact that the workers are strangers in a foreign environment are the causes of the good work records. In addition, the owners argue that only the superior workers are selected for employment in the United States. Union leaders, on the other hand, argue that good wages, good supervision, and power equipment would remove the association of estate employment with slavery. There has been no difficulty in recruiting workers for industrial employment. Workers adjust to the tempo of industry rather than increasing the level of absenteeism even though industrial wages are higher than agricultural wages.

Government as a Wage Pace Maker

In the smaller colonies wage bargaining is complicated by the fact that the government is the largest single employer of labor.[3] Traditionally, the wage set by the government tended to be the going rate. When there was a limited franchise and no unions, wage leadership by the government presented no problem because the legislature represented the employer class. Now that the union-political party controls the governments of many smaller colonies special difficulties arise. The union-dominated legislature under universal franchise set government wage rates which by tradition should be the wage patterns for the colonies. Private employers are now at a disadvantage in bargaining with union representatives, who argue that the wage pattern set by the government should be maintained.

On the other hand, responsible union-leader–politicians are placed in a difficult position because they must resist worker pressure for higher wages on government jobs in order to protect private employers and the public treasury. The civil service as part of the nationalist colored middle class is usually the backbone of the political party. Public-works employees are usually the strongest section of a blanket union.[4] Conflict between the public interest and the particular interests of government employees probably will lead to a sharper distinction between political parties and trade unions. A clearer differentiation between union and political party will end the anomaly of employers bargaining with union leaders who, as representatives of the government, are the largest employers in the colony.

Task Rates

Two problems are created by the prevalence of task-work rates in estate employment. First, all observers agree that the variation in these rates for the same type of work between one estate and another within the same colony is a source of discontent. Because of the complexity of the problem of working out standard task rates many unions have avoided the issue and instead concentrated on general wage increases. While a general wage increase is a simple way to win membership approval, the dissatisfaction caused by wage-rate inequities remains. Those unions which are most successful in agriculture are also those who have faced this problem. Where some contracts merely record agreements to a general wage increase, leaving individual rates to custom on each estate, more successful and aggressive unions outline each rate and work standard in a lengthy contract. The union-management agreement in Antigua, for instance, contains tables of rates for each job on each estate *in each field* with wage adjustments equated to variations in conditions in individual fields. Second, specific task rates open the door to continual bargaining over the quantity of work to be done. While unorganized laborers were unable to raise wages by individual bargaining, they have lowered the task standard over the years, thus providing jobs for a growing population in a static economy. Even when the task standard is clearly understood by custom or union agreement, however, negotiations between the work gang and the driver take place to allow adjustment for local conditions. For example, work is harder after a rain than when the land is dry, so adjustments must be made in sizes of tasks depending upon the condition of the ground. To gather cocoa in a poor season requires more work than in a good season, so the price per basket of cocoa must be adjusted accordingly. As the amount of labor to be sold is subject to continual negotiations, the elimination of job-rate inequities will not entirely eliminate all other inequities.

Wages and Technological Unemployment

The threat of technological unemployment, along with the marginal nature of West Indian industry, are factors limiting union pressure for higher wages. Higher prices and price stability since the war have encouraged technological change, but they have not displaced labor. Likewise, improved sugar factories, fertilizers, and plant varieties have not displaced labor. The substitution of tractors for bullocks has caused some unemployment, but this is offset in part by the conversion of pasturage land to cane land. It is generally agreed, however, that further wage increases must in general be financed from technological improvements of a type which will create unemployment. Most union leaders and employers interviewed by the writer were opposed to a wage scale that would bring about technological unemployment. They argued that there were not enough job opportunities in an agricultural economy already suffering from overpopulation to permit technological unemployment. Although employers are criticized for general backwardness, many interviewed by the writer were sincere in considering technological change as socially irresponsible. A secretary of a waterfront employer's association agreed that half of the work force could be eliminated through the use of fork-lift trucks but he was horrified at the idea of putting so many men out of work. For the same reason most union leaders consider excessive wage demands as irresponsible.

Only a very few union leaders interviewed took the traditional

American trade-union view favoring high wages to force technological change. They argued that high wages would create middle-class attitudes among workers. In this manner women and children would be removed from the labor market, as workers with middle-class values would marry and become financially responsible for their children. Instead of increasing unemployment, high wages would then reduce the supply of labor. Furthermore, they argued that high-wage labor in agriculture would create purchasing power which would permit the development of secondary service industries. A few union leaders argued that a conservative wage policy resulted in workers sharing poverty by sharing jobs; that the creation of technological unemployment would force the government to assume greater responsibility for economic development.

Maximizing the Total Wage Bill

The fear of unemployment causes most unions in the West Indies to behave differently than American unions regarding wage standards. While American unions fight for a standard rate in each industry, West Indian unions pursue a policy of charging what the market will bear so as to maximize the total wage bill without jeopardizing employment opportunities. In this regard, unions are merely following traditional wage policies of the West Indies. For example, domestic servants in upper-class homes are paid top wages which enable them to hire maids in their own homes at lower rates of pay. The maid's maid in some instances has been known to hire another maid at a still lower rate of pay. Where unemployment is endemic, workers accept the proposition that wage differentials between employers should be based on their ability to pay. Consequently, the Jamaica sugar agreement classifies estates into three categories of efficiency and has three sets of wage rates. Workers on estates producing a variety of crops may do exactly the same type of work but receive different rates of pay depending on whether the work is in cane fields, banana plantations, or citrus groves. Observing the confused wage pattern of Jamaica, the World Bank Mission called the union policy short-sighted in that it protected current jobs by harming long-run job opportunities. According to the bank's report, protecting inefficient employers on the one hand while demanding higher wages from the efficient has the long-run effect of discouraging both investment and efficiency.[5]

An exception to the general rule illustrates the problem of a standard wage rate. In Grenada the wage rate is the same for nutmeg and cocoa, the principal crops of the island. Here estate owners complain of the unreasonableness of the workers, arguing that wage rates should fluctuate with swings in the prices of the two crops. During World War II when the supply of nutmeg from Java was cut off, prices soared and workers demanded wage rates commensurate with the increased profits of nutmeg producers. Estates that were predominantly in cocoa and had few nutmeg trees complained that they could not afford to pay such high wages because of the depressed price of cocoa as a result of the rationing of luxury foods. With the ending of the war the price of nutmeg fell and that of cocoa sky-rocketed. Workers on cocoa estates then demanded higher wages commensurate with the increased incomes of the cocoa estates. Nutmeg estates complained that they could not pay higher wages because of the ruinous prices of nutmeg.

Wages, Productivity, and Foreign Capital

All political parties in the West Indies are committed to a platform of attracting foreign capital and pioneer industries. Unions closely identified with political parties must take this fact into consideration in wage negotiations. Lacking in resources, public services, and skilled labor, it is argued that the one attraction of the West Indies is its cheap labor. Accordingly, unions should develop a colony-wide wage rate for comparable labor grades, and foreign companies investing in the West Indies should not be expected to pay more than the going rate. Citing of the going wage for the area was the successful argument of the Jamaica bauxite companies in their wage arbitration case of 1953. In addition, two other arguments for a standard rate were advanced, namely that wage differentials would create labor unrest and disrupt the labor market, and that higher wages would be inflationary in an economy where consumer goods were in short supply. The unsuccessful arguments of the bauxite worker's union at this time were that they were employees of North American companies and allied to North American unions; that they were part of a gigantic industrial complex covering the North American continent; that the productivity of Jamaican workers was equal to that of North American aluminum workers; and that differentials within the bauxite and aluminum industries should be abolished.

While on a "goodwill mission" to British Guiana, Nick Zonarich, International Representative of the United Steelworkers of America, "expressed surprise that wealthy North American companies paid sub-standard wages in British Guiana." [6] The bauxite company representative replied that they were paying the highest wage rate in British Guiana. This exchange of viewpoints again illustrates the difficulty of reconciling the ability-to-pay doctrine with the going-rate-in-the-area doctrine.

The bauxite workers' union won its 1955 wage-arbitration case and strengthened its position on wage differentials with the argument that wage differentials between industries, and especially between agriculture and manufacturing industries, exist in the more advanced industrial countries; and agricultural economies must adjust to the agricultural–manufacturing wage disparity found in economically developed countries. Rejecting the idea that wage differentials would disrupt labor markets, the union pointed to traditional wage differentials within agriculture itself which do not cause unrest. The union did not deny that wage differentials would be inflationary, but claimed this to be the inevitable result of economic development. The union held that inflation, rather than being undesirable, placed new purchasing power in the hands of workers and thus would create a greater demand for consumer goods, thereby encouraging the growth of local secondary industries. The argument for wage differentials was stated by the National Workers Union as follows:

We believe that for the purpose of securing employment, workers will have to tolerate standards of wages in industries of low profitability which wages do not afford a desirable standard of living. Notwithstanding the foregoing, we believe that the worker should get the maximum possible from any industry compatible with the continuance of that industry. We reject the unfounded theory that 'high wages upset the economy,' and, therefore insist on standards of wages in keeping with the profitability of such industries. [7]

Only one trade-union leader interviewed by the writer favored a uniform standard wage rate. It was his belief that the issue of ability to pay should be held in abeyance until after foreign investment had been well established.

Caribbean-wide Wage Standards

Until 1956 unions in each colony bargained individually with their employers, and wages for the same job varied from one colony to another. The formation of the Caribbean Federation of Bauxite and Allied Workers Unions may have marked the beginning of a trend toward area-wide bargaining. The bauxite companies have argued that, as subsidiaries of the parent aluminum company, they competed with other subsidiaries in other colonies and that higher wages would cause the parent company to buy its bauxite elsewhere. The aim of the Federation of Bauxite Unions is to eliminate this type of shadow competition and standardize the wage rate. Waterfront workers in each colony also have bargained with the same shipping companies, and these unions have met to consider the possibility of joint bargaining for area-wide standard wage rates. Under the leadership of the Cuban Sugar Workers Union, the sugar workers' unions of the Caribbean also have met to consider the possibility of area-wide bargaining. Although uniform wage rates in the sugar industry of the Caribbean would not influence world costs and prices significantly, the meeting has been part of an ambitious plan of the Cuban Sugar Workers Union to eliminate competition based upon wage differentials in the entire world-wide sugar industry. With the federation of the British West Indies we may expect increased collaboration in wage bargaining among unions in the various colonies.

Summary

Union-management relations in industrial employments are similar to those in industrial nations. In estate agriculture, however, union-management relations tend to be vague and lacking in formal procedures. The more successful and enduring unions of estate workers have established more formal relationships with employer's associations, in which the terms of employment are described in the contract in some detail and worker grievances are given prompt attention. Contrary to the view held by most employers and many union leaders, estate workers do have grievances. Although various commission reports have stated that the cause of spontaneous strikes has been the lack of efficient bargaining machinery, and although the defining of the work relationship and the adjudication of day-to-day disputes are recognized by labor-relations specialists as being vital union functions, they are not now effectively carried out by most BWI unions. Gradually, however, the quasi-feudal relationship is being replaced by a negotiated contract of rights and duties. The influences of the personnel policies of foreign corporations operating in the BWI and of ICFTU officers, and the success of job-oriented unions are factors causing union-management relations in the BWI to become patterned after those of industrial nations.

At present, wage bargaining predominates over all other union-management issues. Although wage increases won by unions since 1939 have only just kept pace with the cost of living, the relative stability of wage rates before unionism made possible by the large reserve of unemployed and underemployed suggests that the rates would not have advanced as rapidly in the absence of unions. The rising cost of living has been used as the prime argument in wage bargaining, which has meant that workers have been unable to better their real incomes. With greater price stability it has been increasingly difficult to win further wage increases. The marginal position of estate agriculture, the fear of technological change, general unemployment, and the need to attract foreign capital for economic development place severe limitations on union bargaining ability.

Most interviewed employers and union leaders believed that unemployment was so severe that wages could not be raised to a level which would encourage technological change of the type that substitutes capital for labor. All agree, however, that unions must ask for higher wages in order to keep their membership and that ultimately wage demands will lead to technological change, increased labor productivity, and technological unemployment.

A more serious dispute rages over wage differentials based on ability to pay. The traditional view held by workers and many employers is that the prevailing wage rate is below a health-and-decency standard, which creates a moral obligation for employers to pay above-minimum rates according to their ability. Since unemployment is endemic and most business is marginal, it is understood that wage differentials should exist to maximize both employment opportunities and the total wage bill. Such a wage policy, however, is not conducive to managerial efficiency, encouragement of economic development, or attraction of foreign capital. The ability-to-pay formula is even more difficult to apply to a major American corporation enjoying monopolistic profits. Consequently, it appears that a compromise will emerge in which wage differentials will be similar to those of industrial nations. Each industry will pay a standard wage rate, but differentials between industries will develop which will be based on the ability of the industry to pay. This ability to pay, in turn, is related to the productivity of labor, ratio of capital to labor, and degree of monopoly enjoyed by each industry.

As the government is a major, and often dominant, employer of labor, it is traditionally the pace setter in wage standards. Since the labor vote is essential to political success and, in addition, middle-class nationalist support is strong within the civil service, there is pressure for wages to be established by majority vote. Unscrupulous politicians and union leaders take advantage of the situation by promising higher wages if elected to office. Responsible leaders, concerned with taxes, balanced budgets, and economic development, must resist popular clamor for higher wages in government services. Two problems develop from this situation: First, both responsible union leaders and politicians may have their positions undermined by opportunists; and second, government wage policy will be a source of conflict between trade unionists and middle-class nationalists, which will prevent unity in political action.

The argument of employers that higher wages reduce the supply of labor is correct in relation to agricultural employment. On the other hand, the present low wages have increased the supply of labor by forcing women, children, and the aged into the labor market. A more socially desirable arrangement would be a high enough wage to permit a man to marry and support his family. The supply of labor would be reduced to the extent that women would become homemakers and children remain in school. The supply of labor would increase as men who would become responsible for the support of their families would change from voluntary underemployment to a full work day, week, and year. Modest wage increases would not bring about such a radical social change, but substantial ones would make it worthwhile for men to assume family obligations and middle-class values. Another reason that higher wages reduce the supply of field hands is the workers' dislike of the indignity of beast-of-burden jobs associated with slavery. A small wage increase is not enough to overcome this distaste for field labor, nor enough to enable purchasing of significant quantities of consumer goods. Small wage increases can only purchase a little more rum, cigarettes, or cinema tickets, and these benefits are not as attractive as a reduction in hours of distasteful labor. A substantial wage increase, however, would put a worker in a different income bracket, opening the way to a whole new order of consumer purchases, such as table radios—making work worthwhile. Finally, apart from the issue of the wage-policy problem, improved supervisory practices and better tools and equipment could remove much of the stigma of agricultural employment.

Chapter IX	*Union Attitudes*
	Toward Basic Economic
	Problems

Economic development is, and to an increasing degree will be, a vital political issue. Since unions will play an important role in the political life of the Federation of the West Indies (even with greater separation between parties and unions), a knowledge of the attitudes of union leaders toward basic economic issues is therefore necessary to an understanding of the political issues in an economic-development program.

Immature Thinking

Union leaders have been critical of the employer class and of government for so many years that they have not yet adjusted to assuming their proper responsibilities as labor leaders or politicians. As a consequence, many interviewed union leaders appeared to be handicapped by fuzzy thinking. First, there is a popular feeling (shared by many union leaders) among the people of the West Indies that they are in no way responsible for the present state of economic affairs and that "someone else should clean up the mess." It is argued that the "lazy, rich estate owners" have exploited the working people for centuries and that now it is time for the estate owners to pay them back. A common expression is that "the ancestors of the estate owners brought our forefathers here against their will from Africa as slaves and therefore estate owners are now responsible for our welfare." In part this attitude stems from the responsibility which estate owners have traditionally assumed for slaves and indentured servants and which survives under present quasi-feudal employee-employer arrangements. In commenting on this point, Professor Simey observes that an obstacle to the reconstruction of the West Indies is the belief that all remedial measures are compensation for past wrongs.[1] One example serves to illustrate such irresponsibility on the part of a few union leaders. When it was suggested to one trade unionist that the program for economic reform did not appear to be feasible, this man replied: "This is no problem of the working classes. All we have to do is raise hell, and if the white people are so smart, they can figure out some way to keep us satisfied."

Many West Indians, including some union leaders, believe that the British have exploited the West Indian colonies for centuries, and that now that the colonies are no longer profitable the British wish to pull out, leaving the people without economic development or experience in self-government. They regard the subsidies provided by the local government, the British Parliament, the Colonial Development and Welfare Corporation, and the Colonial Industrial Development Corporation as just payments long overdue. It is argued that every business should plow back some of its earnings into social and economic development of the community; until recently the British had failed to do so. Blaming the government for past failures, some union leaders concluded that the proper step toward economic action was to demand even bigger subsidies from the British government. Such a move would eliminate the need for facing squarely the issues of self-government and the responsibilities of the peoples of the West Indies for their own welfare. This thinking no doubt has its roots in the paternalistic colonial policy practiced in the past when West Indians were treated as children.

When it is pointed out that the British have serious problems of their own at home and are unable to subsidize the BWI, another popular thesis is argued—namely, that the obligation to supply subsidies then rests with the United States. In interviews with the writer many trade unionists argued that in a world of poverty no nation has the moral right to be so rich as the United States without sharing some of its "good fortune." Moreover, they

---

[1] For notes to chapter ix, see pp. 203–204.

hold it immoral to spend billions on armaments without spending a few millions, "which would never be missed," for the development of the BWI. Many union leaders told with some emotion what a million dollars would mean to the people of his colony— a million dollars that Americans could painlessly give away. They argue that the United States "squanders" billions of dollars all over the world on economic development to fight communism but will not spend anything on the poverty-stricken friends in its own backyard. Many leaders suggested to the writer that the BWI should cease being friendly to the United States and should pretend to be pro-Communist in order to get their share of the "loot." One may sympathize with such sentiments as good politics and even recognize an element of truth in them, but one must also recognize the fact that this reasoning is in keeping with the tendency to shift the responsibility of their problems to someone else.

Another example of the naïve thinking prevalent among many trade unionists is the belief that their particular ideology could prove to be a panacea. Self-government, socialism, or Catholic doctrines in British Honduras once achieved would set off a chain reaction which would automatically lead to a happy conclusion. It is understandable that unions and political parties should concentrate on immediate objectives; but it is unfortunate that there is so much fuzzy thinking on what to do after the immediate objectives are achieved. The more sophisticated people claim that self-government and socialism (as an ideal rather than as a plan of action) will endow the people with a new spirit of nationalism, pride, and brotherhood which will overcome the inertia of despair and the self-pity which now characterize the people of the BWI. It is argued that once self-government is granted people will have the pride and ambition to build a stable and secure economy. On the other hand, many West Indians sincerely argue that self-government is impossible unless founded upon a secure economic base, and that this economic base will not be forthcoming until the people themselves gain the skill, the work habits, the self-discipline, and thrift for capital accumulation necessary to build a sound economy.

There are other union leaders who came under the spell of bulldozers on United States army bases in the Caribbean and who now avoid facing economic problems by espousing the belief that West Indians "can do anything" if they adopt the "American way." Workers and the lower middle class of St. Lucia, Trinidad, and British Guiana in particular were inordinately impressed with American operations. This group has joined the "cult of the bulldozer," arguing that with American equipment and American know-how anything can be done, and disregarding the lack of resources in the West Indies. It is argued that with American methods the natural resources can be found. A British Guiana businessman—opposed to the British, opposed to the local government, pro-union—said: "I saw the Americans build a modern city in our jungles; I have driven down the Pennsylvania turnpike; I have seen the Hoover Dam; and I have stood atop the Empire State Building. Anyone who can do these things can make British Guiana a wonderful place in which to live whether it has resources or not." American construction methods have changed the perspectives of many West Indians but it has also caused some unrealistic thinking on the potential development of what they now like to refer to as "our country."

The Problem of Overpopulation

Population growth[2] is a fundamental problem which threatens to negate efforts toward full employment and a higher standard of living. The population grows at an estimated rate of 2½ per cent a year, doubling every forty years. (See chapter i.) The economy must keep pace with the population growth in order to provide new jobs and thus supply the economic necessities of life and give the government a growing revenue with which to meet the need for social services. Commenting on this problem, Sir Steven Luke said:

At the end of 1952 the total population of the British Caribbean territories was estimated at 3,293,000 or nearly one-half million more than the figures recorded only six years before in the 1946 census. Each year the net increase of the living is between 70,000 and 75,000 souls, so that by the time these words appear in print the population will have increased by a further 110,000 persons or the total will be about 3,400,000. For those to whom figures mean little it may be profitable to look upon the facts another way. Each year there is added to the population of the British territories a mass of people equivalent to the total population of one of the Windward Islands or twice that of the Island of Antigua or one-third the population of Barbados. Translated into human needs this represents an impressive quantity of houses, schools, churches, hospitals, roads, vehicles, clothing, food, occupation and wages.[3]

Substantial emigration out of the West Indies is not possible. Neither North America nor South America wants unskilled labor, least of all Negroes. The opportunity to migrate to the United Kingdom is limited. The population problem is further complicated by the fact that improved technology reduces the number of opportunities for labor in agriculture, and union pressure for higher wages hastens the process of technological change on estates. Industrialization and restriction of population growth are the only answers to the central problem facing the BWI. An inescapable conclusion therefore is that an ambitious industrial development program could just about hold its own against population growth, maintaining poverty, unemployment, and underemployment at the present high levels. As prospects for industrialization are limited, improvement in the West Indian standard of living in reality depends on restriction of population growth.

Most unionists agree that the population problem is critical; that it does affect the opportunity of workers to find jobs; and that the stability of unions and political parties is endangered by population pressure. Both as union leaders and as politicians, however, they feel it unwise to raise the issue, holding that this problem is not a union matter and that they would only make enemies by advocating measures to restrict population growth. A few Catholic and Anglican trade unionists prefer to ignore the population issue altogether claiming that economic development and migration will offset the increased growth. Only in Barbados, the most densely populated agricultural area in the world, is there a plan of education for parenthood. In the last seven years the population of Barbados has increased by an estimated 30,000, which is a greater number than that of the entire labor force in the sugar industry, the principal source of employment there. Scientific research has doubled the yield per acre in the last seven years but employment opportunities in this industry have declined. Income per capita has held steady while job opportunities are becoming increasingly scarce. The unwillingness of union leaders and politicians, except in Barbados, to face the population issue may negate efforts toward economic development.[4]

Attitude Toward Foreign Capital

All trade-union leaders and politicians agree that foreign capital is necessary to economic development because the BWI are too poor for much internal saving. Members of the upper income group who could invest in local enterprise have a high propensity to consume; tend to invest savings in farmland; and invest any surplus income abroad. The bulk of development capital must therefore come from outside. One obstacle to foreign investment, however, is the belief by some of the more unsophisticated West Indian politicians and unionists that the colonies are rich in resources just waiting to be exploited by foreign capitalists. They would set up barriers to prevent the "rape" of their country.[5] Instead of offering incentives to private capital, these politicians would see to it that all earnings on investments remain in the colony. There are even politicians so naïve as to be waiting for an American millionaire who will give them interest-free loans or outright gifts for economic development. The need for foreign capital is recognized but payment for its use is regarded as "exploitation" on the part of the lender. Many unionists and politicians fail to realize that investment opportunities are more secure and attractive in the United States than in the BWI. Instead of behaving as shy and modest maidens doubting the intentions of foreign capitalists, the role must be reversed, with the BWI the active suitor of capital.

West Indian Socialists also fear outside private capital and want direct loans from Great Britain, the United States government, or the World Bank. They point out that many individual companies in the United States and Europe are far more powerful than their small islands and imply that no fair bargain can be reached. They review the past wrongs of foreign investors in corrupting local governments and in exploitation of workers and natural resources. Socialists argue that they cannot have true freedom and self-government if they are subservient to giant corporations. They further point out that labor must gain immediate benefits, but private investors will insist on paying the prevailing substandard wages. Most union leaders and politicians, however, feel that economic development is so important that everything should be done to make the investment of foreign capital as attractive as possible. The Sugar and Plantation Workers Conference held in British Guiana in August, 1955, acknowledged the fact that without large-scale investment the problem of unemployment and underemployment would become more serious as the sugar industry mechanizes to meet world competition. The conference went on record in favor of an over-all development program of the entire Caribbean patterned after the Puerto Rican program.[6] An editorial in the *CAD-ORIT Information Bulletin* stated that trade unionists recognize the need for foreign capital but that unions will demand fair wages.[7] Fair wages mean wages which are above the general level prevailing in the BWI and raise the ability-to-pay issue discussed in chapter vi. Most trade unionists believe that adequate safeguards against foreign exploitation can be developed and that satisfactory wage differentials can be established while at the same time investment of foreign capital is made more attractive.

All West Indian colonies have a pioneer-industry law patterned after Puerto Rico's. The Trinidad law, which is typical, provides for the granting of relief from customs duty and income tax for five years to persons establishing pioneer industries; and for permission to bring to the colony foreigners with technical skills not available in the local labor force.[8] Debate over pioneer-industry laws centers on the issue of protective provisions for workers. A few union officials interviewed by the writer would follow a policy of offering low wages in the hope that the resulting jobs created by foreign investment would make the sacrifice worthwhile, but most unionists complained that more protection for workers was needed in the pioneer-industry laws. They argued that foreign capital should be required to pay a wage providing a minimum standard of health and decency for workers even though such a minimum standard is above prevailing wage rates in the West Indies. Middle-class administrative and technical personnel, even more than unionists, are concerned over the possibility that "importees" will get the top jobs in the pioneer industries. This problem is difficult to solve. On the one hand, the "importees" are disliked because they demand premium pay and home leave in overseas service; often practice racial discrimination; and may assume positions at the apex of local society. On the other hand, local people are lacking in many skills, and even those who have skills are often improperly trained. Local people who do develop real skills migrate to Canada, the United States, and the United Kingdom where pay is higher and job opportunities greater. As the nationalists have learned, once in political office, they must import skills and pay premium wages in order to carry out development schemes.

Attitudes Toward Economic Development

Union leaders and politicians place great stress on the need for economic planning; it is a favorite topic in speech-making. They claim that the British have failed in economic development, and that with greater self-government their particular political party will go forward toward economic planning for rapid industrialization. Commenting on this reasoning, Professor Simey describes the tendency of these leaders to place the blame for all economic troubles of the West Indies on the colonial office "importees" as a dangerous piece of escapism.[9] Actually few West Indians have carefully-thought-out solutions for the problems of economic development.[10]

The following frequently reiterated points, however, are well taken. First, industrial development is absolutely necessary. The suggestion of the Moyne Report, which must be taken in its depression-era context, that the BWI can offer only a humble, but healthy, subsistence living, is rejected by most West Indians. Studies made by the World Bank, which stress agricultural development as the quickest, cheapest way to increase national income are rejected for emotional reasons. Nationalists relate industry to independence, power, and wealth. Unionists relate industry to better jobs, regular work, higher wages, and a new way of life. The BWI will try for industrialization in spite of the great difficulties. The Moyne Report and the Colonial Development and Welfare Corporation have been criticized for advocating welfare programs before economic development. Investment in capital goods must precede social-welfare programs, it is argued, in order to provide an economic base to support social welfare. Workers are impatient, however. Union leaders find it popular to advocate bigger appropriations for schools, housing, medical care, and social security. A major political issue shaping up concerns a balancing of expenditures between immediate welfare benefits and investment in long-run economic development.[11]

Second, the government must secure capital to develop harbor facilities, roads, and cheap electric power before private capital can be attracted to the West Indies. At the present time, even if profitable industry could be started, an industrialist would be hesitant to establish a plant in the West Indies where power supply is expensive and uncertain, water supply uncertain, transportation expensive, and harbor facilities nonexistent or inadequate. Social investment must precede private investment.

Third, there is general agreement for the need of a research program. Little is known about the mineral wealth or the soil chemistry of the West Indies. Although certain staple tropical crops have formed the foundation of West Indian economy for generations, little research has been done in the growing, handling, and use of these crops except for sugar cane. As has been dramatically demonstrated in the sugar industry, research is a worthwhile investment.

Fourth, although wages are very low, labor in the West Indies is very expensive,[12] because labor lacks skill and training and is unaccustomed to industrial discipline. Other reasons for low labor productivity are poor supervision, lack of tools, small lot production, and poor health. Although West Indians prefer industrial employment to agricultural labor, they lack experience in industry. Accordingly, an apprenticeship program to be synchronized with economic growth is advocated.[13] The present problem is due to the fact that industry is hesitant to locate new plants where skilled labor is lacking while graduates of apprenticeship training programs find themselves without any call for their particular skills. Putting it another way, the report of the British Guiana and British Honduras Settlement Commission stated that the greatest obstacle to economic development was human inefficiency, with the result that labor costs were dangerously high compared with those of competitors in the Orient. The Commission did not believe that under present circumstances private capital would be attracted to the area. Rejecting a laissez-faire program, a government building program was justified by the Commission in the hope that employee skills, ambition, and self-respect might develop to a point where public subsidy became unnecessary.[14]

Fifth, the entrepreneurial spirit and drive required in private industry are lacking among the people of the West Indies. The historical reasons for this were examined in chapter i. Accordingly, it is accepted that the local government must enter more industries and businesses. This policy does not stem from Socialist ideology but from the absence of an entrepreneurial class.

Certain other important points are generally overlooked by union leaders and politicians in their discussion of economic planning: When they hope for the discovery and development of mineral resources they overlook the fact that the exploitation of these resources not only requires large amounts of capital and cheap electric power but provides few direct employment opportunities. The development of mineral resources may add substantially to the revenue of the colony—this is all to the good and the multiplier effect will create further employment, but resources are limited relative to the magnitude of the employment problem.

Besides, economic planners in the West Indies fail to visualize the workers themselves as a potential market. Traditionally, the West Indies have exported agricultural produce in return for the importation of food supplies and manufactured consumer goods. They are not accustomed to thinking of the local population as a market. Wartime shipping shortages followed by postwar inflation has given consumer-goods industries a good start, and if it is possible to raise the income of the working class these industries should benefit substantially.

Further, union leaders place great emphasis on the industrialization of the West Indies in spite of the World Bank reports for Jamaica, British Honduras, and British Guiana, which stress the improvement of agriculture. Nationalists the world over, it appears, identify a high standard of living, political independence, and national pride with industrialization. They suspect that their country has remained underdeveloped as a result of colonial policies and international monopolies. They know that agriculture everywhere is in a poor position to bargain with manufacturing industry. As noted elsewhere, West Indian workers have an intense distaste for estate agriculture and a liking for industrial jobs. Consequently, union leaders tend to brush aside any analysis recommending the improvement of existing agriculture as the quickest and easiest way to raise national income.

In addition, planners fail to see that the civil-service bureaucracy is an obstacle to economic development. For a poor country, the civil service is overstaffed and its methods are grossly inefficient. The civil service is not noted for its spirit of service to business and the public, but rather is notorious for its buck-passing ability. Equally serious is the fact that the civil service is guilty of favoritism and corruption in its dealings with business.[15] Such a bureaucracy is an impediment to economic development, but as civil-service employees are usually the backbone of middle-class nationalist parties, politicians will be reluctant to reform the civil service.

In discussing the civil-service bureaucracy, the World Bank Report for British Guiana stated that a major problem for both government and industry is the need for trained personnel. The Report observed that the economic-development programs of the government were sound and well conceived but lacking in qualified personnel to carry them out. Among other things, turnover of personnel in British Guiana was so high that development programs were hampered by a lack of continuity of staff. Instances were cited in which a new department head would start a program only to quit before he finished his plan and his replacement would repeat the process with a different set of plans. The Bank Report attributed the poor quality of the civil service to: Political agitation to give preference to Guianese although they lack training and ability; the emigration of qualified Guianese for areas offering higher pay and greater opportunities; the fact that imported personnel require a salary out of line with the general salary levels of British Guiana; the high turnover of imported personnel.[16]

Also, planners fail to see the possibility of developing industries which would import raw materials to be processed for export.[17] As stated above, the exploitation of existing raw materials does not provide great employment opportunities and the market for consumer goods within the West Indies is too small to provide large-scale employment opportunities. The importation of raw materials requiring large amounts of labor in the process of fabrication, however, would solve the employment problem, provided markets could be found for these goods. Since such a scheme raises many problems, its potentialities are generally overlooked by economic planners in the West Indies.

Finally, most West Indian trade unionists fail to realize the extent to which trade-union instability is in itself a deterrent to economic development. Employers wish to deal with unions that have a stable membership; they wish to deal with responsible unions whose members do not indulge in wildcat strikes; and they do not wish to be the victims of jurisdictional disputes.[18] Prospective investors do not like the "ability to pay" wage-differential policy of many unions and feel insecure because of apparent antagonism to foreign capital.[19] Employers and investors do not like collective-bargaining demands to coincide with election campaigns in which union leaders are running for office; and they do not like to become entangled in labor disputes in which union officers and government ministers are the same people.[20] Sir Alfred Savage, governor of British Guiana, in his broadcast on the suspension of the constitution, after listing instances in which capital had fled the country in fear of political instability, said:

To the trade unionists of this country I would say you have a great responsibility and opportunity to restore confidence in this country. In the months that lie ahead your words and actions will be closely watched overseas. On you will depend to a large extent whether industrialists who are interested in the development of the resources of this country will feel that if they come here they will be given a fair deal by you as well as by the Government.[21]

At the present stage of political development, politicians denounce the British for their failure to develop the colonies; they criticize them for the inadequacy of present development programs; and these same politicians make exaggerated promises as to economic development that will take place when their political parties are in office. Once in office, however, lack of tangible economic development is blamed by the parties on existing limitations on complete self-government. Colonial administrators despair of this fuzzy-mindedness of many West Indian politicians and members of the legislature. However, they readily admit that, once brought to grips with the problems of economic development, West Indians have learned fast; and that they are becoming more realistic in their study of the problem. Recent economic development in Jamaica, for example, is indicative of what can be accomplished by nationalist leaders with zeal and determination.

Summary

Union leaders in the West Indies can speak eloquently on the need for economic development and the failure of the British. A greater measure of self-government coupled with economic development have been twin issues in every campaign. Most union leaders, however, are hazy as to how to go about economic development and are overoptimistic as to the economic potential of their colonies. As a greater measure of self-government has been granted and as unionists have found themselves in responsible positions, they have learned rapidly the real problems encountered in economic development. Once the slogans of imperialism and colonial exploitation are abandoned, union leaders and nationalist politicians find the interest, enthusiasm, and determination necessary for economic development. Neither union leaders nor politicians can become responsible, however, if the working-class electorate chooses to support those making the wildest promises.

Overpopulation and continued rapid population growth are basic economic and political problems. In the face of continued population growth, even the most ambitious development program can only keep poverty and endemic unemployment from worsening. Unions cannot function effectively in the midst of large-scale general unemployment. On the one hand, a union strategy favoring job security at the expense of wage standards would obstruct economic development and fail to satisfy worker demands. On the other hand, if unions follow traditional job-oriented goals, a minority will hold the jobs while the majority of workers will be unemployed. Finally, the possibility of political stability is doubtful if a large mass of the electorate is unemployed and underemployed. In spite of the seriousness of the population problem, however, most union leaders and politicians are unwilling to face the issue.

BWI leaders agree on the need for foreign capital, but disagree whether (a) private foreign capital is welcome; and (b) the wage policies and limitations on "importees" should be pursued. These are not insurmountable problems. Safeguards for foreign capital and local welfare can be worked out.

Economic planners agree on the need for government social investment, long overdue, in order to provide a climate for private investment. Beyond this, planners are uncertain; agricultural development is promising, but lacks appeal; natural-resource development and consumer-goods industries have appeal but are insufficient fully to employ the labor force. Only through the importation of raw materials to be processed for export can the BWI make genuine headway against poverty and unemployment.

Union instability and irresponsibility are themselves obstacles to economic development. If unions cannot hold their membership against the appeals of opportunists; cannot resolve jurisdictional disputes; and cannot keep politics out of collective-bargaining issues, economic progress will be made more difficult. Union stability, on the other hand, will contribute to economic development if it creates a disciplined work force which does not follow any Pied Piper into wildcat strikes. By channelizing worker aggressions into union goals, passive resistance to employers may be overcome. Union stability may also promote the political stability necessary to attract foreign capital.

Chapter X | Conclusions

For almost a century after emancipation, British West Indian workers lived in a socioeconomic system dominated by an estate system of agriculture which differed little from conditions prevailing under slavery. Estate owners, the colored middle class, and the colonial government were not interested in a positive program for economic development, and the former slaves were not equipped to do anything about the situation. The workers, confronted with limited employment opportunities in beast-of-burden jobs at low wages, responded by developing passive and submissive personalities. Dissatisfaction with existing conditions was, and continues to be, expressed in absenteeism, leaving a job without notice, refusal to assume initiative, and passive insubordination. By limiting wants to a subsistence level, workers could, and do, withhold their labor, thereby creating a labor shortage in agricultural employment in the midst of general underemployment. Consequently, an employment relationship developed that left the duties and rights of employees and employers exceedingly vague.

Such an economic system functioned when BWI workers were relatively better off than workers in the sweatshops and industrial slums of countries going through the pains of industrial revolution. Even today most West Indians, except in the big cities, have adequate though unbalanced nourishment and none suffer from the cold for want of clothing and shelter because the climate is warm. Gradually, however, living standards and employee status in the industrial nations of the world pulled far ahead of the almost static socioeconomic system of the BWI. The depression, population pressure, and exposure to modern management and technology during World War II brought about a dramatic change in worker attitudes and personality traits. Labor unrest and union development followed.

Labor unrest in the BWI did not come from disruption of the traditional way of life caused by rapid industrialization. Instead, it sprang from the failure of the BWI to develop industrially. West Indian workers do not like the beast-of-burden jobs in agriculture which are associated with slavery. They want industrial employment, preferably with power equipment, which gives them a dignity and status not accorded field hands. West Indian workers do not like the estate system of agriculture because of the undignified type of employee-employer relationship it engenders. They prefer the independence of a job where they are subservient to an employer only during working hours and only in matters directly pertaining to the job. Moreover, they prefer the personnel and supervisory practices associated with modern industry. Although productivity is notoriously low in the BWI, West Indian workers have proved themselves capable of skill, initiative, and discipline when given opportunity in industry. Middle-class European values and ways of life are not foreign to West Indian workers, but they cannot assume these values as underemployed, casual laborers. West Indian workers want jobs with a security and rate of pay that will permit them to break with the social order of peasant communities.

Union leaders and middle-class nationalists alike reject economic studies which recommend further development of agriculture as the logical plan for raising living standards. "Realists" may argue that industrialization is impracticable for the BWI. "Romanticists" may argue that the urban, industrial wage earner has an ugly way of life compared with the happy-go-lucky, out-of-doors life of the field hand. BWI workers prefer industrial employment and nationalists demand it. Labor protest is against the continuance of a type of feudalism rather than against capitalism and industrialization.

Workers throughout the BWI have common problems based on a similar history and socioeconomic background, but these identical problems have been explained by various union leaders with differing ideological frameworks. In different parts of the BWI workers have heard their problems explained in terms of Communist, Socialist, radical Catholic, and pragmatic union ideology as well as in terms of unionism blended with primitive religions. Workers will adopt the ideology that explains their difficulties and offers a program of action *provided* the leadership is successful in winning tangible benefits. Union ideology in the BWI is largely the reflection of the ideology of the successful union leader. During the 1940's, and to a lesser extent even today, the psychic satisfaction of striking and of the "repetitive drama" were sufficient outlets, but eventually workers became more sophisticated and want more tangible gains.

A union that has close contact with workers and offers a program for winning immediate benefits, can win worker support irrespective of the ideology used as a frame of reference. Workers are not interested in complicated economic analyses or utopian schemes, but they will go along with these schemes if their on-the-job needs are catered to. Communism or Peronism, for example, could win worker support if only the ideology was coupled with effective unionism. Middle-class nationalists' slogans denouncing colonialism and demanding greater measures of self-government receive worker endorsement when tied to effective unionism and are rejected when the appeal of nationalism stands by itself. Unionism of the type found in most affiliates of the International Confederation of Free Trade Unions has been the most successful because it is best suited to the needs of the workers.

West Indians, particularly of the upper class, frequently express the opinion that BWI workers are incapable of union organization. To support their contention they point to the general lack of community organization in rural areas. Left to their own devices, agricultural workers expend considerable energy in unions created by political opportunists, mystics, and grafters. With outside aid and advice, however, stable, job-oriented unions can be established. A review of successful unions, regardless of ideology, shows that they have one characteristic in common—the willingness of the leadership to work hard in the interests of employees. Communist, socialist, nationalist, Catholic, mystic, and racketeering leadership has received worker support so long as it has remained close to the workers. Agricultural workers in Antigua, St. Kitts, Jamaica, and British Guiana have been organized by leaders willing to go to the country districts to do the organizing. Workers in the jungles of British Honduras and British Guiana, where roads are nonexistent, have been organized by men with the determination and willingness to face hardships. Since rank-and-file leadership is not now generally available, union failures are due to neglect of union duties for personal goals, politics, or utopian ideologies by outside leaders.

From a broad viewpoint, labor protest in the BWI has expressed itself in two ways. The first is a blind, emotional, and irrational one, whose extreme expression is pocomania and obeah, and to a lesser degree in Garveyism and the Messiah complex. In unionism, emotionalism is expressed in the multitude of unions formed by leaders skilled in fiery oratory. These unions are also weak in internal organization and in their dealings with employers. Consequently, unions of this type do not last. A large part of BWI union history has been a cycle beginning with an orator-showman gaining a large following which he calls a union, then precipitating a strike which results in no tangible gains or union contract, but probably wins political office for the showman. A new showman then appears on the scene, jurisdictional strife ensues, and the cycle is repeated. From the material presented in chapters i and ii, describing the nature of the estate system, and pointing out the lack of traditions and social structure, it may be understood why labor protest finds its expression in this form. Unfortunately, however, this sort of labor protest does not solve the problems of the worker. Instead, it promotes union and political instability and is a serious obstacle to economic development.

A second type of labor protest is expressed by unions pursuing traditional job-oriented goals. This type of unionism did not spring from the BWI environment but is an importation—as are many BWI institutions—which has been adjusted to fit conditions in the West Indies. The type of unionism found in the United States and the United Kingdom does not find fertile ground among agricultural workers who are semiliterate and superstitious, lacking in worker leadership, poorly paid, and underemployed. Nevertheless, this unionism is slowly and steadily gaining ground. Part of the gain is due to the technical and financial assistance supplied by the International Confederation of Free Trade Unions, British and American unions, and the colonial government, but job-oriented unionism also progresses because it satisfies the needs of workers.

As concluded by the British government after the riots of 1935–1939, this type of unionism promotes the social good. It gives the worker a voice in the employment relationship without recourse to passive insubordination and spontaneous riots. It prevents legitimate grievances from being exploited by leaders whose motives are open to question. It forces lethargic management to assume its responsibilities and to become more efficient. In this manner job-oriented unionism is contributing to political stability and to a basis for economic development.

A trend in union development in the BWI seems to be emerging. Agricultural workers were the first to engage in spontaneous uprisings. These disturbances were capitalized upon by leaders with oratorical, negotiating, and organizing ability, but did not necessarily lead to the development of trade unionism. For a time, emotional release and psychological uplift were enough. Next, workers supported leaders who won the biggest wage increases. Finally, with the industrial workers leading the way, workers' loyalty shifted to those unions which developed an apparatus for orderly negotiation over terms of employment, and which maintained a close contact with workers concerning their on-the-job problems.

Traditional theories of the labor movement do not readily describe the reasons for the development of the BWI union movement. Neither capitalistic nor colonial exploitation can altogether explain labor unrest or union development. West Indian workers do not think in these terms. Labor protest was against poverty, lethargy of management, and lack of status. Although Marxist analysis is used by some to explain the problems of the BWI, the worker revolution is against the continuation of a type of feudalism. Likewise, union development cannot be called a reaction against capitalism, for West Indian capitalism is of a rather primitive variety. Workers seem to prefer the modern capitalism of the oil and bauxite companies. Once again, BWI unionism appears to be a protest against feudalism rather than the "child of capitalism" proposition.

It would be difficult to hold that BWI unionism developed to protect workers against the "higgling of the market," or against the "perils of a self-regulating market." Wages were low but stable. Employment opportunities were scarce but equally shared, so that underemployment became more serious than unemployment. Estate owners were saddled with fixed costs of a house spot, garden spot, public utilities, and a crude sort of social security for a growing labor force they could not fully utilize. In short, custom governed the employment relationship. Status and poverty rather than higgling and uncertainty led to labor unrest. Had a free market existed, wages would probably have been lower, unemployment greater, and the aged and infirm would have starved. Most unions in the BWI do not fit the pattern described by Perlman as "job-conscious" unionism. Here workers have been dissatisfied but inarticulate. Outside leadership has explained worker dissatisfaction in many different ways.

BWI unions in general are not oriented toward bargaining over terms of employment and grievance handling. Most unions lack local organization and leadership; they are engaged in politics and advocate programs that offer little direct benefit to workers. Nevertheless, those unions that have stressed local organization with local leadership; are equipped to handle grievances; negotiate contracts which define terms of employment; and place union goals above political goals appear to be well suited to the problems of agricultural workers on BWI estates. Job-conscious unionism is an importation and is in the minority, but is making progress and gaining stability for the BWI labor movement.

It would be improper to compare the labor movements of the United States and the United Kingdom with a labor movement which is twenty years old. It is understandable that the young BWI labor movement should experiment with many different forms of unionism. It is also understandable that it should borrow heavily from established and mature labor movements and it is not surprising that proved methods of trade unionism should prove successful in the BWI.

Some social scientists take the position that our values should not be imposed on foreign cultures, that different societies have different values, prefer their own way of doing things, and resent the interference of outsiders. It is proper for social scientists to maintain the role of impersonal observers of social phenomena and to point out that social change and foreign ideas increase conflict and confusion; but to hold that outsiders should not interfere in union development of other cultures is itself a value judgment. Workers are protesting against their present way of life, which is not a foreign importation. Moreover, interference began with the institution of slavery. A common complaint of West Indians is the lack of enough outside assistance in the transition from slavery to freedom. Granting of freedom to organize and to bargain collectively without giving aid, advice, and direction would be as irresponsible as the policy pursued after emancipation. Left to themselves, BWI unions would have had a long and painful process of development. Strange values may be imposed upon workers by a local demagogue, and Communists are eager to give struggling young labor movements "advice," "assistance," and "liberation." The question is not whether to "impose values," but whose values should be imposed.

The BWI labor movement has made great strides in its brief history. There are many reasons for serious instability, yet there are hopeful signs pointing to improvement. West Indian unions are now in a critical stage—a stage in which even the strongest union could be destroyed or taken over by opportunists who combine stirring oratory with administrative ability. Only the lack of the latter skill has thus far prevented such opportunists from exploiting worker unrest. If international communism should invest time and money in infiltrating West Indian unions, communism might enjoy a large measure of success. The greatest threat to the BWI labor movement, however, is the possible emergence of some self-appointed Messiah who will play Pied Piper to the workers for his own self-aggrandizement. Threats of such a development should not be confused with interesting customs or vagaries of 'natives' whose values are different from ours.

Coincident with union development, BWI colonies have been granted an increasing measure of self-government and will soon be given dominion status. The birth of the new nation will put an end to colonial interference, but the new federation will need aid and assistance in establishing a self-governing democracy. Privately, many responsible West Indians fear that outside interference will end too soon. In the new federation, unions and political parties must be closely related because of the nature of the BWI electorate. Although interrelated, the political stability of the new federation will depend on a stable union movement. On the one hand, responsible politicians must have the support of a unified and stable union movement in order to have stable political parties. On the other hand, if unions can be easily taken over by any opportunist, these self-seekers will use the union movement as an instrument to undermine established political parties. Accordingly, union stability may hold a key to the future of this newest of nations.

Notes

Notes to Chapter I | General Background

1. For detailed historical background see W. L. Burn, *The British West Indies;* Eric Williams, *Capitalism and Slavery;* William M. MacMillan, *Warning from the West Indies;* Lowell J. Ragatz, *The Fall of the Planter Class in the British Caribbean, 1763–1833;* Philip D. Curtin, *Two Jamaicas.*

2. See Ronald Sires, "Government in the BWI—An Historical Outline," *Social and Economic Studies,* VI, 2 (June 1957), 109–122.

3. Burn, *op. cit.,* p. 147.

4. Eric Williams, *The Negro in the Caribbean,* p. 16.

5. William G. Sewell, *The Ordeal of Free Labor in the British West Indies.*

6. Kenneth Sterling, "A Changing Caribbean," *Facts and Figures,* VI, 5–6 (September–October 1957), 4.

7. S. Daniel Neumark, "The Importance of Agriculture in the Caribbean Economy," *Caribbean Economic Review,* III, 1–2 (October, 1951), 12.

8. *The Sugar Industry of British Guiana,* Report of Commission, John A. Venn, Chairman, p. 5. (Hereinafter referred to as the Venn Report.) See also R. R. Follett Smith, "B. G. Sugar Industry," *The Caribbean,* XI, 10 (May, 1958).

9. *Trinidad and Tobago Disturbances, 1937,* Report of Commission, Sir John Forster, Chairman, p. 13. (Hereinafter referred to as the Forster Report.)

10. W. Arthur Lewis, "The Industrialization of the British West Indies," *Caribbean Economic Review,* II, 1 (May, 1950), 5.

11. *The Sugar Industry of Trinidad,* Report of Commission, Lord Herwald R. Soulbury, Chairman. (Hereinafter referred to as the Soulbury Report, Trinidad); *Sugar Industry of St. Kitts,* Report of Commission, Lord Herwald R. Soulbury, Chairman. (Hereinafter referred to as the Soulbury Report, St. Kitts); *West India Royal Commission Report,* Report of Commission, Lord Walter E. G. Moyne, Chairman, p. 18. (Hereinafter referred to as the Moyne Report); Venn Report, p. 5.

12. Sterling, *op. cit.,* p. 4; *London Times,* January 28, 1958.

13. Mary Proudfoot, *Britain and the United States in the Caribbean,* p. 52.

14. Praedial pertains to land and farming. A praedial slave was a field hand. Hence praedial larceny relates both to subject and object of thievery, that is, field hands are accustomed to helping themselves to edible crops.

15. A. L. Jolley, "Agriculture," *The Caribbean,* X, 4 (November 1956), 80.

16. *West Indies Yearbook, 1956–1957,* p. 346 and *1957–1958,* p. xxxiii.

17. Sterling, *op. cit.*, p. 2.

18. *West Indies Yearbook, 1956–1957*, p. 337.

19. "Tourism Survey," *The Caribbean*, XI, 7 (February, 1958).

20. Lewis, *op. cit.*, p. 1.

21. Mary Proudfoot, *op. cit.*, p. 314.

22. Venn Report, p. 16.

23. International Bank for Reconstruction and Development, *Economic Development of Jamaica*, p. 196. (Hereinafter referred to as the World Bank Report, Jamaica.)

24. Malcolm J. Proudfoot, *Population Movements in the Caribbean*, p. 74.

25. The disproportional growth of cities appears characteristic of underdeveloped areas everywhere. See "The Lure of the City," *ILO News*, 97 (June, 1956). Also Katherin Bauer, "Urban Growth in Underdeveloped Areas," *Annals of the American Academy of Political and Social Sciences*, CCCV (May, 1956), 60–69.

26. Mary Proudfoot, *op. cit.*, pp. 76–77.

27. Leonard Broom, "The Social Differentiation of Jamaica," *American Sociological Review*, XIX, 2 (April, 1954), 121; George Crumper, "Social Structure of the British West Indies," *Caribbean Affairs*, Part I, p. 34; Simon Rottenberg, "Labor Relations in an Underdeveloped Economy," *Economic Development and Cultural Change*, I (December, 1952), 250–51.

28. Mary Proudfoot, *op. cit.*, p. 69; Madeline Kerr, *Personality and Conflict in Jamaica*, pp. 1, 93–113, 172.

29. Curtin, *op. cit.*, p. 55, calls the feeling of exile one of the most important psychological characteristics of white Jamaicans.

30. *CAD-ORIT Information Bulletin* (January, 1955), p. 7.

31. Rottenberg, *op. cit.*, p. 253.

32. For further discussion of the historical development of the colored class, see Curtin *op. cit.*, pp. 23, 42, 54.

33. The story is told of a colored man who was refused admission to a hotel in Barbados (Barbados is the only place in the West Indies having a declared color bar), when he noticed a much darker complexioned gentleman registering at the desk. In response to his complaint, the room clerk informed him that the gentleman registering was not colored. On the contrary, he was a member of one of the island's best families.

34. For a discussion of middle-class attitudes and the West Indian class-color structure see *Labour Conditions in the West Indies*, Report of Commission, Major Orde Browne, Chairman, pp. 38–39. (Hereinafter referred to as the Orde Browne Report.) International Labor Organization, *Labour Policies in the British West Indies*, p. 18. (Hereinafter referred to as the ILO Report.) Annette Baker Fox, *Freedom and Welfare in the Caribbean*, pp. 89, 116; T. S. Simey, *Welfare and Planning in the B.W.I.*, pp. 75, 94, 101, 104; Mary Proudfoot, *op. cit.*, pp. 66–75; Kerr, *op. cit.*, p. 101; Paul Blanchard, *Democracy and Empire in the Caribbean*, pp. 51–59; Williams, *The Negro in the Caribbean*, pp. 57–69.

35. Blanchard, *op. cit.*, p. 57; George T. Daniel, "Labor and Nationalism in the British Caribbean," *Annals of the American Academy of Political and Social Sciences*, CCCX (March, 1957), 164–165.

36. Kerr, *op. cit.*, p. 172.

37. The Forster Report, pp. 76–81, concluded that racial issues were not an underlying factor in the 1937 disturbances in Trinidad, though white South Africans were deeply resented.

38. Simey, *op. cit.*, p. 96.

39. Kerr, *op. cit.*, pp. 96–97.

40. Mary Proudfoot, *op. cit.*, p. 74.

41. Fernando Henriques, *Family and Colour in Jamaica*, p. 59.

42. Kerr, *op. cit.*, pp. 163–164.

43. Simey, *op. cit.*, p. 18; Venn Report, p. 141; Blanchard, *op. cit.*, pp. 58–59,

113, 114, 130; Meville J. and Frances S. Herskovits, *Trinidad Village*, pp. 19–20.

44. For historical background, see Curtin, *op. cit.*, pp. 3–23, describing conditions following emancipation, which are not too dissimilar from conditions before unionism.

45. Crumper, *op. cit.*, Part III, p. 24.

46. Department of Labor, Jamaica, *Annual Report*, 1945, p. 2.

47. See Venn Report, pp. 14, 50.

48. *Ibid.*, p. 59.

49. *Ibid.*, pp. 12, 59, and Ragatz, *op. cit.*, for discussion of the historical position of the driver in relation to the work force.

50. Venn Report, pp. 11–12.

51. Blanchard, *op. cit.*, p. 126.

52. Crumper, *op. cit.*, Part I, p. 17.

53. Simon Rottenberg and Nora Siffleet, *Unemployment in Antigua*, pp. 15–17.

54. Department of Labor, Antigua, *Annual Report*, 1951, p. 4.

55. Department of Labor, Jamaica, *Annual Report*, 1945, p. 2.

56. Venn Report, p. 74.

57. Orde Browne Report; see also Blanchard, *op. cit.*, p. 48.

58. Kerr, *op. cit.*, p. 107.

59. Mary Proudfoot, *op. cit.*, pp. 88, 135–151, 224–272; Blanchard, *op. cit.*, pp. 38–39, 60–67; Kerr, *op. cit.*, pp. 20–80, 109–147, 174; Kerr, "The Study of Personality Deprivation Through Projection Tests," *Social and Economic Studies*, IV, 1 (March, 1955), 85; Department of Labor, Jamaica, *Annual Report*, 1945, p. 2; Fox, *op. cit.*, p. 64; Yehudi Cohen, "The Social Organization of a Selected Community in Jamaica," *Social and Economic Studies*, II, 4 (March 1954), 110–131; Raymond T. Smith, *General Report of Anthropological Study Carried Out in Three Negro Villages in the Coastal Area of British Guiana, S.A.*, unpublished manuscript; Fernando Henriques, "West Indian Family Organization," *Caribbean Quarterly*, II, 1 (1951), 16–26; Fernando Henriques, *Family and Colour in Jamaica*, ILO Report, p. 18; Orde Browne Report, p. 36; Simey, *op. cit.*, pp. 36–37; C. V. D. Hadley, "Personality Patterns and Aggression in the British West Indies," *Human Relations*, II, 4 (October, 1949), 349–362.

60. Daniel, *op. cit.*, pp. 162–171.

61. Fox, *op. cit.*, pp. 168–170.

62. The Forster Report, p. 81, concluded that the desire for self-government was not an underlying cause for the 1937 disturbances in Trinidad.

63. Mary Proudfoot, *op. cit.*, p. 91.

64. Kerr, *Personality and Conflict*, p. 106.

Notes to Chapter II | *Recent Background*

1. International Labor Organization, *Labour Policies in the British West Indies*, p. 156. (Hereinafter referred to as the ILO Report.) Annette Baker Fox, *Freedom and Welfare in the Caribbean*, pp. 27–28. Paul Blanchard, *Democracy and Empire in the Caribbean*, also describes rioting in Puerto Rico in 1935 and 1937 (p. 27).

2. *West India Royal Commission Report*, Report of Commission, Lord Walter E. G. Moyne, Chairman. (Hereinafter referred to as the Moyne Report.)

3. For further discussion of this point see chapter v.

4. The founders of West Indian labor unions who had had occasion to discuss their problems with Sir Walter Citrine emphasized in interviews his important role in giving them confidence and courage to go ahead with what had at

first appeared to be a hopeless task. See also Eric Williams, *Capitalism and Slavery*, p. 96.

5. Although the labor disturbances of the late 1930's together with economic activities coincident with World War II mark a turning point in BWI history, care should be taken not to overstate the abruptness of the change. Many of those interviewed look upon the 1930–1940 period as the fruition of a movement begun by those returning from the Canal Zone and from World War I during the 1920's. Although they were a small group and not directly concerned with trade-union organization, they laid the groundwork in establishing new ideas and familiarizing West Indian workers with unionism. For further discussion of this point see Williams, *op. cit.*, pp. 89–93.

6. J. E. Heesterman, "Jamaica, Report on Industry," *The Caribbean*, VIII, 6 (January, 1955), 109, 111, 127–128. ILO Report, p. 51. The Earl of Listowel (F. W. Hare), Rita Hinden, Rawle Farley, and Colin Hughes, *Challenge to the British Caribbean*, p. 13. Blanchard, *op. cit.*, p. 29.

7. For further discussion of the impact of economic development see chapter iv.

8. Fox, *op. cit.*, p. 67.

9. Department of Labor, Barbados, *Annual Report*, 1952, p. 5.

10. See Annual Report of the Colonial Development and Welfare Corporation, *Development and Welfare in the West Indies*, 1952, by Sir Stephen Luke, pp. 91–92.

11. For further discussion of arbitration in the West Indies see chapter v.

12. For example, see *Report of the Third Conference of BWI Labour Officers*, May 16–19, 1950, p. 7.

13. International Bank for Reconstruction and Development, *The Economic Development of Jamaica*, p. 82. (Hereinafter referred to as the World Bank Report, Jamaica.)

14. *CAD-ORIT Information Bulletin* (January, 1955), p. 11.

15. Speaking at the Second Annual Conference of the Caribbean Area Division of ORIT, Hans Gottfurcht of the International Confederation of Free Trade Unions condemned government favoritism in board appointments while F. C. Catchpole of the Development and Welfare Corporation of the West Indies, representing the government, denied the charges. CAD-ORIT, *Proceedings of the Second Annual Conference of CAD-ORIT*, Trinidad (1955), p. 63.

16. *General Industrial Conditions and Labour Relations in Trinidad*, Report of Commission, F. W. Dalley, Chairman, pp. 119–124. (Hereinafter referred to as the Dalley Report, 1954.)

17. CAD-ORIT, *Proceedings of the Second Annual Conference*, p. 64.

18. T. S. Simey, *Welfare and Planning in the B.W.I.*, p. 104. Philip D. Curtin, *Two Jamaicas*, p. 84, notes that the fear of a slave revolt was always with the white minority, and the successful revolt in Haiti gave the white community constant feelings of insecurity.

19. Central Bureau of Labour Statistics, *Trade Unionism in Jamaica, 1918 to 1946*, p. 16.

20. Williams, *op. cit.*, pp. 83–85, points out that the slaves were far from docile.

21. See Dalley Report, 1954, p. 45.

22. *Sugar Industry of Antigua*, Report of Commission, Lord Herwald R. Soulbury, Chairman, p. 76. (Hereinafter referred to as the Soulbury Report, Antigua.)

23. Dalley Report, 1954, pp. 20–25, 139–141.

24. Simon Rottenberg, "Labor Relations in an Underdeveloped Economy," *Economic Development and Cultural Change*, I (December, 1952), 253. Madeline Kerr, *Personality and Conflict in Jamaica*, p. 106, also makes this point.

25. ILO Report, p. 127.

26. Rottenberg, *op. cit.*, p. 254. This writer recalls also the same problem when the steel industry in the United States was first organized. If Mexicans from one

village joined the union, those who came from a feuding village quit it. If one Southern European ethnic group joined the union, rival ethnic groups dropped their memberships. Workers brought all their problems to the union organizer, who acted as social worker and father confessor. Although the Steelworkers Union is job-oriented, international representatives continue to spend much of their time in counseling workers. West Indian unions probably will go through the same stage.

27. Fernando Henriques, *Family and Colour in Jamaica*, p. 61.
28. Kerr, *op. cit.*, p. 147.
29. Meville J. Herskovits, *Myth of the Negro Past*, p. 186. (There is no seventh book of Moses.)
30. Kerr, *op. cit.*, p. 160.
31. Fox, *op. cit.*, p. 68.
32. *Trade Union Organization and Industrial Relations in Trinidad*, Report of Commission, F. W. Dalley, Chairman, pp. 13, 34. (Hereinafter referred to as the Dalley Report, 1947.)
33. Kerr, *op. cit.*, 156–164.
34. For details of the Garvey movement see Edmund Cronon, *Black Moses*. See also Henriques, *op. cit.*, p. 60; Herskovits, *op. cit.*, p. 265; Williams, *op. cit.*, pp. 92–93.
35. For historical background see Curtin, *op. cit.*, pp. 29–35.
36. Henriques, *op. cit.*, pp. 79–85, 117. Simey, *op. cit.*, pp. 37–39; Kerr, *op. cit.*, pp. 137–149, 213–215.
37. Herskovits, *op. cit.*, p. 345.
38. Kerr, *op. cit.*, pp. 111–113.
39. *Ibid.*, p. 174.
40. *Ibid.*, pp. 172–173.
41. *Sugar Industry of British Guiana*, Report of Commission, John A. Venn, Chairman, p. 90. (Hereinafter referred to as the Venn Report.)
42. Central Bureau of Labour Statistics, *op. cit.*, p. 12.
43. Kerr, *op. cit.*, pp. 156–160.
44. World Bank Report, Jamaica, p. 82.
45. Dalley Report, 1954, p. 38.
46. Fox, *op. cit.*, p. 81.
47. *Report of Commission of Inquiry St. Lucia Sugar Strike*, Sir Clement Malone, Chairman. (Hereinafter referred to as the Malone Report).
48. Rottenberg, *op. cit.*, p. 256.
49. Listowel (Hare), *et al.*, *op. cit.*, p. 8; Simey, *op. cit.*, pp. 189–190.

Notes to Chapter III | *Union Development in the Larger Colonies*

1. See J. E. Heesterman, "Jamaica, Report on Industry," *The Caribbean*, VIII, 6 (January, 1955), 109–111, 127–128. In spite of the diversity of products, however, sugar still predominates. One firm, Tate and Lyle, owns 60,000 acres and produces one-third of the crop, while 28 other estates, averaging 8,000 acres, produce most of the balance. See Paul Blanchard, *Democracy and Empire in the Caribbean*, pp. 87–91.
2. For a detailed chronology of early union developments, see Central Bureau of Labour Statistics, *Trade Unionism in Jamaica, 1918 to 1946*.
3. Blanchard, *op. cit.*, p. 95.
4. Ronald Sires, "Government of the BWI—An Historical Outline," *Social and Economic Studies*, VI, 2 (June, 1957), 125.

5. *Ibid.*, pp. 98–99.
6. See Madeline Kerr, *Personality and Conflict in Jamaica*, p. 156.
7. Blanchard, *op. cit.*, pp. 95–96.
8. *CAD-ORIT Information Bulletin* (March, 1957), p. 17.
9. The present general secretary of the National Workers Union is Michael Manley, son of Norman Manley, a fact which causes some to conclude that the Manley family is not far different from Bustamante in their control of a union-political party. As stated previously, Norman Manley has never attempted to be a union officer. Michael Manley, on the other hand, has refused to run for political office or to hold office in the People's National party. Instead, he has devoted his energies entirely to building a strong, well-run union.
10. *Proceedings of the Second Annual Conference of CAD-ORIT*, Trinidad (1955), p. 38.
11. Eric Williams, *Capitalism and Slavery*, p. 94, calls Bustamante a rich labor demagogue. Bustamante was knighted for his services to Crown and Empire in 1955.
12. *Sugar Industry of Trinidad*, Report of Commission, Lord Herwald R. Soulbury, Chairman, p. 6. (Hereinafter referred to as the Soulbury Report, Trinidad.)
13. Robert M. Hallett in an article in the *Christian Science Monitor* states: [The East Indians] are striving to improve their position politically, socially and economically, which brings them into conflict with the Negro elements in the society, which are dominant. A wide gulf yawns between the almost completely Westernized culture of the Negroes and the Asian background of the East Indians." Hallett, "East Indians Learning to Become West Indians," *Christian Science Monitor*, February 1, 1957.
14. *Trade Union Organization and Industrial Relations in Trinidad*, Report of Commission, F. W. Dalley, Chairman, p. 5. (Hereinafter referred to as the Dalley Report, 1947.) International Labor Organization, *Labour Policies in the British West Indies*, p. 156. (Hereinafter referred to as the ILO Report.)
15. *Trinidad and Tobago Disturbances, 1937*, Report of Commission, Sir John Forster, Chairman, p. 57. (Hereinafter referred to as the Forster Report.)
16. *Ibid.*, pp. 47–53.
17. *Ibid.*, pp. 76–81.
18. Dalley Report, 1947, p. 7.
19. Serafino Romualdi, "Free Labor in the Caribbean," *Marine Guide* (June, 1953), p. 5.
20. *CAD-ORIT Information Bulletin* (September, 1954), p. 12.
21. *Ibid.* (November, 1957), p. 10.
22. Dalley Report, 1947, p. 13; *General Industrial Conditions and Labour Relations in Trinidad*, Report of Commission, F. W. Dalley, Chairman, p. 6. (Hereinafter referred to as the Dalley Report, 1954.)
23. The writer would describe the West Indian Independence party as pro-Communist, based in part on the opinions of informed Trinidadians and in part on his experience in attending mass meetings of the party. See also Dalley Report, 1954, pp. 37–39.
24. The merger of the Railway Employees Union, Government Farm and Nursery Workers Union, and Hydraulics Industrial Workers Union into the National Union of Government Workers, February, 1958, is a step toward unity. *CAD-ORIT Information Bulletin* (March, 1958), p. 19.
25. Dalley Report, 1954, p. 30; *CAD-ORIT Information Bulletin* (September, 1954), p. 12.
26. Dalley Report, 1954, p. 25.
27. This summary is based on interviews with Labor Department officers and union leaders in the sugar industry, and an interview with the secretary of the sugar-producers' association. See also Dalley Report, 1954, pp. 7, 8, 11–13, 121–124.

28. Soulbury Report, Trinidad, pp. 4–6; Dalley Report, 1947, pp. 19-23.

29. Dalley Report, 1954, p. 9. In addition, Robert M. Hallett, writing in the *Christian Science Monitor,* quotes a local newspaper which characterized Maraj as "the biggest menace Trinidad has ever faced." (See note 13.)

30. *Proceedings of the Second Annual Conference of CAD-ORIT,* p. 17.

31. *CAD-ORIT Information Bulletin* (September, 1956), p. 4.

32. *Ibid.* (March, 1957), p. 16.

33. Dalley Report, 1954, pp. 32–33; see also pp. 18–19, 62–63.

34. *Ibid.,* pp. 13–18, 22–25, 31–33.

35. *Ibid.,* p. 38.

36. On this point see Blanchard, *op. cit.,* pp. 113–115.

37. Sires, *op. cit.,* p. 127.

38. *Sugar Industry of British Guiana,* Report of Commission, John A. Venn, Chairman, p. 6. (Hereinafter referred to as the Venn Report.)

39. International Bank for Reconstruction and Development, *The Economic Development of British Guiana,* p. 6.

40. See Blanchard, *op. cit.,* pp. 121–129.

41. *Ibid.,* pp. 10, 11, 59.

42. See W. H. Knowles, "What Personnel Men Face in a South American Jungle," *Personnel Journal,* XXXIII, 10 (March, 1955).

43. *Ibid.,* p. 90; ILO Report, p. 143; Blanchard, *op. cit.,* p. 130.

44. British Guiana, Bureau of Public Information, *Order Suspending the Constitution and a White Paper Issued by Her Majesty's Government,* pp. 28–29, 32–35. (Hereinafter referred to as the White Paper.)

45. Venn Report, pp. 99–101. *Report of the Enmore Enquiry Commission,* pp. 26–42. White Paper, p. 23.

46. White Paper, pp. 32–34.

47. *Ibid.,* pp. 23–25.

48. *Ibid.,* p. 20.

49. Robert J. Alexander, "Communist Power Cracks in British Guiana," *The International Free Trade Union News,* XI, 10 (October, 1955), 8.

50. Harry Pollak, "Mission to the Caribbean," *Inter-American Labor Bulletin,* VIII, 5 (May, 1957), 3.

51. Blanchard, *op. cit.,* p. 128.

52. These conclusions are based on the writer's own observations. The Venn Report gives the Joint Estate Councils more credit than the writer is willing to concede. See Venn Report, pp. 94–96.

53. See *Sugar Industry of British Guiana,* Report of Commission, John A. Venn, Chairman, p. 70. *Report of the Enmore Enquiry Commission,* pp. 29–39.

| *Notes to Chapter IV* | *Union Development in the Smaller Colonies* |

1. International Bank for Reconstruction and Development, *The Economic Development Program of British Honduras,* pp. 1–3.

2. See Paul Blanchard, *Democracy and Empire in the Caribbean,* pp. 196–197.

3. Shortly before this book went to press, a split took place between rival factions of the General Workers Union. From brief mention of this split in the reports of the International Confederation of Free Trade Unions, the writer concludes that it is neither serious nor extensive. *CAD-ORIT Information Bulletin* (November-December 1956), p. 11.

4. *Report of an Inquiry Held by Sir Reginald Sharpe, Q.C., into Allegations of Contacts Between the Peoples' United Party and Guatemala. The Peoples'*

United Party also won the majority of seats in the 1957 elections against the opposition of a splinter group.

5. *Inter-American Labor Bulletin*, VII, 6 (June, 1956), 4.

6. CAD-ORIT, *Secretary's Report*, Third Biennial Conference, Trinidad (1957), p. 5.

7. Blanchard, *op. cit.*, pp. 180–181.

8. In 1956 an opposition party within the labor union was formed, but its candidates did not win enough votes to entitle them to a rebate of their election deposit.

9. Blanchard, *op. cit.*, pp. 185–186.

10. London, Colonial Office, *Colonial Reports, Barbados, 1954–1955*, p. 21.

11. *West Indies Yearbook, 1956–1957*, p. 163.

12. Blanchard, *op. cit.*, p. 152.

13. *Ibid.*, pp. 26, 147–152.

14. Some union officers have split from the Labour party and run as independents while still holding union office. See *The Beacon* (Progressive League weekly; Bridgetown, Barbados), December 14, 1956; *CAD-ORIT Information Bulletin* (August, 1956), p. 2.

15. *Ibid.* (March, 1957), p. 2; (July, 1956), p. 6; (July, 1957), p. 16.

16. Blanchard, *op. cit.*, p. 169.

17. For a detailed analysis of the rise of Gairy's union see Simon Rottenberg, "Labor Relations in an Underdeveloped Economy," *Economic Development and Cultural Change*, I (December, 1952).

18. *Proceedings of the Second Annual Conference of CAD-ORIT*, Trinidad (1955), p. 13.

19. *Ibid.*, pp. 15–16; *CAD-ORIT Information Bulletin* (August, 1956), p. 3 and (August, 1958), p. 21.

20. Jim Bury, "Observations on a Recent Mission," *Inter-American Regional Organization News Bulletin*, VIII, 9 (September, 1957), 4.

21. *Ibid.*, p. 2.

22. *CAD-ORIT Information Bulletin* (September, 1957), p. 11.

Notes to Chapter V | *Survey of Trade Unionism*

1. *CAD-ORIT Information Bulletin* (June, 1955), p. 1.

2. *Ibid.* (May-June 1956), p. 9.

3. International Labor Organization, *Labour Policies in the British West Indies*, p. 132; *Proceedings of the Second Annual Conference of CAD-ORIT*, Trinidad (1955), p. 5.

4. The General Workers Union of British Honduras is affiliated with the Inter-American Regional Division of the International Confederation of Free Trade Unions (ORIT-ICFTU), but as it does not consider British Honduras in the Caribbean sphere it is not affiliated with the Caribbean Area Division of ORIT.

5. For further discussion of CAD-ORIT and federations of British West Indian unions by industry see chapter vi.

Notes to Chapter VI | *External Factors Influencing Union Development*

1. Fab A. Hojas, Barbadian historian, in an unpublished manuscript, *Black Democracy,* writes that left-wing Harlem influence made such headway in the West Indies in the latter part of the 1930's that Grantley Adams prevailed upon the colonial government to undertake the Moyne Commission study. See also Eric Williams, *Capitalism and Slavery,* pp. 42, 97, and T. S. Simey, *Welfare and Planning in the B.W.I.,* pp. 76–78, 190.

2. Eric Williams, "Race Relations in Puerto Rico and the Virgin Islands," *Foreign Affairs* (January, 1945).

3. For some negative reactions to the American "occupation" see Paul Blanchard, *Democracy and Empire in the Caribbean,* pp. 100, 116, 132.

4. International Labor Organization, *Labour Policies in the British West Indies,* p. 118. Annual Report of the Colonial Development and Welfare Corporation, *Development and Welfare in the West Indies, 1946,* by Sir John MacPherson, p. 21.

5. Annual Report of the Colonial Development and Welfare Corporation, *Development and Welfare in the West Indies, 1952,* by Sir Stephen Luke, p. 11.

6. Milton Plumb, "Report on British West Indies Labor Program," *Inter-American Labor Bulletin,* VII, 4 (April, 1956), 3–4.

7. Ferdinand C. Smith was expelled from office in the National Maritime Union and deported from the United States for alleged Communist activities. Ferdinand C. Smith, "Why I am a Communist," *Spotlight,* XIV, 6–7 (June-July 1953), 16–17.

8. Robert J. Alexander, "Communist Power Cracks in British Guiana," *International Free Trade Union News,* XI, 10 (October, 1955), 8. *CAD-ORIT Information Bulletin* (March-April 1956), pp. 4–5. Communist influence in Trinidad was limited to the personal sympathies of two important union leaders toward Russia and the Russian interpretation of international affairs. Under pressure from the government, employers, and their own executive board they withdrew from the World Federation of Trade Unions in 1954. *General Industrial Conditions and Labour Relations in Trinidad,* Report of Commission, F. W. Dalley, Chairman, pp. 33–37.

9. In 1954 the writer attended meetings of the West Indian Independence party which were virtually without an audience. Holmes Alexander, syndicated newspaper columnist, reports the position of this party unchanged in 1956. Holmes Alexander, "Up, Barbados," *Berkeley Daily Gazette,* November 28, 1956.

10. *Report of an Inquiry Held by Sir Reginald Sharpe, Q. C., into Allegations of Contacts Between the Peoples' United Party and Guatemala.*

11. *CAD-ORIT Information Bulletin* (August, 1954), p. 5.

12. *Ibid.* (February, 1957), p. 3.

13. *Ibid.* (February, 1955), p. 5.

14. See Kenneth Sterling, "Inside Jamaica," *The Canadian Mineworker,* XIII, 8 (October, 1953), 4.

15. *CAD-ORIT Information Bulletin* (January, 1958), p. 11.

16. CAD-ORIT, *Caribbean Area Division of ORIT, What it is and What it Stands For.*

Notes to Chapter VII | Unions and Political Parties

1. See Eric Williams, *Capitalism and Slavery*, pp. 89–94, for a discussion of the 1918–1924 revolt of the middle class in contrast with the 1939–1946 laboring-class revolt.
2. The Peoples' United party of British Honduras is distinct, on paper, from its ally the General Workers Union, but in practice they are closely tied together as would be expected in a small colony.
3. Annual Report of the Colonial Development and Welfare Corporation, *Development and Welfare in the West Indies, 1946*, by Sir John MacPherson, p. 22; Colin A. Hughes, "Semi-Responsible Government in the BWI," *Political Science Quarterly*, LXVIII, 3 (September, 1953).
4. *CAD-ORIT Information Bulletin* (August, 1954), p. 8.
5. Hughes, *op. cit.*, p. 351.
6. *Proceedings of the Second Annual Conference of CAD-ORIT*, Trinidad (1955), pp. 10–19.
7. *Ibid.*, p. 11.
8. *CAD-ORIT Information Bulletin* (May, 1955), p. 8.
9. Statement made by the Honorable John Gutch, chief secretary, and Sir Alfred Savage, governor, over Radio Demerara, British Guiana, October 9, 1954.
10. National Workers Union, *Proceedings of the Third Annual Conference*, Jamaica (1955).
11. *CAD-ORIT Information Bulletin* (April, 1958), p. 18 and (August, 1958), p. 19.
12. *Ibid.* (May-June 1958), p. 3.
13. *Ibid.* (October-November 1957), p. 2.
14. CAD-ORIT, Officers Report, *CAD-ORIT's Role in a Changing Caribbean*, Third Biennial Conference, Trinidad (1957).
15. See British Information Services, Reference Division, *West Indian Federation*, ID, 1185 (January, 1955), for a complete summary and background of the plans for West Indian federation.
16. Robert M. Hallett makes similar observations in a series of articles in the *Christian Science Monitor*, December 22, 24, 26, 27, 28, 29, 1956.
17. *CAD-ORIT Information Bulletin* (October-November 1957), pp. 1–3.
18. Morely Ayearst, "Political Prospects of Federation," *Social and Economic Studies*, VI, 2 (June, 1957), 248–257.
19. For stories on the first federal election see *New York Times*, March 27 and March 30, 1958; *Christian Science Monitor*, March 26, March 28, April 23, and May 2, 1958; *London Times*, March 28 and April 19, 1958.

Notes to Chapter VIII | Union Management Relations

1. See W. H. Knowles, "Supervision in the British West Indies: Cause of Industrial Unrest," *Industrial and Labor Relations Review*, VIII, 4 (July, 1955).
2. Eric Williams, *Capitalism and Slavery*, pp. 22–25.
3. Simon Rottenberg, "Labor Relations in an Underdeveloped Economy," *Economic Development and Cultural Change*, I (December, 1952), 256, also stresses this point.

4. In its third annual convention the National Workers party of Jamaica criticized the Peoples' National party to which it is allied for its failure to raise wages of government employees.

5. International Bank for Reconstruction and Development, *The Economic Development of Jamaica*, p. 81.

6. *CAD-ORIT Information Bulletin* (March, 1957), p. 5.

7. National Workers Union, *Statement of Policy*, Third Annual Conference, Jamaica (1955).

Notes to Chapter IX | *Economic Problems Union Attitudes Toward Basic*

1. T. S. Simey, *Welfare and Planning in the B.W.I.*, p. 53. See also Madeline Kerr, *Personality and Conflict in Jamaica*, p. 173.

2. See *The British Guiana and British Honduras Settlement Commission*, Report of Commission, Sir Geoffrey Evans, Chairman. (Hereinafter referred to as the Evans Report.) Although this report is out of date as the population has increased even more rapidly than predicted, it does give a good review of the nature and magnitude of the population problem. For more recent estimates of population growth, unemployment, and underemployment see Douglas Manley, "Post-War Migration of West Indians to Great Britain," *International Labor Review*, LXXIV, 2 (August 1956), 191–196. See also G. W. Roberts, "Some Demographic Considerations of West Indian Federation," *Social and Economic Studies*, VI, 2 (June, 1957), 269–275.

3. Annual Report of the Colonial Development and Welfare Corporation, *Development and Welfare In the West Indies, 1952*, by Sir Stephen Luke, p. 47. See also Simey, *op. cit.*, pp. 151–152.

4. Members of the white upper classes who were interviewed stressed the population problem far more than did those of any other group. Often denying the possibility of poor personnel policies, they analyzed labor unrest as a population problem alone. They showed a feeling of futility about plans for economic development, believing that any efforts to increase the national income would be canceled out by a growing population. Believing the population problem to be insoluble, several employers expressed the opinion that the best thing to do was to move out of the West Indies and let the masses multiply until they starved to death.

5. W. Arthur Lewis, "The Industrialization of the British West Indies," *Caribbean Economic Review*, XI, 1 (May, 1950), 37, criticizes this view.

6. *CAD-ORIT Information Bulletin* (August, 1955), p. 5.

7. *Ibid.* (June, 1955), p. 2.

8. Department of Labor, Trinidad and Tobago, *Annual Report*, 1949, p. 8.

9. Simey, *op. cit.*, preface, p. x.

10. Annette Baker Fox, *Freedom and Welfare in the Caribbean*, chap. viii.

11. Dudley Seers, "Federation of the BWI: The Economic and Financial Aspects," *Social and Economic Studies*, VI, 2 (June 1957), 198.

12. International Bank for Reconstruction and Development, *The Economic Development of Jamaica*, p. 208. (Hereinafter referred to as World Bank Report, Jamaica.)

13. Luke, *op. cit.*, pp. 21–22.

14. Evans Report, *op. cit.*, pp. 3–4.

15. Simey, *op. cit.*, p. 80. World Bank Report, Jamaica, pp. 245–249.

16. International Bank for Reconstruction and Development, *The Economic Development of British Guiana*, pp. 84–85.

17. See Lewis, *op. cit.*
18. Fox, *op. cit.*, p. 69.
19. World Bank Report, Jamaica, p. 81.
20. Fox, *op. cit.*, p. 66.
21. Reprinted by the Bureau of Public Information, British Guiana, October, 1953.

Bibliography

Books

Blanchard, Paul. *Democracy and Empire in the Caribbean*. New York: Macmillan, 1947.

Burn, W. L. *The British West Indies*. London: Hutchinson House, 1951.

Cronon, Edmund. *Black Moses*. Madison: University of Wisconsin Press, 1955.

Curtin, Philip D. *Two Jamaicas*. Cambridge: Harvard University Press, 1955.

Fox, Annette Baker. *Freedom and Welfare in the Caribbean*. New York: Harcourt Brace, 1949.

Henriques, Fernando. *Family and Colour in Jamaica*. London: Eyre and Spottiswoode, 1953.

Herskovits, Meville J. *Myth of the Negro Past*. New York: Harper, 1941.

————, and Frances S. *Trinidad Village*. New York: Alfred A. Knopf, 1947.

Hojas, Fab A. *Black Democracy*. Barbados. (Unpublished manuscript.)

Kerr, Madeline. *Personality and Conflict in Jamaica*. Liverpool: Liverpool University Press, 1952.

Lewis, Arthur W. *Labour in the West Indies*. London: Fabian Society, 1939.

Listowel, The Earl of (W. F. Hare), Rita Hinden, Rawle Farley, and Colin Hughes. *Challenge to the British Caribbean*. London: Fabian Publications, 1952.

MacMillan, William M. *Warning from the West Indies*. Middlesex: Penguin Books, 1938.

Proudfoot, Malcolm J. *Population Movements in the Caribbean*. Trinidad: Caribbean Commission, 1951.

Proudfoot, Mary. *Britain and the United States in the Caribbean*. New York: Frederick A. Praeger, 1953.

Ragatz, Lowell J. *The Fall of the Planter Class in the British Caribbean, 1763–1833*. New York: The Century Company, 1928.

Rottenberg, Simon and Nora Siffleet. *Unemployment in Antigua*. Puerto Rico: University of Puerto Rico, Labor Relations Institute, 1952.

Sewell, William G. *Ordeal of Free Labor in the British West Indies*. New York: Harpers, 1861.

Simey, T. S. *Welfare and Planning in the B.W.I.* Oxford: Clarendon Press, 1946.

Smith, Raymond T. *General Report of an Anthropological Study Carried Out in Three Negro Village Communities in the Coastal Area of British Guiana, S. A.* (Unpublished manuscript.)

Williams, Eric. *Capitalism and Slavery*. Chapel Hill: University of North Carolina Press, 1944.
———. *The Negro in the Caribbean*. Washington, D. C.: Associates for Negro Folk Education, 1942.

Articles

Alexander, Holmes. "Up, Barbados," *Berkeley Daily Gazette,* Berkeley, California, November 28, 1956.
Alexander, Robert J. "Communist Power Cracks in British Guiana," *The International Free Trade Union News*, XI, 10 (October, 1955).
Anonymous. "Second Caribbean Labour Congress, September 2–9, 1947," *New World* (Masses Supplement, Jamaica: October, 1947).
———. "Labour," *Spotlight*, XIV, 1 (Jamaica: August, 1953).
———. "Lure of the City," *ILO News*, 97 (Geneva: June, 1956).
———. "Moses at the Crossroads," *Spotlight*, XIV, 9 (Jamaica: September, 1953).
———. "Political Periscope," *Spotlight*, XIV, 9 (Jamaica: September, 1953).
———. "Tourism Survey," *The Caribbean*, XI, 7 (Trinidad: February, 1958).
———. "TUC Outs Hart," *Jamaica Daily Gleaner*, August 31, 1953.
———. "Wages, Rates and Productivity," *Jamaica Daily Gleaner*, October 17, 1953.
———. "Women," *Spotlight*, XIV, 8 (Jamaica: August, 1953).
Ayearst, Morely, "Political Aspects of Federation," *Social and Economic Studies*, VI, 2 (June, 1957).
Bauer, Katherine. "Urban Growth in Underdeveloped Areas," *Annals of the American Academy of Political and Social Sciences*, CCCV (May, 1956).
Braithwaite, Lloyd. "Federal Associations and Institutions in the West Indies," *Social and Economic Studies*, VI, 2 (June, 1957).
———. "Social Stratification in Trinidad," *Social and Economic Studies*, II, 2–3 (October, 1953).
Broom, Leonard. "The Social Differentiation of Jamaica," *American Sociological Review*, XIX, 2 (April, 1954).
Bury, Jim. "Observations on a Recent Mission," *Inter-American Regional News Bulletin*, VIII, 9 (September, 1957).
Cohen, Yehudi A. "The Social Organization of a Selected Community in Jamaica," *Social and Economic Studies*, II, 4 (March, 1954).
Crumper, George. "Social Structure of the British West Indies," *Caribbean Affairs*, Part I (no date).
Daniel, George T. "Labor and Nationalism in the British Caribbean," *The Annals of the American Academy of Political and Social Sciences*, CCCX (March, 1957).
Garlin, Winnifred. "British Guiana is Still Red on the Map," *Jamaica Daily Gleaner*, Jamaica, October 18, 1953.
Hadley, C. V. D. "Personality Patterns and Aggression in the British West Indies," *Human Relations*, II, 4 (October, 1949).
Hallett, Robert M. "East Indians Learning to Become West Indians," *Christian Science Monitor*, February 1, 1957.
———. "Caribbean Chiefs Gird for Top Jobs," *Christian Science Monitor*, December 26, 1956.
Henderson, Julia. "Foreign Labor in the United States During the War," *International Labour Review* (Geneva: December, 1945).
Henriques, Fernando. "West Indian Family Organization," *Caribbean Quarterly*, II, 1 (Trinidad: 1951).
Heesterman, J. E. "Jamaica, Report on Industry," *The Caribbean*, VIII, 6 (Trinidad: November, 1956).

Hughes, Colin A. "Semi-Responsible Government in the BWI," *Political Science Quarterly*, LXVIII, 3 (September, 1953).

Jolley, A. L. "Agriculture," *The Caribbean*, X, 4 (Trinidad: November, 1956).

Kerr, Madeline, "The Study of Personality Deprivation Through Projection Tests," *Social and Economic Studies*, IV, 1 (March, 1955).

Knapland, Paul. "Federation of the West Indies," *Social and Economic Studies*, VI, 2 (June, 1957).

Knowles, W. H. "Supervision in the British West Indies: Cause of Industrial Unrest," *Industrial and Labor Relations Review*, VIII, 4 (July, 1955).

———. "What Personnel Men Face in a South American Jungle," *Personnel Journal*, XXXIII, 10 (March, 1955).

Lewis, Arthur W. "Issues in Land Settlement Policy," *Caribbean Economic Review*, III, 1–2 (Trinidad: October, 1951).

———. "The Industrialization of the British West Indies," *Caribbean Economic Review*, XI, 1 (Trinidad: May, 1950).

Manley, Douglas. "Post-War Migration of West Indians to Great Britain," *International Labour Review*, LXXIV, 2 (Geneva: August, 1956).

Matthews, Cedric. "Agricultural Labour and Mechanization," *Caribbean Economic Review*, III, 1–2 (Trinidad: October, 1951).

Neumark, S. D. "The Importance of Agriculture in Caribbean Economy," *Caribbean Economic Review*, III, 1–2 (Trinidad: October, 1951).

Plumb, Milton. "Report on British West Indies Labor Program," *Inter-American Labor Bulletin*, VII, 4 (April, 1956).

Pollak, Harry. "Mission to the Caribbean," *Inter-American Labor Bulletin*, VIII, 5 (May, 1957).

Richardson, Henry J. "Social Security Problems, with Special Reference to the British West Indies," *Social and Economic Studies*, V, 2 (June, 1956).

Roberts, G. W. "Population Trends in the British Caribbean Colonies, 1948–61," *Caribbean Economic Review*, III, 1–2 (Trinidad: October, 1951).

———. "Some Demographic Considerations of West Indian Federation," *Social and Economic Studies*, VI, 2 (June, 1957).

Romualdi, Serafino. "Free Labor in the Caribbean," *Marine Guide* (Trinidad: June, 1953).

Rottenberg, Simon. "Labor Relations in an Underdeveloped Economy," *Economic Development and Cultural Change*, I (December, 1952).

———. "Income and Leisure in an Underdeveloped Economy," *Journal of Political Economy*, LX, 2 (April, 1952).

———. "Management and the Agricultural Tradition in Puerto Rico," *Caribbean Quarterly*, II, 3 (Trinidad: 1951).

Schwarz, Ernst. "Progressive Government in Jamaica: 'The Manley Plan,'" *Facts and Figures*, IV, 3–4 (March-April, 1955).

Seers, Dudley. "Federation of the BWI: The Economic and Financial Aspects," *Social and Economic Studies*, VI, 2 (June, 1957).

Simpson, George E. "Political Cultism in West Kingston, Jamaica," *Social and Economic Studies*, IV, 2 (June, 1955).

———. "Culture Change and Reintegration Found in the Cults of West Kingston, Jamaica," *Proceedings of the American Philosophical Society*, XCIX, 2 (April, 1955).

Sires, Ronald. "Government of the BWI—An Historical Outline," *Social and Economic Studies*, VI, 2 (June, 1957).

Smith, Ferdinand C. "Why I am a Communist," *Spotlight*, XIV, 6–7 (Jamaica: June-July, 1953).

Smith, R. R. Follett. "B. G. Sugar Industry," *The Caribbean*, XI, 10 (Trinidad: May, 1958).

Smith, Raymond. "Family Organization in British Guiana," *Social and Economic Studies*, I, 1 (February, 1953).

Sterling, Kenneth. "Inside Jamaica," *Canadian Mineworker,* XIII, 8 (Edmonton, Alberta: October, 1953).
———. "A Changing Caribbean," *Facts and Figures,* VI, 5–6 (September-October, 1957).
Williams, Eric. "Race Relations in Puerto Rico and the Virgin Islands," *Foreign Affairs* (January, 1945).

Trade-Union Publications

The *Beacon.* Weekly of the Progressive League. Bridgetown, Barbados.
Bustamante Industrial Trade Union. *Labor Day Annual* (celebrating the anniversary of the union). Kingston, Jamaica: 1951, 1952, 1953.
CAD-ORIT. *Caribbean Area Division of ORIT, What it is and What it Stands For.* Barbados: 1954. (Pamphlet.)
CAD-ORIT. *CAD-ORIT Information Bulletin.* Barbados: September, 1954—December, 1956; Trinidad: January, 1957—September, 1958.
———. Officers' Report. *CAD-ORIT's Role in a Changing Caribbean,* Third Biennial Conference. (Trinidad: 1957. Mimeographed.)
———. *Proceedings of the Second Annual Conference of CAD-ORIT.* Trinidad: 1955.
———. *Secretary's Report,* Third Biennial Conference. Trinidad: 1957. (Mimeographed.)
General Workers Union. *Resolutions for Discussion,* Tenth National Congress. 1950. (Unpublished.)
(The Labour Party, *Progress Report.* Antigua. N.d., m.p.
National Workers Union. *Proceedings of the Third Annual Congress,* November 1, 1954—November 15, 1955. (Unpublished.)
———. *Statement of Policy,* Third Annual Conference. Jamaica: November 20, 1955.
ORIT-ICFTU. *Inter-American Labor Bulletin.* Washington, D. C.: 1954–1958. (Monthly.)
———. *West Indian Workers Organization Conference.* Barbados: 1952. (Mimeographed report.)
Peoples' United Party, Executive Committee. *Resolutions adopted by PUP Convention,* September 30, 1953. (Unpublished.)
West Indian Independence Party. *Provisional Statement and Provisional Fundamental Programme.* Trinidad: Hill's Printery, October, 1952.

Government Commissions

Antigua. *Sugar Industry of Antigua.* Report of Commission, Lord Herwald R. Soulbury, Chairman. Antigua: Government Printing Office, 1949.
British Honduras. Department of Information and Communications. *The P.U.P. and Guatemala.* Belize, British Honduras: Government Printing Office, 1954.
———. *Report of an Inquiry Held by Sir Reginald Sharpe, Q.C., into Allegations of Contacts Between the Peoples' United Party and Guatemala.* London: H.M.S.O., 1954.
Great Britain. Colonial Office. *Report of the Enmore Enquiry Commission* in Appendix to the Report on British Guiana (1950). British Guiana: Government Printery, August, 1948).
———. *Labour Conditions in the West Indies.* Report of Commission, Major Orde Browne, Chairman. London: H.M.S.O., 1939.
———. *The British Guiana and British Honduras Settlement Commission.* Report of Commission, Sir Geoffrey Evans, Chairman. London: H.M.S.O., 1948.
———. *Trade Union Organization and Industrial Relations in Trinidad.* Report of Commission, F. W. Dalley, Chairman. London: H.M.S.O., 1947.

———. *Trinidad and Tobago Disturbances, 1937.* Report of Commission, Sir John Forster, Chairman. London: H.M.S.O., 1938.
———. *West India Royal Commission Report.* Report of Commission, Lord Walter E. G. Moyne, Chairman. London: H.M.S.O., 1945.
———. *Sugar Industry of British Guiana.* Report of Commission, John A. Venn, Chairman. London: H.M.S.O., 1949.
———. *Sugar Industry of St. Kitts.* Report of Commission, Lord Herwald R. Soulbury, Chairman. London: H.M.S.O., 1949.
St. Lucia. *Report of Commission of Inquiry St. Lucia Sugar Strike.* Report of Commission, Sir Clement Malone, Chairman. St. Lucia: 1951.
Trinidad. *Sugar Industry of Trinidad.* Report of Commission, Lord Herwald R. Soulbury, Chairman. Trinidad: 1949.
———. *General Industrial Conditions and Labour Relations in Trinidad.* Report of Commission, F. W. Dalley, Chairman. Trinidad: Government Printing Office, 1954.

Publications of International Organizations

International Bank for Reconstruction and Development. *The Economic Development of British Guiana.* Report of World Bank Mission. Baltimore: Johns Hopkins Press, 1953.
———. *The Economic Development Program of British Honduras.* Belize, British Honduras: Government Printing Office, 1954.
———. *The Economic Development of Jamaica.* Baltimore: Johns Hopkins Press, 1952.
International Labor Organization. *Labour Policies in the British West Indies.* ILO Report. Geneva: 1952.
The Caribbean Commission. (Commission established by the governments of England, France, the Netherlands, and the United States.) *The Caribbean.* Port-of-Spain, Trinidad. (Monthly.)

Annual Reports of Departments of Labor in BWI

Department of Labor. Barbados. *Annual Report.* 1951, 1952.
———. British Guiana. *Annual Report.* 1938–1952.
———. British Honduras. *Annual Report.* 1950, 1951.
———. Grenada. *Annual Report.* 1938–1952.
———. Jamaica. *Annual Report.* 1938–1952.
———. St. Lucia. *Annual Report.* 1938–1952.
———. St. Vincent. *Annual Report.* 1938–1952.
———. St. Kitts, Nevis, Anguilla. *Annual Report.* 1952.
———. Trinidad and Tobago. *Annual Report.* 1938–1952.

Government Publications

British West Indies. Barbados. *Third Conference of BWI Labour Officers, May 16–19, 1950.* Bridgetown, Barbados.
———. British Guiana. Bureau of Public Information. *Order Suspending the Constitution and a White Paper Issued by Her Majesty's Government.* Georgetown, British Guiana, 1953.
———. Jamaica. Central Bureau of Labour Statistics. *Trade Unionism in Jamaica, 1918 to 1946.* Kingston, Jamaica, 1946.
———. Central Bureau of Statistics. *Digest of Statistics.* Kingston, Jamaica: Government Printer, 1953.
———. *Blue Book for Island of Jamaica, 1945.* Kingston, Jamaica: Government Printer, 1948.

————. Trinidad. *Caribbean Statistical Digest.* Port-of-Spain, Trinidad: February, 1952.

————. *Trinidad and Tobago Year Book, 1957.* Port-of-Spain, Trinidad: 1957.

————. St. Vincent. *Plan for Development of St. Vincent.* Kingstown, St. Vincent: Government Printer, 1948.

————. *British West Indies Sugar Association.* Yearbook, 1952. Barbados.

Canada. *West Indies Yearbook, 1956–1957 and 1957–1958.* Montreal: Thomas Skinner of Canada, 1957 and 1958.

Great Britain. Colonial Development and Welfare Corporation. *Development and Welfare in the West Indies, 1943–1944,* annual report by Sir Frank Stockdale. London: H.M.S.O., 1945.

————. *Development and Welfare in the West Indies, 1952,* annual report by Sir John MacPherson. London: H.M.S.O., 1947.

————. *Development and Welfare in the West Indies, 1947,* annual report by Sir George Seel. London: H.M.S.O., 1951.

————. *Development and Welfare in the West Indies, 1952,* annual report by Sir Stephen Luke. Barbados: H.M.S.O., 1953.

————. British Information Services, Reference Division. *West Indian Federation.* ID, 1185 (revised). January, 1956. (Mimeographed newsletter.)

————. London: Colonial Office. *Colonial Reports, Barbados, 1954–1955.* London: H.M.S.O., 1954.

————. *Colonial Reports, British Guiana, 1955.* London: H.M.S.O., 1955.

————. *Colonial Reports, British Honduras, 1955.* London: H.M.S.O., 1956.

————. *Colonial Reports, Grenada, 1953–1954.* London: H.M.S.O., 1955.

————. *Colonial Reports, Jamaica, 1954.* London: H.M.S.O., 1955.

————. *Colonial Reports, Leeward Islands, 1954–1955.* London: H.M.S.O., 1956.

————. *Colonial Reports, St. Lucia, 1953–1954.* London: H.M.S.O., 1954.

————. *Colonial Reports, St. Vincent, 1953–1954.* London: H.M.S.O., 1954.

————. *Colonial Reports, Trinidad and Tobago. 1954.* London: H.M.S.O., 1956.

Index

Ability to pay argument, 164, 177
Adams, Grantley, 29, 109–111, 152
Agriculture: collective bargaining in, 155–158; economics of, 11–16; employment, 36–37; mechanization of, 35, 163; unionization, 118; wage determination, 158; working conditions, 31–38, 82, 89
Alexander, Cecil, 81, 82
All-Trinidad Sugar Workers Union, 83–85
American Committee for West Indian Federation, 129
American military bases, influence of, 129–130
American union influence in BWI unionism, 136–137
Anticolonialism, 40–41
Antigua, 106, 135, 148
Antigua Labor Party, 107
Antigua Trades and Labour Union, 106–107
Arbitration, 51, 55–56, 75

Barbados, 19, 107–110, 134
Barbados Labour Party, 109–111
Barbados National Party, 109
Barbados Progressive League, 109–111, 129, 142, 146
Barbados Workers Union, 109–111, 146
Bauxite industry, 17, 76, 88, 166
Belize Estate and Produce Co., 101
Blanket unions, 123, 144
Booker Brothers, McConnell and Company, 31, 88, 100, 156
British Empire and Rate Payers Union, 85-86
British Guiana: economic background, 88–89; politics, 47; population growth, 19; racial groups, 22; race issue, 29; sugar industry, 12; union development, 91–100; working conditions, 89–90
British Guiana Bauxite Miners Union, 99
British Guiana Labour Union, 95–96
British Guiana Trade Union Council, 93, 94, 100
British Guiana Timber Co., 100
British Guiana Timber, Saw Mill and Quarry Workers Union, 100

British Guiana and British Honduras Settlement Commission, 179
British Guiana and West Indian Trade Union Congress, 125
British Guiana Workers League, 96
British Honduras, 14, 15, 101–104, 135
British Trade Union Congress, 85, 98, 136, 147
British Transport Workers Union, 82
Brown, Orde, 32, 44, 102
Brown, W. G., 64, 115
Burnham, L. Forbes S., 94, 95, 147
Bury, Jim, 114
Bustamante, Alexander, 59, 61, 69, 71, 111, 145, 152
Bustamante Industrial Trade Union, 71, 123, 145, 156
Butler, Uriah, 59, 77–78, 80, 83, 85, 86, 87

Carasco, F. J., 61, 116
Caribbean Area Division of ORIT, 53, 74, 85, 125, 136, 144, 149, 177
Caribbean Federation of Aluminum and Allied Workers, 99, 136, 167
Caribbean Federation of Labour, 125–126
Caribbean Trade Union Congress, 125, 129
Caribbean-wide wage standards, 164
Catholic influence, and union ideologies, 103, 135, 175
Charles, George, 113
Chicleros, 102
Cipriani, Captain, 77, 113, 142, 149
Citrine, Walter, 106, 110, 136
Citrus bulk-purchase agreement, 14
Civil service, inefficiency of, 8, 181
Class structure of BWI, 23
Collective bargaining, 156–158
Colonial Development and Welfare Corporation, 172, 178
Colonial Industrial Development Corporation, 172
Colonialism, 8–9, 40–41
Communication Workers of America, AFL-CIO, 137, 146
Commonwealth Sugar Agreement, 13–14
Communism, 72, 79, 80–81, 92, 94, 103–104, 125, 129, 133–134, 156

Union shop, government attitude toward, 51
Unions: attitude toward foreign capital, 176–177; attitude toward Federation of BWI, 149–153; and economic development, 46–47; employer attitudes toward, 54–57; ideology, 187–192; influence of American military bases, 47–48, 129–130; jurisdictional disputes, 121–122; obstacles to growth, 57–60; and politics, 141–154; role of government, 49–54; statistics, 124; structure, 122–124
United States Farm Labor Recruitment Program, 131–132
United States military bases, influence of, 47–48, 114, 129–130
United Steelworkers of America, AFL-CIO, 73, 99, 113, 136
University College of the West Indies, 53

Venn Report, 11, 19, 34, 61, 89, 90

Wage boards, 53
Wage determination: ability to pay, 164; in agriculture, 158; Caribbean-wide standards, 167; and the government, 161; and labor supply, 160;

productivity and foreign capital, 165; task rates, 162; and technological change, 163
Wage rates, bauxite industry, 99, 166
Washington, Booker T., 128
Waterfront Workers Union, Grenada, 113
West Indian Defense Committee, 128
West Indian Independence Party, 80, 133
Williams, Eric, 29, 87, 131, 146, 147, 152
Wolcott, Frank, 111
Working class: leadership, 61–62; nationalism, 40–41; personality patterns, 39; racial attitudes, 27–28; social disorganization, 38–40
Working conditions on estates, 31–38, 82–83, 89–90
World Bank Report, British Guiana, 89, 181
World Bank Report, Jamaica, 19, 52, 62
World Federation of Christian Trade Unions, 73
World Federation of Trade Unions, 72, 79, 93, 113, 133
Woodcock, George, 25, 98

Zonarich, Nick, 166